SPIEGEL & GRAU

# CONFESSION
## *of a*
# BUDDHIST
# ATHEIST

# CONFESSION

*of a*

# BUDDHIST ATHEIST

## STEPHEN BATCHELOR

SPIEGEL & GRAU

NEW YORK

2010

Published in the United States by Spiegel & Grau,
an imprint of The Random House Publishing Group,
a division of Random House, Inc., New York.

SPIEGEL & GRAU and Design
is a registered trademark of Random House, Inc.

Library of Congress Cataloging-in-Publication Data

Batchelor, Stephen.
Confession of a Buddhist atheist / Stephen Batchelor.
p. cm.
ISBN 978-0-385-52706-4
eBook ISBN 978-1-58836-984-0
1. Batchelor, Stephen. 2. Buddhists—Biography. 3. Spiritual biography—
Great Britain. I. Title.
BQ942.A689A3 2010
294.3'923092—dc22
2009037937

Printed in the United States of America on acid-free paper

www.spiegelandgrau.com

2 4 6 8 9 7 5 3 1

First Edition

Book design by Jo Anne Metsch

There are not only one hundred, or five hundred, but far more men and women lay followers, my disciples, clothed in white, enjoying sensual pleasures, who carry out my instruction, respond to my advice, have gone beyond doubt, become free from perplexity, gained intrepidity and become independent of others in my teaching.

—Siddhattha Gotama

———————

Stories are impossible but it's impossible to live without them. That's the mess I'm in.

—Wim Wenders

# PREFACE

*Confession of a Buddhist Atheist* tells the story of a thirty-seven-year journey through the Buddhist tradition. It begins with my encounter in India at the age of nineteen with the Dalai Lama and the teachings of Tibetan Buddhism, and concludes with the reflections of a fifty-six-year-old secular, nondenominational lay Buddhist living in rural France. Since I was not raised as a Buddhist, this is a story of conversion. It tells of my fascination with Buddhism as well as my struggle to come to terms with doctrines—such as reincarnation—that I find difficult to accept, and authoritarian religious institutions that resist criticism and innovation. My personal struggles may also reflect a broader cultural conflict between the worldview of a traditional Asian religion and the intuitions of secular modernity.

My encounter with traditional forms of Buddhism led me to ask with increasing urgency: Who was this man Siddhattha Gotama, the Buddha? What sort of world did he live in? What was distinctive and original in his teaching? I began to realize that much of what was presented to me in good faith as "Buddhism" were doctrines and practices that had evolved many centuries after the Buddha's death, under very different circumstances from those in which he lived. Throughout its history Buddhism has displayed a remarkable ability to adapt to novel situations and reinvent itself in forms appropriate to the needs of its new adherents. Yet this very ability to present itself in another guise has also served to obscure the origins of the tradition and the figure of its founder. In many schools of Buddhism today, the discourses of Siddhattha Gotama are rarely studied, while the man himself is often elevated to the status of a god.

My quest to trace the origins of Buddhism led me to the study of the Pali Canon: the body of teachings attributed to Siddhattha Gotama in the ancient Pali language. While these texts are not verbatim transcripts of what the Buddha said, they preserve the earliest elements of his teaching and provide glimpses into the fraught social and political milieu of his world. This quest also took me back to India to visit those places mentioned in the Pali Canon where the Buddha lived and taught nearly twenty-five hundred years ago. These studies and field trips, together with G. P. Malalasekera's invaluable *Dictionary of Pali Proper Names,* have enabled me to reconstruct an account of the Buddha's life that is embedded in his relations with his benefactors, family, and disciples and formed by the political and social tensions of his time.

Many of the people who appear in this book are or were Buddhist monks. Yet the term "monk" (or "nun") in Buddhism does not mean quite the same thing that it does when used in a Christian context. The Pali word for "monk" is *bhikkhu,* which literally means "beggar." ("Nun" is *bhikkhuni*, which means the same.) A *bhikkhu* or *bhikkhuni* is one who has dropped out of mainstream society in order to devote him- or herself to the practice of the Buddha's teaching. On receiving ordination, *bhikkhus* and *bhikkhunis* take more than two hundred vows (many of them minute behavioral conventions). They commit themselves to a life of chastity and poverty but—traditionally at least—are encouraged to lead a wandering life and survive by begging alms. In addition to pursuing a life of simplicity, solitude, and contemplation, the *bhikkhu* or *bhikkhuni* will also teach when invited to do so, and provide counseling and pastoral care to those in need. Buddhism makes no distinction between a monk and a priest.

I was a Buddhist monk (initially a novice, then a *bhikkhu*) for ten years; since disrobing, I have lived as a married layman. Because I do not belong to any Buddhist institution or tradition, I have no "home" in the Buddhist world. I have become a freelance itinerant teacher, traveling to wherever in the world I am invited to share what I have learned.

*Confession of a Buddhist Atheist* is written from the perspective of a committed layperson who seeks to lead a life that embodies Buddhist values within the context of secularism and modernity. I have no interest in preserving the dogmas and institutions of traditional Asian forms of Buddhism as though they possessed an intrinsic value independent of the conditions under which they arose. For me, Buddhism is like a living organism. If it is to flourish outside self-enclosed ghettos of believers, it will have to meet the challenge of understanding, interacting with, and adapting to an environment that is strikingly different from those in which it has evolved.

Since this book is intended for the general reader, I have omitted all diacritical marks on Pali terms. These are, however, included in the notes, appendixes, and glossary.

STEPHEN BATCHELOR
*Aquitaine*
*September 2009*

# CONTENTS

# Contents

# part one

# MONK

# 1

# A BUDDHIST FAILURE

# ( I )

MARCH 10, 1973. I remember the date because it marked the four-teenth anniversary of the Tibetan uprising in Lhasa in 1959, which triggered the flight of the Dalai Lama into the exile from which he has yet to return. I was studying Buddhism in Dharamsala, the Tibetan capital in exile, a former British hill-station in the Himalayas. The sky that morning was dark, damp, and foreboding. Earlier, the clouds had unleashed hailstones the size of miniature golf balls that now lay fused in white clusters along the roadside that led from the village of McLeod Ganj down to the Library of Tibetan Works and Archives, where the anniversary was to be commemorated.

A white canvas awning, straining and flapping in the wind, was strung in front of the Library. Beneath it sat a huddle of senior monks in burgundy robes, aristocrats in long gray *chubas,* and the Indian su-perintendent of police from Kotwali Bazaar. I joined a crowd gathered on a large terrace below and waited for the proceedings to begin. The Dalai Lama, a spry, shaven-headed man of thirty-eight, strode onto an impromptu stage. The audience spontaneously prostrated itself as one onto the muddy ground. He read a speech, which was barely audible above the wind, delivered in rapid-fire Tibetan, a language I did not yet understand, at a velocity I would never master. Every now and then a drop of rain would descend from the lowering sky.

I was distracted from my thoughts about the plight of Tibet by the harsh shriek of what sounded like a trumpet. Perched on a ledge on the steep hillside beside the Library, next to a smoking fire, stood a bespectacled lama, legs akimbo, blowing into a thighbone and ringing a bell. His disheveled hair was tied in a topknot. A white robe, trimmed in red, was slung carelessly across his left shoulder. When he wasn't blowing his horn, he would mutter what seemed like imprecations at the grumbling clouds, his right hand extended in the threatening mudra, a ritual gesture used to ward off danger. From time to time he would put down his thighbone and fling an arc of mustard seeds against the ominous mists.

Then there was an almighty crash. Rain hammered down on the corrugated iron roofs of the residential buildings on the far side of the Library, obliterating the Dalai Lama's words. This noise went on for several minutes. The lama on the hillside stamped his feet, blew his thighbone, and rang his bell with increased urgency. The heavy drops of rain that had started falling on the dignitaries and the crowd abruptly stopped.

After the Dalai Lama left and the crowd dispersed, I joined a small group of fellow *Injis*. In reverential tones, we discussed how the lama on the hill—whose name was Yeshe Dorje—had prevented the storm from soaking us. I heard myself say: "And you could hear the rain still falling all around us: over there by the Library and on those government buildings behind as well." The others nodded and smiled in awed agreement.

Even as I was speaking, I knew I was not telling the truth. I had heard no rain on the roofs behind me. Not a drop. Yet to be convinced that the lama had prevented the rain with his ritual and spells, I had to believe that he had created a magical umbrella to shield the crowd from the storm. Otherwise, what had happened would not have been that remarkable. Who has not witnessed rain falling a short distance away from where one is standing on dry ground? Perhaps it was nothing more than a brief mountain shower on the nearby hillside. None of us would have dared to admit this possibility. That would have brought us perilously close to questioning the lama's prowess and, by implication, the whole elaborate belief system of Tibetan Buddhism.

For several years, I continued to peddle this lie. It was my favorite (and only) example of my firsthand experience of the supernatural powers of Tibetan lamas. But, strangely, whenever I told it, it didn't *feel* like a lie. I had taken the lay Buddhist precepts and would soon take monastic vows. I took the moral injunction against lying very seriously. In other circumstances, I would scrupulously, even neurotically, avoid telling the slightest falsehood. Yet, somehow, this one did not count. At times, I tried to persuade myself that perhaps it was true: the rain had fallen behind me, but I had not noticed. The others—albeit at my prompting—had confirmed what I said. But such logical gymnastics failed to convince me for very long.

I suspect my lie did not feel like a lie because it served to affirm what I believed to be a greater truth. My words were a heartfelt and spontaneous utterance of our passionately shared convictions. In a weirdly unnerving way, I did not feel that "I" had said them. It was as though something far larger than all of us had caused them to issue from my lips. Moreover, the greater truth, in whose service my lie was employed, was imparted to us by men of unimpeachable moral and intellectual character. These kind, learned, enlightened monks would not deceive us. They repeatedly said to accept what they taught only after testing it as carefully as a goldsmith would assay a piece of gold. Since they themselves must have subjected these teachings to that kind of rigorous scrutiny during their years of study and meditation, then surely they were not speaking out of blind conviction, but from their own direct knowledge and experience? Ergo: Yeshe Dorje stopped the rain with his thighbone, bell, mustard seeds, and incantations.

The next morning, someone asked the teacher at the Library, Geshe Dhargyey, to say something about the practices involved in controlling the weather. Geshe-la (as we called him) belonged to the scholarly Geluk school, in which the Dalai Lama had been trained. Not only did he possess an encyclopedic knowledge of Geluk orthodoxy, he radiated a joyous well-being that bubbled forth in mirthful chuckles. The question seemed to disturb him. He frowned, then said in a disapproving voice: "That was not good. No compassion. It hurts the *devas*." The *devas* in question belonged to a minor class of gods who manage the weather. To zap them with mantras, mudras, and mustard seeds were acts of violence. As an advocate of universal compassion, this was not something Geshe-la was prepared to condone. I was surprised by his willingness to criticize Yeshe Dorje, a lama from the Nyingma (Ancient) school of Tibetan Buddhism. And why, I wondered, would the Dalai Lama—the living embodiment of compassion—tolerate the performance of a ritual if it injured *devas*?

Tibetan lamas held a view of the world that was deeply at odds with the one in which I had been raised. Educated in the monasteries of old Tibet, they were ignorant of the findings of the natural sciences. They knew nothing of the modern disciplines of cosmology, physics, or biology. Nor did they have any knowledge of the literary, philosophical, and religious traditions that flourished outside their homeland. For them, all that human beings needed to know had been worked out centuries before by the Buddha and his followers and was preserved in the Kangyur and Tengyur (the Tibetan Buddhist canon). There you would learn that the earth was a triangular continent in a vast ocean dominated by the mighty Mount Sumeru, around which the sun, moon, and planets revolved. Driven by the force of good and bad deeds committed over beginningless former lifetimes, beings were repeatedly reborn as gods, titans, humans, animals, ghosts, and denizens of hell until they had the good fortune to encounter and put into practice the Buddha's teaching, which would enable them to escape the cycle of rebirth forever. Moreover, as followers of the Mahayana (Great Vehicle), Tibetan Buddhists vowed to keep taking birth out of compassion for all sentient beings until every last one of them was freed. Of the world's religions, they believed that Buddhism alone was capable of bringing suffering to an end. And of the various kinds of Buddhism, the most effective, rapid, and complete of them all was the form of the religion as preserved in Tibet.

I believed all this. Or, more accurately: I *wanted* to believe all this. Never before had I encountered a truth I was willing to lie for. Yet, as I see it now, my lie did not spring from conviction but from a lack of conviction. It was prompted by my craving to believe. Unlike some of my contemporaries, whom I envied, I would never achieve unwavering faith in the traditional Buddhist view of the world. Nor would I ever succeed in replacing my own judgments with uncritical surrender to the authority of a "root" lama, which was indispensable for the practice of the highest tantras, the only way, so it was claimed, to achieve complete enlightenment in this lifetime. No matter how hard I tried to ignore it or rationalize it away, my insincerity kept nagging at me in a dark, closed recess of my mind. By the lights of my Tibetan teachers, I was a Buddhist failure.

# 2

# ON THE ROAD

FROM THE MONK'S cell, hewn out of the sandstone cliff centuries earlier, where I spent my days idly smoking a potent blend of marijuana, hashish, and tobacco, a narrow passage led to a dark inner staircase that I would illuminate by striking matches. The steep rock steps climbed to an opening that brought me out, via a narrow ledge, onto the smooth dome of the giant Buddha's head, which fell away dizzily on all sides to the ground one hundred and eighty feet below. On the ceiling of the niche above were faded fragments of painted Buddhas and bodhisattvas. I feared looking up at them for too long lest I lose my balance, slip, and plummet earthward. As my eyes became used to the fierce sunlight, I would gaze out onto the fertile valley of Bamiyan, a patchwork of fields interspersed with low, flat-roofed farmhouses, which lay stretched before me. It was the summer of 1972. This was my first encounter with the remains of a Buddhist civilization, one that had ended with Mahmud of Ghazni's conquest of Afghanistan in the eleventh century.

Like others on the hippie trail to India, I thought of myself as a traveler rather than a mere tourist, someone on an indeterminate quest rather than a journey with a prescribed beginning and end. Had I been asked what I was seeking, I doubt my answer would have been very coherent. I had no destination, either of the geographical or spiritual kind. I was simply "on the road," in that anarchic and ecstatic sense celebrated by Jack Kerouac, Allen Ginsberg, and other role models I revered at the time.

I enjoyed nothing more than simply being on the way to somewhere else. I was quite content to peer for hours through the grimy, grease-smeared windows of a rattling bus with cooped chickens in the aisle, observing farmers bent over as they toiled in fields, women carrying babies on their backs, barefoot children playing in the dust, old men seated in the shade smoking hookahs, and all the shabby little towns and villages at which we stopped for sweet tea and unleavened bread. Yet as soon as we entered the telltale suburban sprawl of the city of our destination, my stomach would contract and I would feel anxious and restless again. I did not want to stop. My craving to keep moving was like an addiction.

My first memory is that of sitting on my mother's lap, nestled in the folds of her fur coat while peering through an airplane window at the miniature houses and cars of Toronto. I was three years old. My parents had emigrated from Scotland to Canada in 1957 in an attempt to save their marriage. They separated a year later and I returned to England with my mother and younger brother, David, where we grew up in Watford, a charmless suburb on the outer rim of London. My mother did not remarry and raised my brother and me alone. I had no further contact with my father.

We were initially supported by my mother's father, Alfred Craske, a businessman who had a photoengraving firm in Covent Garden. Alfred had rejected the God-fearing atmosphere of his childhood and considered all religion humbug, while his wife, Mabel—my grandmother— was the demure daughter of the local Wesleyan minister. My mother adopted her father's views on religion and considered herself a humanist. Emotionally she remained close to her mother and her mother's sister Sophie, a nurse who had served in the Dardanelles and Flanders, never married, and faithfully attended chapel. In the background hovered the enigmatic shadow of Alfred's younger brother Leonard, who had renounced a promising medical career and a young wife to pursue his passion for theater and sculpture in the United States. The Craskes had nothing further to do with him. A weathered bronze statue of a dancing nymph called "Joy" in our back garden was the only evidence of Leonard's existence.

As a child I did not attend church. I was exempted from "Scripture" classes at the schools I attended, so I did not receive the basic instruction in Christianity that was part of the British educational curriculum. When I was eight or nine, I remember being struck by a BBC radio program that mentioned how Buddhist monks avoided walking on the grass in order not to kill any insects. I have often wondered whether this first positive impression of Buddhist monks played a role in my later adopting Buddhism, or whether I chose to remember it because in retrospect it helped me rationalize the unconventional decision I made to become a Buddhist monk myself.

From an early age I was troubled by how rarely I experienced genuine contentment. I was conscious of how niggling worries were constantly present either in the center or at the periphery of my self-awareness. I remember lying awake at night trying to stop the incessant outpouring of anxious thoughts. I was perplexed by the failure of teachers at school to address what seemed the most urgent matter of all: the bewildering, stomach-churning insecurity of being alive. The standard subjects of history, geography, mathematics, and English seemed perversely designed to ignore the questions that really mattered. As soon as I had some inkling of what "philosophy" meant, I was puzzled as to why we were not taught it. And my skepticism about religion only grew as I failed to see what the vicars and priests I encountered gained from their faith. They struck me either as insincere, pious, and aloof or just bumblingly good-natured.

As the 1960s unfolded, I was magnetically drawn into the counterculture that mocked and rejected the "straight" society of bourgeois, middle-class Britain. For the first time I heard kindred voices express their frustrations and hopes in wistful songs that called for love and freedom and in poorly printed manifestos that incited revolution. And then there were the drugs. Cannabis and LSD provided a more intense and rapturous consciousness than I had ever experienced before. Rather than the dull information gleaned from textbooks, they seemed to offer a direct portal to the shimmering, fractal-unraveling play of life itself. As a pastoral (rather than a cosmic) hippie, I would wander for hours through Whippendell Woods, high on acid, minutely studying spiderwebs and the delicate tracery of leaves, marveling at how a beetle clambered over blades of grass, then lie in meadows gazing at the swirling, paisley-haloed clouds.

My absorption in these extracurricular activities made me more or less abandon my schooling. I nonetheless read voraciously: *The Doors of Perception* by Aldous Huxley; *Steppenwolf, The Glass Bead Game,* and *Siddhartha* by Hermann Hesse; *The Way of Zen* by Alan Watts—while dabbling in the Bhagavad Gita, the Tao Te Ching, and the Tibetan Book of the Dead. I grew my hair long, wore beads, and attended all-night rock concerts with liquid light shows on Parliament Hill Fields, where I would listen to the Soft Machine, Pink Floyd, and the Edgar Broughton Band.

In April 1971, I had a dream within a dream. I had just turned eighteen and was halfheartedly preparing for my A-levels at grammar school. I dreamed that I was camping in France in the rain. When I fell asleep in my tent, I dreamed that I dreamed another dream. This is what I wrote about it:

> A grayish carpet in a never ending hallway started going up, the slope became steeper, soon there were banisters, each made from brass mounted on polished wood. The further it continued, the more difficult it became, until it was nearly perpendicular. It [took] an agonizing force to reach the top, but through determination and self-will he managed to hoist himself up. All there was was a small hallway but the light was strange—it was very white and clean, around him were beautiful vases

all over the floor and in the corner a white spiral staircase, made from wood. He [climbed] it and there was yet another landing, only this time the light was even whiter and more intense, the air remained beautifully pure but began to compress him and overpower him.

He entered a room; in this room there was one bed. He pulled back the coverlet and saw a girl lying there, she was young, not fully developed and naked, the expression on her face was blank and her hair a mouse brown. He put the coverlet back and went out of the room.

He made his way past oriental vases and jewels, past naked eastern princesses, past all forms of earthly temptation and decided to ascend to the next level. This level was more or less the same as the others in appearance, except that the floor was less profusely garnished. There were three or four simple wooden doors. He went into one of these rooms and here the air was practically unbearable, it was deafeningly sweet and intense. The air seemed to be colored crème de menthe and it possessed about an equivalent consistency. The walls were colored with exceedingly pale but naturally bright colors, everything was slightly out of focus and the light and the air seemed to be alive with millions of molecules trying their utmost to split.

Slowly the source of this energy was made apparent, one of the four walls began to open like a massive door, through the ever increasing crack a shaft of golden sun came, until the opening was about three feet wide, then there appeared a man, at least it resembled a man. But this being was amazingly tall and he radiated a kind of supernatural power and glowing radiance of life and light. He was dressed in flowing white robes and a saffron cloak. His hair was tied like Botticelli's Venus.

For some reason, possibly because I submitted this as a writing assignment at school (hence the third person "he"), I did not record what this strange tall man said to me. Yet his words have echoed in my mind as a riddle ever since. They haunt me still, nearly forty years later. He said: "I am making your double." Then I woke up.

I failed all my A-levels except French, thereby losing the place I had been offered at the Regent Street Polytechnic in London to study photography. My mother was distraught. Suddenly I found myself freed from the prospect of returning to the drudgery of another educational institution that autumn. I could still take photographs, yet without the constraint of their having to be judged by an academic system for which I had little respect. I decided to spend a year traveling in Europe, ostensibly to study art and culture, before returning to England to retake the A-levels I needed in order to pursue the course in photography. But I dreaded the idea of further classroom studies and exams. The very thought of pursuing a conventional career depressed me.

Later that summer, an American friend of a friend flew in from California and gave me a copy of the just published *Be Here Now* by "Baba" Ram Dass. Ram Dass, a.k.a. Richard Alpert, had been expelled from Harvard with Timothy Leary in 1963 for providing students with psilocybin. In 1967 he went to India, where he lived for two years with Neem Karoli Baba and other gurus, before returning to the United States and writing an account of his journey from psychedelics to the yogic and devotional practices of Hinduism. For many of my generation, this accessible text, written in comic-book form, provided an important bridge from the mind-scrambled aspirations of the drug culture to the spiritual traditions of Asia.

For the next six months I worked as a cleaner in an asbestos factory until I had saved enough money to be able to flee the British Isles, which I then regarded as the exclusive source of my discontent. I took a map of Europe, closed my eyes, and let my finger fall where it would. It landed near Toulouse in southwest France. I booked a flight there and departed in February 1972. I hitchhiked to Italy, where I dutifully visited famous churches and art galleries in Florence and Rome, but despite the beauty of what I saw, the entire exercise felt hollow and false. I soon abandoned the conceit of pursuing any lofty cultural goals and simply went wherever the next ride was heading. Inevitably, perhaps, I started drifting eastward. From Athens I went to Istanbul, then via southern Turkey into Syria, Lebanon, Israel, and Jordan. I crossed the desert to Baghdad, went south to Basra, then hitched into Iran. I passed through Shiraz, Isfahan, Teheran, and Meshed until I finally reached Afghanistan in June.

The farther east I went, the further I entered into a time that was no longer that of twentieth-century Europe. At two crucial points—when I crossed the Bosporus into Anatolia and the Afghan border into the town of Herat—it felt as though centuries were erased in less than an hour. The retreat from my homeland became a flight into the past, as though the past were a place where nothing could ever go wrong. In Herat, I lay on my hotel bed, delighting in the clip of ponies pulling tongas that rang with a shimmer of bells, the cries of street vendors, and the joyous shrieks of little boys, all entirely cleansed of the background cacophony of motorized traffic. By Western standards the Afghans were poor and "backward," but they possessed a dignity—they did not flinch when you looked them in the eye, they seemed to have nothing to conceal or be ashamed of—that somehow, despite my privileged upbringing, I had never really known.

After seeing the giant Buddhas of Bamiyan, I returned to Kabul and continued east into Pakistan. From Peshawar, my traveling companion Gary Zazula and I rode in a jeep, piled high with swaying bodies and backpacks, to Chitral, a hill town in the Hindu Kush that was still home to a prince, who let us camp in his palace grounds beside the tumultuous river that came down from Mount Tirich Mir. From Chitral, we hiked all day until we reached the remote valleys of Kafiristan, a tribal area without roads, electricity, or Islam, whose people were said to be descendants of the Greeks who passed through there with Alexander the Great. But we miscalculated how long it would take and ran out of water in the heat of midday, just as we reached the pass that looked down on the thin green valley of Bumburet, far below, which wiggled through the barren mountains. After we stumbled and slid down scree to the valley, we were too parched for caution and drank copiously from an irrigation channel. By evening we were violently ill.

There were no doctors, no clinics, no clean water, no sanitation, and hardly any food available in Kafiristan. For days we lay sweating, feverish in a dark, filthy room, getting weaker by the day. We would emerge from our lair only in the cool of evening and sit beneath a mulberry tree, the eagle eye of a mountain peering down upon us, to watch the girls and young women of the valley link arms and sway together, intoning songs, while goitered crones crouched along a mud wall, glancing at us suspiciously. We wondered how on earth we would get out of the place. We lacked the strength to climb back up to the pass. The only alternative was to follow the river downstream to Chitral, but a crucial bridge had been swept away in a recent storm. One morning, a trio of hippies in flowing silks and turbans, their eyes blackened with kohl, appeared in the doorway of our room. The local people had told them that the river path was now passable. To give us the energy to walk back, they handed each of us a small purple pill of LSD, laced with "quite a bit" of speed.

When we reached where the bridge should have been, only the stanchions remained on each bank. The river churned and frothed blithely past toward a narrow defile between two perpendicular walls of rock. We grinned foolishly and stumbled around, trying to gather our splintered senses. As though out of nowhere, a wiry man with sunburnished skin, dressed in a short woolen smock and rough leather sandals, manifested before us. He laughed and beckoned with his staff for us to follow him. He walked straight to the rock face and started climbing nimbly up a barely visible crevice. We dumbly followed. Halfway up, I paused and looked straight down at the river far below. Its waters made only a faint hiss now. I looked up and our guide was gone. We were alone, like two flies with red nylon backpacks stranded on a wall. Then the rock to which I was clinging began to feel very rubbery. I found it hard to distinguish my hands and feet from the cliff face. I was fascinated to see how my limbs seemed to be merging with the stone. Then, with a sickening jolt, I knew that I was just about to die. I saw myself peel away from the cliff and slip downward, mouth agape.

After what felt like an eternity, our savior's head reappeared. He climbed down and helped each of us, step by trembling step, to reach the top. Still shaking with fear, we thanked him profusely. He smiled, waved, and trotted off ahead of us. It was shortly after this, as we were walking slowly back to Chitral, that Zazula remarked, "It's like the Buddha said. Life is suffering." Despite all we had just been through, I was troubled. My limited reading about Buddhism had somehow failed to impress this point upon me. I found the remark puzzling and shocking, true but unacceptable. It aroused in me, for the first time, a curiosity to know what this man, the Buddha, had meant.

I arrived in India at the end of August. From the border city of Amritsar, I went straight up into the mountains, to Dharamsala, where I had heard the Dalai Lama lived in exile with his community of fellow Tibetans. It was still monsoon season. Clouds drifted up from the plains, enveloping the trees and paths in mist. As I walked into the quiet, sleepy village of McLeod Ganj, the white dome of a stupa, from which clanged an intermittent bell, loomed into view. Stooped Tibetan women with colorful aprons and plaited braids of wispy hair circumambulated this architectural symbol of enlightenment, turning creaking prayer wheels mounted in its wall.

A couple of days later, I attended the weekly audience with the Dalai Lama. About fifteen of us lined up before the steps of his green-roofed residence on a hillock below McLeod Ganj. There were some Tibetans from other settlements in India, dressed in all their finery and holding silk scarves to offer to His Holiness, along with a cluster of fidgeting, unkempt Westerners. The young Dalai Lama suddenly appeared and came down to greet us, arms outstretched, smiling and chuckling. His eyes darted from person to person. He seemed intensely curious about each one of us. Having accepted and returned the scarves to the Tibetans, some of whom were now sobbing uncontrollably, he turned to the foreigners. "Where you come from?" he asked. We dutifully mumbled the name of a country until the long-haired man with a stoned grin at the end of the line blurted: "That's what I came here to find out, man!" Puzzled, the Dalai Lama asked for a translation, then erupted with laughter as he clasped the hippie's hands in his own. "Ho! ho! Very good. Very good." I was smitten. I had imagined that he would be a remote and severe prelate, not this joyous vortex of intelligent calm.

My wanderings came to a halt. My brush with sickness and death had unnerved me. I had a disquieting need to think about what this brief, fragile existence was for. On September 4, I enrolled in Geshe Dhargyey's two-month introductory class on Buddhism at the Library of Tibetan Works and Archives.

My conversion to Buddhism was more or less immediate. I did not have to be persuaded either by philosophical arguments or religious polemics. Geshe Dhargyey radiated a kindness that was neither pious nor patronizing. He could be stern one moment, only to burst into peals of laughter the next. He seemed to care unconditionally about me, a complete stranger from a distant land about which he knew nothing. What I heard him say, often in a garbled translation, instinctively rang true. I had found someone who talked without reservation or embarrassment about what mattered most to me. The word *dharma,* he explained, came from the Sanskrit root *dhr-:* "to hold." The teachings of the Buddha were like a safety net that "held" one from falling into hell and other painful realms. I may have had doubts about the literal existence of hell, but I had little doubt that my life was in a kind of free fall.

Throughout this time my camera and lenses had lain untouched in the bottom of my rucksack. The journey to India had opened my eyes to the world in ways that I could not capture on film. With Geshe Dhargyey's encouragement, I found myself peering into the invisible regions of my soul, where art appeared to have little purchase. So I decided to sell my photographic equipment in order to help finance my studies in Dharamsala. I shot off a last roll of film, then gave the camera to my friend Ray James to sell on the black market in Delhi. Before he could find a buyer it was stolen from his room in a cheap hotel in Pahar Ganj.

It was not only Geshe Dhargyey who impressed me. I was moved by the faith and courage of the ordinary Tibetan men and women, who lived in shacks made from discarded slats of wood and flattened cooking-oil cans and survived by working on road gangs and selling sweaters donated by Western charities to the Indians. They had followed the Dalai Lama over the Himalayas into India with little more than the clothes they wore, many were sick and exhausted, all had found it hard to tolerate the heat and humidity of the plains. Now they lived in poverty in one of the poorest countries of the world. But despite all of this, they radiated an extraordinary warmth, lucidity, and joie de vivre.

Much of what animated me in those days I now recognize as the romantic yearnings of an idealistic, alienated, and aimless young man. I endowed these strange, exotic people, about whom I knew little, with all the virtues that my own culture seemed to lack. Having been raised by a single mother, I suspect I was also searching for an absent father. Yet at the core of my muddled quest lay a quiet certainty that I had stumbled across something authentic and true, which I could neither doubt nor adequately name. For the first time in my life, I had encountered a path: a purposive trajectory that led from bewilderment and anguish to something called "enlightenment." Although I had only the dimmest idea of what "enlightenment" might mean, I embraced the path toward it.

# 3

# THE SEMINARIAN

I RENTED A disused cowshed with a slate roof and crumbling walls on a terrace below Glenmore, a grand but neglected Raj-era house in the forest near McLeod Ganj. I cut off my shoulder-length hair, which had become infested with lice, reduced my consumption of hashish, bought a set of prayer beads, and started to decipher the Tibetan alphabet. I made an altar out of an old fruit box, on which I placed a cheap Buddha statue and, propped up alongside it, curling black-and-white photographs of the Dalai Lama, his senior and junior tutors, and Geshe Dhargyey. Each morning I would fill seven brass bowls with water and offer these, together with a butter lamp and stick of incense, to the Buddhas and bodhisattvas of the ten directions. I became, almost overnight, a rather devout and serious seminarian. Reciting mantras, with books and a wooden writing board in a bag slung over one shoulder, I would skip down the steep, stony path to the Library and sit cross-legged all morning before Geshe Dhargyey, frantically transcribing whatever he said. Each afternoon I would trade English for Tibetan lessons in the village, then return to my cowshed to study my notes by the sooty light of a kerosene lamp, memorize vocabulary, and experiment with meditation.

I learned that human life was exceedingly rare to come by. According to Geshe-la, the chance of taking a human rebirth was as remote as that of a blind turtle who surfaces only once in a hundred years inserting its neck through a golden yoke being tossed about on the surface of the oceans. Of all the possible forms in which one can be reborn, the human is the most precious, since it alone provides the leisure and opportunity to practice the Dharma, which shows the path that leads to the end of suffering. Yet this human life is short and can end abruptly at any moment. There is thus an urgent need to gather all one's energies and focus them unwaveringly on the task of achieving enlightenment, not just for yourself, but for all living creatures who suffer just as you do.

The passionate conviction with which Geshe Dhargyey delivered these teachings instilled in me a fervor to realize their truth for myself. The Dharma revealed new and unsuspected vistas. My existence was so much more than this brief, tragic span of life on earth. The consciousness that animated me had been drifting through the rounds of birth and death since beginningless time. I had been a god, a titan, an animal, a man, a woman, a bird, an insect, a ghost, a hell-being incalculable times. Now I had met, perhaps for the first time in eons, a teacher who could show me the way out of this cycle of repetitive existence, which, despite all its highs and lows, in the end leads nowhere. One needs, therefore, not only to abandon all interest in the transient joys of this life, but also in the rewards of heaven that come from living virtuously. Thus one aspires for nirvana, the final "blowing out" of the ignorance and craving that trigger the acts that propel one through the frustrating rounds of rebirth.

By meditating daily on these ideas, by turning them around in my mind and considering them from different angles, I was encouraged to ask in all seriousness what this life is for, what matters most for myself and others, what non-negotiable values I might even be willing to die for. At the same time, I started to notice the poignant ephemerality of things. I sensed the immanence of death in my bones. I felt the urgency of knowing that this day on earth might be my last. Yet rather than making me gloomy and morbid, such reflections intensified my sense of being alive. They induced a kind of rapture, which snapped me out of the dull routines of the familiar and confronted me with the miracle of life as it unfolds and vanishes each instant. I imbibed the teachings like a man parched with thirst would drink fresh water. Never before had I been asked to dwell on these existential and moral issues. Now I had encountered a tradition that not only gave them great importance but provided a systematic methodology to focus upon them in such a way that they penetrated to the core of my self-awareness.

Geshe Dhargyey taught that each living creature had, at one moment or other in the course of its infinite lifetimes, been my mother. How could I contemplate freeing myself from the round of repeated existence if those who had nourished me as a baby, sacrificed their well-being for my sake, still remained trapped in the vicious cycle of birth and death? Surely I had an obligation to repay such kindness, and how better to do that than by attaining enlightenment not for my sake but for *theirs*. For if I genuinely wished to alleviate their suffering, I needed to show them a path that leads to the end of rebirth and hence the end of pain. Yet to be able to guide someone else along such a path required that I had reached its goals myself. Therefore, I needed to dedicate my life to realizing enlightenment for "all mother sentient beings" and not relax my efforts until each one of them, without exception, was liberated from birth and death. This is the bodhisattva vow, the altruistic commitment that animates Mahayana (Great Vehicle) Buddhism as opposed to the Hinayana ("Inferior Vehicle"), which leads merely to one's own personal salvation.

I was humbled and inspired by this vision of universal, selfless compassion. It gave me a deep sense of purpose, a vocation that extended infinitely beyond the confines of this existence into the myriad lifetimes that lay ahead. So in the presence of Geshe Dhargyey, I took the bodhisattva vow and pledged myself to banish a self-cherishing attitude and dedicate myself eternally to the welfare of others.

It was this selfless commitment, I realized, that had given the Tibetans the courage to face and overcome the hardships of their recent history. They did not seem unduly oppressed by their exile. They had lost everything, but they were far from defeated. They were sustained by a grander, vaster vision of what life could be. No matter how unbearable at times were the travails of this unjust world, they faded to insignificance when compared to the sufferings of all beings throughout endless time and space.

In order to become a Buddha as quickly and effectively as possible, the Tibetans practice a unique body of teachings inherited from India called the "Diamond Vehicle" (Vajrayana, i.e., tantric Buddhism). Unlike the Buddha's sutras, which were discourses given to the general public, the tantras were taught only to select disciples. These were secret teachings, which to receive and practice one had to be "empowered" by a qualified tantric master, who in turn had been empowered by an unbroken lineage of teachers going back to the Buddha himself. The highest class of tantra entailed imagining oneself as "a god" at the heart of a resplendent mandala, thereby replacing one's "ordinary perception" of being a mundane ego with the "divine pride" of being a fully enlightened Buddha. Once this perceptual transformation was achieved, one could then proceed with the actual transformation of oneself into a Buddha by means of yogic practices involving subtle energies, nerve channels, and chakras. Having taken the bodhisattva vow and come to an adequate understanding of the sutra teachings, we were strongly encouraged to receive a tantric empowerment in order to enter the "swift path" to complete enlightenment.

After I had been a year or so in Dharamsala, Geshe Dhargyey arranged for a group of us to receive the tantric empowerment of Yamantaka from Tsenshap Serkong Rinpoche, one of the senior advisors to the Dalai Lama. Serkong Rinpoche was a serene old lama with sparkling eyes set in a face like cracked earth, who lived in a bungalow below the McLeod Ganj post office with two attendants and a cook. The empowerment took several hours and entailed much visualization, chanting, ringing of bells, and rattling of hand drums. Once initiated into the mandala of Yamantaka, I solemnly undertook to recite daily for the rest of my life the text that described the generation of myself into this tantric god. Henceforth, every morning I would become the glorious and mighty bull-headed Yamantaka:

> with a dark azure body, nine faces, thirty-four arms, and sixteen legs, of which the right are drawn in and the left extended. My tongue curls upward, my fangs are bared, my face is wrinkled with anger, my orange hair bristles upward. . . . I devour human blood, fat, marrow, and lymph. My head is crowned with five frightful dried skulls and I am adorned with a garland of fifty moist human heads. I wear a black snake as a brahmin's thread. I am naked, my belly is huge and my penis erect. My eyebrows, eyelashes, beard, and body hair blaze like the fire at the end of time.

Over the following months, I received further empowerments from Serkong Rinpoche, Trijang Rinpoche—the Dalai Lama's junior tutor— and the Dalai Lama himself. I soon had to spend at least an hour a day reciting ritual texts in order to honor the commitments I had taken.

I became totally absorbed in the world of Tibetan Buddhism. The Dharma was the one thing that mattered to me. I had convinced myself that this path was the only way to realize the full potential of a human life. In order to receive these empowerments, I had to regard the officiating lama not as an ordinary human being, but as a living Buddha, a perfect embodiment of enlightenment, who had taken birth in this world solely out of compassion for deluded creatures like myself. I had to acknowledge any fault I saw in him as my own negative projection, the consequence of my impure view that obscured his radiant perfection. I took a vow never to disparage such a teacher. To break my tantric commitment to him would result in rebirth in the worst of all possible hells. For solely through the inspiration and blessings of these extraordinary men was progress along the path to enlightenment made possible.

My decision to become a monk was a natural outcome of this passionate dedication to Buddhism. For a young man without any ties or responsibilities, who wanted to focus his life entirely on the Dharma, a life of monastic simplicity, celibacy, and abstinence provided the optimal environment for study, reflection, and meditation. When I first asked Geshe Dhargyey to ordain me shortly after my twentieth birthday, he refused. He sent me away to reflect more carefully before taking such a step. A year later, I asked him again. This time he accepted. So I shaved my head, leaving a little tuft to be symbolically cut off during the ceremony, and had a set of robes made by a tailor in McLeod Ganj. In the presence of five fully ordained monks, I was ordained as a novice (*sramanera*) at three p.m. on June 6, 1974, in Geshe Dhargyey's private quarters at the Library of Tibetan Works and Archives. I had just turned twenty-one. I had been a Buddhist for less than two years. Now I was a shaven-headed, red-robed, celibate renunciant.

Although I wrote to my mother regularly from Dharamsala, I said nothing about my deepening personal engagement with Buddhism. As far as she knew, I was pursuing a rather eccentric course of academic field study in a Tibetan refugee settlement in India. She was glad that I had at last found something to engage my interest and relieved that I was no longer drifting through Asia taking drugs. Her main concern was where these studies would lead in terms of my finding a respectable career. She had no inkling at all of what I was planning to do. A couple of days before receiving ordination, I wrote her a long letter explaining the step I was about to take, justifying myself in the jargon of Buddhist doctrine, which I guiltily knew would mean little if anything to her. By the time she received the letter, I was already in robes. On hearing the news, she said: "My heart sank into my feet."

But I was a monk without a monastery. Except for the Namgyal Dratsang, the elite monastic community that served the Dalai Lama, there were no monasteries in Dharamsala. Each monk had to fend for himself. Apart from my change in dress and hairstyle, outwardly my daily life remained much the same as before. Once I was used to my new role and others ceased to comment on it, I realized that little had changed inside as well. I was still the same person, subject to the same emotions, longings, and anxieties. Unshaven and unwashed, I would walk through McLeod Ganj with grim determination, my eyes nailed to a point on the ground six feet in front of me, desperately trying not to notice the hippie girls in their diaphanous dresses. The inwardness of monasticism appealed to me; it seemed to legitimate my growing tendency toward introspection and solitude.

Three months after becoming a monk, I participated in a ten-day Vipassana retreat conducted by the Indian teacher S. N. Goenka, which was held in the Library. Mr. Goenka, a successful businessman who had been born and raised in Mandalay, had learned Vipassana meditation from U Ba Khin, a minister in the first independent Burmese government. He was fifty years old, with heavy jowls and a deep bass voice, and sat cross-legged in a sarong beside his wife, who never said a word. I have no idea why this "Hinayana" meditation course came to replace the daily classes at a Mahayana Buddhist institute, but it seemed to have had the backing of the Dalai Lama. Geshe Dhargyey took the opportunity to go to the hot springs in Manali for the duration of the retreat.

For the first three days, we concentrated on the inflow and outflow of breathing, gradually narrowing attention to the sensation of the breath as it touched the upper lip. This served to focus concentration. For the remaining seven days we slowly "swept" the body for sensations, going from the crown of the head to the tips of the toes and then back again. When doing this "body-sweeping," we gave particular attention to the impermanence of every sensation. After doing this exercise for several hours a day in an atmosphere of complete silence, with only one pithy talk each evening, I came to experience myself in a way I never had before.

Without relying on any deities, mantras, or mandalas, without having to master the intricacies of any doctrine or philosophy, I vividly understood what it meant to be a fragile, impermanent creature in a fragile, impermanent world. The mindfulness sharpened my attention to everything that was going on within and around me. My body became a tingling, pulsing mass of sensations. At times when I sat outside I felt as though the breeze were blowing through me. The sheen of the grass was more brilliant, the rustling leaves were like a chorus in an endlessly unfolding symphony. At the same time there was a deep stillness and poise at the core of this vital awareness. The experience did not last in all its intensity for very long. Once the course was finished, more mundane habits of mind took over again. But I had been shown a way to know what I would now understand as the contingent ground of life itself. For this, I am forever grateful to Mr. Goenka.

My encounter with Vipassana was entirely fortuitous. Had it not been presented on my doorstep in the Tibetan institution where I was studying, I doubt that at the time I would have sought it out elsewhere. The retreat opened up the first crack in the edifice of my faith in Tibetan Buddhism. Mr. Goenka had been trained in the Burmese Theravada school, which is based on the teachings of the Pali Canon. It soon became clear that the Tibetan canon, which, I had been assured, contained every single discourse the Buddha ever gave, lacks the majority of texts preserved in Pali, including *The Discourse on the Grounding of Mindfulness (Satipatthana Sutta)*, on which Mr. Goenka based his teaching.

After my encounter with Vipassana, I briefly considered going to a monastery in Burma, Thailand, or Sri Lanka to develop this practice further. Yet my commitment to the tradition in which I had been ordained as a monk and initiated into the Vajrayana remained strong, as did my devotion to my Tibetan teachers. I also realized that the effectiveness of Mr. Goenka's mindfulness practice was to some extent due to all the reflections I had done on the foundations of Buddhism under the guidance of Geshe Dhargyey. Before going off to explore another form of Buddhism, I realized that I needed to be more fully grounded in the one to which I already belonged. Nonetheless, the worm of doubt had started quietly burrowing its way inside me.

Those of us who ended up in Dharamsala in the early 1970s found ourselves transported back to an intact pocket of medieval Tibet, a society
almost untouched by modernity, which had preserved entire traditions
of Indian Buddhist logic, epistemology, philosophy, psychology, meditation, medicine, astrology, and art. It was as though a group of Italian
hippies had wandered off into the Apennines and discovered in a remote valley a fully functioning papal court of the fourteenth century
that had somehow been bypassed by history. The axis of the entire
community was the Dalai Lama himself, who was charged with the
daunting task of overseeing the settlement of one hundred thousand
refugees in India, while bringing the tragic plight of Tibet to the world's
attention.

But the world ignored him. When I arrived in Dharamsala in 1972
he had been neither to Europe nor America. After President Nixon's
historic visit to China in February of that year, what little support the
United States had provided to the Tibetans was cut off. Stranded in
India, with no influential friends, the Dalai Lama could only listen in
horror as news trickled across the border of the wanton destruction of
his country at the hands of the Red Guards. Although he was invited to
London and other European capitals in 1974, he had to wait until
1979—a full twenty years after fleeing Tibet—before the U.S. State
Department, under the Carter administration, agreed to issue him a
visa and face the wrath of China for "interfering in the internal affairs
of the Motherland."

In the autumn of 1974, I was among a small group of students
from the Library who met with the Dalai Lama to seek his advice on a
project to translate Shantideva's eighth-century *A Guide to the Bodhisattva's Way of Life (Bodhicaryavatara)*, a classic text of Indian Mahayana Buddhism much loved by the Tibetans. His Holiness was
enthusiastic about the idea and encouraged us to go ahead. For the
next year, Geshe Dhargyey went painstakingly through this text in Tibetan, explaining each word and line, thus providing a solid foundation
on which to produce an English translation.

Little is known about Shantideva, the enigmatic and anarchic author of this text. He probably lived during the eighth century CE in India and is believed to have composed his *Guide* while he was a monk at the renowned monastic university of Nalanda, the greatest center of Buddhist learning in Asia at the time. According to legend, Shantideva was reputed to be an idler, whose only activities were "eating, sleeping and shitting." In order to purge the monastery of such wastrels a public examination was held to test the knowledge and competence of each monk. Those who failed would then be expelled. When it came to Shantideva's turn, he mounted the teaching podium and, to everyone's surprise, recited by heart this highly original and poetic Sanskrit text. As he neared the end of his recitation he began to levitate until, his voice growing fainter, he disappeared into the clouds. Although the monks from Nalanda eventually tracked him down, he refused to return to the monastery and lived the rest of his life in obscurity as a layman.

Unlike many classical Buddhist writings, which tend to be somewhat dry and abstract, Shantideva's *Guide* is an intensely personal account of a struggle to understand and practice the Dharma. Speaking in the first person, Shantideva has no illusions about his own shortcomings. Rather than presenting the path as a trajectory of incremental self-improvement, he appreciates how it swerves unevenly from joy to despondency, how the darkest confusion can be illuminated by moments of clarity, how the pain of a stranger can suddenly feel as real as your own—yet a moment later be forgotten in a fresh surge of narcissism. I found this reassuring. It corresponded to my own experience, which sat uncomfortably with the calibrated hierarchy of "spiritual development" as propounded in most Buddhist texts. Vacillation and doubt seemed locked in a perennial struggle with faith and conviction. As a monk, I had very few avenues of escape from this dilemma. I was obliged to stay seated on this bucking horse, no matter how much it tormented and exhausted me.

Shantideva's *Guide,* in its verses and through the author's own example, offers a vision of the kind of human character best suited to the task of responding effectively to one's own and others' suffering. This character is a sensibility that eludes simple definition, and it is precisely what had struck me most about the Dalai Lama. On reflection I realized that I admired him not because he possessed a particular spiritual quality, such as "compassion" or "wisdom." I had observed how he had a capacity to respond to diverse situations with an integrity and spontaneity that issued from the totality of who he was. At the heart of this sensibility lay a deep empathy for the plight of others, which seemed to pour forth from him effortlessly and abundantly. According to Shantideva, such empathy requires that one undergo a radical emptying of self, so that instead of experiencing oneself as a fixed, detached ego, one comes to see how one is inextricably enmeshed in the fabric of the world.

The self does not exist "from its own side," as the Tibetans say, as an object that can be isolated and defined. The more you search for it, whether through meditation, philosophical inquiry, psychological analysis, or dissection of the brain, you will not, in the end, discover any "thing" that corresponds to it. Nonetheless, this is not to deny that a self exists. It exists, but not in the way we instinctively feel it to exist. An empty self is a changing, evolving, functional, and moral self. In fact—and this is the twist—if the self were *not* empty in this way, it would be unable to do anything. For such a hypothetical self would be utterly disassociated from everything in the living world, existing in a purely metaphysical sphere, incapable of either acting or being acted upon.

I spent much of my last year in Dharamsala studying the Buddhist doctrine of emptiness in Shantideva's *Guide* and its Tibetan commentaries. I could theoretically grasp what "emptiness" meant, but this had little if any impact on the actual experience of being me. Then one hot afternoon after class I was sitting cross-legged in the shade of a tree beneath the Library, alternately gazing out over the hazy plains and trying to meditate. All of a sudden I found myself plunged into the intense, unraveling cascade of life itself. That opaque and sluggish sense of myself, which invariably greeted me each time I closed my eyes to meditate, had given way to something extraordinarily rich and fluid. It was as though someone had released a brake that had been preventing a motor from turning and suddenly the whole vehicle sprang into throbbing life. Yet it was utterly silent and still. I was collapsing and disintegrating, yet simultaneously emerging and reconstituting. There was an unmistakable sense of proceeding along a trajectory, but without any actual movement at all. Whether during or shortly after this experience, which may not have lasted more than a few seconds, I recall saying to myself: "I will never arrive at something. I will never arrive at nothing. Emptiness is the infinity of things."

It reminded me of a time—I would have been five or six years old— at the edge of the Sarratt village pond, holding my mother's hand. "Imagine there is a frog three feet from the bank," she said. "If each jump it takes is always half as long as the one before, how many jumps would it take the frog to reach the water?" This child's version of Zeno's paradox, enhanced by Mr. Goenka's collapsing impermanence and the Buddhist doctrine of emptiness, was, I now realized, a premonition of "the infinity of things."

By this time I was living in an outbuilding of Elysium House, a former British estate high up on the forested ridge of hills above McLeod Ganj. I loved the bracing mountain air, the troops of black-faced langur monkeys, the blue and white Himalayan magpies. Nearby, in a small hut, lived Geshe Rabten, a teacher with whom I had been studying and whom I greatly admired. I would soon follow him to Switzerland in order to pursue a training in Buddhist philosophy. Elysium House was also the base in Dharamsala for a small community of Vipassana meditators with whom I would sit morning and evening, watching my breath and sweeping my body from head to toe.

One evening at dusk, as I was returning to my room along a narrow path through the pine forest, carrying a blue plastic bucket slopping with water that I had just collected from a nearby source, I was abruptly brought to a halt by the upsurge of an overpowering sense of the sheer strangeness of everything. It was as though I had been lifted onto the crest of a great wave that rose from the ocean of life itself, allowing me for the first time to be struck by how mysterious it was that anything existed at all rather than nothing. "How," I asked myself, "can a person be unaware of *this*? How can anyone pass their life without responding to *this*? Why have I not noticed *this* until now?" I remember standing still, trembling and dumb, with tears in my eyes. Then I continued on my way before night fell.

This experience made me uncomfortably aware of a chasm between what I was studying and something that had happened to me in my own life that struck me as vitally important. The Buddhist texts with which I was familiar did not seem to speak about, let alone value, such experiences as the one that had just shuddered through me. I found it difficult to find any words in Tibetan to express it. And when I described it to the English-speaking Lama Yeshe—a charismatic disciple of Geshe Rabten who had a large following of Westerners in Nepal—he seemed neither to grasp what I was talking about nor why I would accord it any significance. To what should I have given greater authority? The sacred writings of Buddhism as taught to me by men for whom I had enormous respect? Or my own visceral intuitions, which rather than providing answers, seemed only to raise more questions? I believed (or wanted to believe) that the apparent conflict between the two would be resolved if only I dedicated myself long and hard enough to my studies and training. As a young Western novice of twenty-three, I was inclined to trust more in the wisdom of the tradition than in my own imperfect understanding.

# 4

# EEL WRIGGLING

GESHE RABTEN HAD a face like chiseled rock. When you entered his room, he would be seated on his bed, swaying slightly from side to side, his fingers turning the beads of a rosary. Then he would look up and his eyes would pierce you like cold steel. He unnerved me; I felt incapable of hiding anything from him. The last word anyone would use to describe Geshe was *empty*. But that is what he taught us: that the person is nothing but a fleeting configuration of the fugitive elements of body and mind; that there is nothing substantial to it, nothing enduring, nothing constant. Yet Geshe was the very embodiment of substance and constancy. This was a man who had endured and gave every impression of intending to endure.

When I asked whether I could come to Switzerland to study Buddhist philosophy with him, he looked at me with a long, quizzical gaze, then grunted his assent. Geshe had a mission. He was going to establish in the materialistic West a monastic community that would uphold the true word of the Buddha as it had been passed down to him through an unbroken lineage of enlightened teachers. We compared him to Atisha, the Indian abbot who had brought Buddhism to Tibet in the eleventh century. Geshe wanted to found a community modeled on his own monastic college of Sera Je in Lhasa, Tibet. I was to be part of a small group of specialists, a Jesuitical vanguard, my mind honed by the subtleties of dialectics, primed to spread the Dharma in Europe and beyond. We would be expected to memorize texts, receive oral instruction, study commentaries, and debate the meaning of it all in Tibetan (a language I was still struggling to master). Geshe had the reputation of a first-class debater. At Sera, he would debate all night until his hands were chapped and bleeding from the cold. In Dharamsala, he had been appointed as the Dalai Lama's philosophical assistant and debating partner.

The scholarly Geluk tradition of Tibetan Buddhism, to which Geshe belonged, maintained that through the study of formal logic and the practice of debate, one could achieve rational certainty about such key Buddhist doctrines as karma and rebirth. I hoped that this training would resolve my remaining doubts about these issues and provide a sound intellectual basis for my vocation as a Buddhist monk. "Just as a goldsmith assays gold, by rubbing, cutting, and burning," says an oft-cited passage attributed to the Buddha, "so should you examine my words. Do not accept them just out of faith in me." This openness to critical inquiry struck me then, as it does now, as central to the entire Buddhist endeavor. Moreover, since such inquiry was seen, together with meditation and ethics, as part of the path to awakening, it ceased to be an academic exercise in logic-chopping. I found this approach highly appealing. Buddhism, it seemed, was a rational religion, whose truth-claims could withstand the test of reason.

I spent five years in Europe under Geshe Rabten's guidance, mainly in Tharpa Choeling, the monastery he founded in the Swiss village of Le Mont-Pèlerin, above the town of Vevey, overlooking Lake Geneva and the mountains of the Rhône Valley. For the first two years our group of a dozen monks and laymen studied a simplified version of the philosophy of Dharmakirti, a seventh-century Indian scholar-monk whose work, in Tibetan monasteries, provides the foundation in logic, epistemology, and critical analysis, upon which one then advances to the Madhyamaka (Middle Way) philosophy of emptiness.

The more I learned of Dharmakirti's approach, the more I appreciated its down-to-earth clarity and rigor. Unlike later Buddhist thinkers, who tended toward a mystical idealism, I found Dharmakirti to be realistic and pragmatic. His philosophy gave me an excellent conceptual framework for interpreting my practice of mindfulness as well as the other experiences I had had in Dharamsala.

Rather than saying that ultimately everything was empty of inherent existence, as I had been taught until then, Dharmakirti maintained that the changing, functional, causal, and conditioned world, present to ordinary sensory and mental experience, was what was ultimately real. To be real, in Dharmakirti's terms, means to be capable of producing effects in the concrete world. Thus a seed, a jug, wind in the trees, a desire, a thought, the pain in one's knees, another person: these are what are real. Emptiness of inherent existence, by contrast, is just a conceptual and linguistic abstraction. It may serve as a strategic idea, but it lacks the vital reality of a rosebud, the beating of one's heart, or a crying child. The aim of meditation, for Dharmakirti, was not to gain mystical insight into emptiness, but to arrive at an unfiltered experience of the fluctuating, contingent, and suffering world.

What prevents you from experiencing the world in such a way? The problem lies in the instinctive human conviction that one is a permanent, partless, and autonomous self, essentially disconnected from and unaffected by flux and contingency. This conviction may provide a sense of security and permanence in an insecure and impermanent world, but the price one pays is that of alienation, disenchantment, and boredom. One feels cut off from the life around oneself, adrift in a self-referring world of one's own imagining. For Dharmakirti, however, the point is not to dwell on the absence or emptiness of such a disconnected ego, but to encounter the phenomenal world in all its vitality and immediacy once such a conception of self begins to fade.

I can best illustrate this with an example. When my wife and I bought our house in France, a large wooden shed stood in the garden just behind the house itself. The shed cut out the light and blocked the view. Moreover, it had become overgrown with honeysuckle and ivy, so that its size increased year by year, darkening the shadow it cast and increasing the rank humidity in the passage between it and the house. It was packed with obsolete German industrial machinery that had not been touched in decades. Its only virtue, and the main argument for keeping it, was that the local feral cats used it as a place to have their kittens.

Finally, we got rid of the shed. Once that year's batch of kittens was gone, we sold the machinery as scrap metal and invited our friend Paco, who needed the wood, to dismantle it. In the course of an afternoon, something that had been such a gloomy presence for so long was suddenly not there anymore. For the next few days, I would stand where it had once stood and consciously delight in its absence. The dark, dank passage it created had vanished. House and garden were transformed. Light poured into the downstairs windows, and hitherto unknown vistas of the garden and surrounding countryside opened up.

After a few days, the rapturous experience of "no shed" faded. I forgot about the shed that had once been there and was no longer struck by its absence. I simply attended to the garden and house as they now were. For Dharmakirti, the experience of "emptiness" or "not-self" is like this. To realize the absence of a permanent, partless, autonomous ego enables hitherto unknown vistas in one's life to open up. The dark, opaque perspective of self-centeredness gives way to a more luminous and sensitized awareness of the shifting, contingent processes of body and mind. Once one gets used to this, one ceases to notice the absence of such a self. It is replaced by another way of living in this world with others, which, after a while, becomes entirely unremarkable. To keep insisting on "emptiness" as something sacred and special would be like erecting a shrine in the garden to the absence of the shed instead of getting on with the gardening.

I greatly enjoyed these studies. Geshe Rabten communicated the ideas clearly and succinctly, then had us divide into pairs to pick apart in debate the details of what he had just taught. This was an excellent intellectual discipline. It made me aware of how much of my thinking was muddled. Without subjecting one's ideas to such scrutiny, it is easy and reassuring to cherish opinions that, in the end, are found to rest on the sloppiest of unexamined assumptions. This training in philosophical analysis, however, was a two-edged sword. It only worked up to a point. As soon as it encountered a Buddhist belief that did not stand up so well to its critique, it risked undermining one's faith. I could not have foreseen then, at the height of my enthusiasm for Dharmakirti, how a few months later I would be waking up in the middle of the night in a cold sweat, agonizing about whether the primary cause of a mental state was necessarily another mental state.

This crisis erupted because, when we finally came to the proof for rebirth, I was not at all convinced by it. Here it is:

> *subject:* the mind of a baby that has just been born
> *predicate:* existed previously
> *reason:* because it is a mind
> *example:* like this mind

Mind, for Dharmakirti, is said to be "clear and knowing." *Clear* means that mind has no material properties: it cannot be seen, heard, smelled, tasted, or touched. Yet the mind is not a mere abstraction either, for it has the capacity to know things, initiate acts, and is thus capable of producing effects in the world. Being by nature immaterial, mind cannot, in principle, be produced by something material, such as a body or a brain. Therefore, the mind of a newborn baby must have come from a previous continuum of mind; it cannot have emerged out of mindless physical causes alone.

I was skeptical. Given current scientific knowledge of the brain, I did not find it difficult to believe that such an organ was capable of producing thoughts, feelings, and perceptions. That seemed an entirely reasonable hypothesis to explain the origin of mental phenomena. Yet

Dharmakirti does not even mention the brain. He has no knowledge of it at all. When pressed as to how one could know with certainty that mind is immaterial and thus only capable of being produced by a previous immaterial mind, Geshe Rabten replied that in advanced states of meditation one came to know this directly, through one's own first-hand experience. Thus the "proof" of rebirth rested on a subjective experience of a non-physical entity in a non-ordinary state of awareness. If you lack such an experience yourself, then you have to trust the word of meditators more accomplished than oneself.

But if the proof of rebirth finally depends on having faith in the reports made by others of their subjective experiences, then how is it any different from claiming that God exists because mystics—why would they lie?—claim to have had direct experience of God? On what grounds should I choose to believe a Buddhist meditator rather than a Christian mystic or, for that matter, someone who claims to have been abducted by aliens and taken to a spaceship docked behind Alpha Centauri? All may be equally moral, sincere, and honest people, passionately convinced in the truth of what they have experienced, but their claims are going to persuade only those who are already predisposed to believe them.

Why does all this matter so much? Why did it cause me so many sleepless nights? It matters because the entire edifice of traditional Buddhist thought stands or falls on the belief in rebirth. If there was no rebirth, then why would one expend any effort in trying to liberate oneself from the cycle of birth and death and attain nirvana, the final aim of Buddhism? If there was no rebirth, then how would moral acts that do not ripen before one's death ever bear their fruits? In such a case, provided you were not caught and punished in this life, you could get away with murder without ever having to face its consequences. If there was no rebirth, why would you vow to attain enlightenment for the sake of all sentient beings, a task that will take endless lifetimes to complete? If there was no rebirth, then what does it mean to say that the Dalai Lama is the fourteenth reincarnation in a line of Tibetan monks, the first of whom was born in 1391? If there was no rebirth, why did generations of supposedly enlightened Buddhist teachers say that there was?

Yet for rebirth to be possible, something must survive the death of the body and brain. To survive physical death, this "something" must not only be non-physical but also capable of storing the "seeds" of previously committed moral acts (karma) that will "ripen" in future lifetimes. Since Buddhists reject the existence of a permanent self that persists from life to life, they posit an impermanent, non-physical mental process to account for what is reborn. This unavoidably leads to a body-mind dualism. Dharmakirti's "clear and knowing mind" that inhabits a material body seems no different from Descartes's *res cogitans* (a knowing entity) that inhabits a *res extensa* (an extended entity, i.e., a body).

How can such an immaterial mind ever connect with a material body? Being immaterial, it cannot be seen, heard, smelled, tasted, or *touched*. If it is untouchable, how can it "touch" or have any contact with a brain? How does it connect to a neuron or a neuron connect to it? In the Hollywood movie *Ghost,* there is a chase sequence in which the hero (a disembodied ghost) leaps through a moving subway train in order to escape his pursuer and lands safely on the opposite platform. But if he can move unobstructed through a train, I wondered, why doesn't he just keep moving unobstructed through the concrete platform? What possible resistance can a material object ever present to an immaterial one? A non-physical mind would have exactly the same difficulty connecting to a physical body as a ghost would have in connecting to a subway platform.

I rebelled against the very idea of body-mind dualism. I could not accept that my experience was ontologically divided into two incommensurable spheres: one material, the other mental. Rationally, I found the idea incoherent. Yet this is what I was being asked (told) to believe. I could not accept that, in order to be a Buddhist, I had to take on trust a truth-claim about the nature of the empirical world, and, having adopted such a belief, that I had to hold on to it regardless of whatever further evidence came to light about the relation of the brain to the mind. Belief in the existence of a non-physical mental agent, I realized, was a Buddhist equivalent of belief in a transcendent God.

As soon as you split the world in two parts—one physical and one spiritual—you will most likely privilege mind over matter. Since mind—even an impermanent Buddhist mind—survives bodily death and is the agent of moral choice, then it is not only more enduring and "real" than mere matter but also the arbiter of one's destiny. The more you valorize mind and spirit, the more you will be prone to denigrate matter. Before long, mind starts to become Mind with a capital *M,* while matter becomes the illusory sludge of the world. The next thing you know, Mind starts to play the role of God: it becomes the ground and origin of all things, the cosmic intelligence that animates all forms of life.

Geshe Rabten told us to subject the texts we studied to rational scrutiny and critique, but he also insisted that the authors of those texts were fully enlightened beings. It dawned on me that we were not expected to use logic and debate to establish whether or not the doctrine of rebirth was true. We were only using them to prove, as best we could, what the founders of the tradition had already established to be truc. If the arguments failed to convince us, that did not really matter. For in the end, reason was subordinate to faith. Geshe encouraged us to keep inquiring into these matters, but as long as we did not arrive at the same conclusion as the tradition, then clearly we had not inquired enough. "Do not accept [my words] just out of faith in me," said the Buddha, but in reality we were expected to do just that. I realized then that to pursue my vocation as a Tibetan Buddhist monk, belief in rebirth was not optional but obligatory.

These issues were not merely academic. They had a direct bearing on my social identity as a monk and my material survival in the world. I could not, without being a hypocrite, present myself in public as a Buddhist monk (Geshe had started asking me to instruct classes of laypeople and younger novices), while privately aware that I could not accept one of the cardinal tenets of Buddhism. I experienced a disconcerting gap between my external persona and my inward state of mind. When I look at photographs of myself taken at Tharpa Choeling, I have a shine in my eyes and a smile on my face, but when I read through my diaries, I am struck by how much time I spent wallowing in anxiety, doubt, insecurity, and unrequited longing.

Then one sleepless night I realized that even if there was no life after death, even if the mind was an emergent property of the brain, even if there was no moral law of karma governing my fate, this would have no effect whatsoever on my commitment to the practice of the Dharma. I had to acknowledge that, although I had been paying lip service to these ideas, I had no interest at all in future lifetimes or liberation from the cycle of birth and death. Yet Tibetan Buddhism taught that one could not even consider oneself a Buddhist if one valued this life more than one's destiny after death. But I did. No matter how hard I tried, I was incapable of giving more importance to a hypothetical, postmortem existence than to this very life here and now. Moreover, the Buddhist teachings and practices that had the most impact upon me did so precisely because they heightened my sense of being fully alive in and responsive to this world.

When I told Geshe Rabten of my difficulty in believing in rebirth, he was shocked. The idea that one might subject such a doctrine to rational analysis simply in order to test whether or not it was true was, for him, *nyon-pa:* "crazy." He furrowed his brow and stared at me with a troubled and uncomprehending expression. He did not seem able to grasp what my problem was. Finally he said: "This is a Buddhist monastery. If you don't believe in rebirth, then how"—he pointed to the window, then swept his arm across the villages and towns that lay far below us along the shores of Lake Geneva—"then how are we any different from all those people out there?" For Geshe, belief in rebirth was not just an intellectual preference. It was an essential part of his moral identity. If you did not believe that your actions would have consequences after your death, then why would you be motivated to behave in anything but a greedy, self-centered way during your brief span of life on this earth?

In the end—though I never dared tell Geshe this—I resolved the dilemma by adopting an agnostic position on rebirth. I recognized that were I to be questioned on the subject, the only honest answer would be to say that I did not know whether there was life after death or not. This agnostic stance had the double advantage of enabling me to escape the charge of hypocrisy while, at the same time, not actually denying what the tradition regarded as an axiomatic article of Buddhist faith. Such self-serving casuistry was what Siddhattha Gotama—the Buddha himself—would have called "eel wriggling," but it allowed me a respite from the turmoil of doubt and enabled me to continue, for the time being at least, with my training as a Tibetan Buddhist monk.

Throughout the month of December 1978, I was able to take a break from this exhausting inner struggle. I was invited to the Manjushri Institute, a Tibetan Buddhist center in the north of England. The resident teacher, Geshe Kelsang Gyatso, a colleague of Geshe Rabten from Sera, needed someone to translate the English transcripts of lectures he had given on Shantideva's philosophy of emptiness back into Tibetan in order for him to arrive at a publishable draft. I was happy to do this. It was the sort of intellectual challenge I enjoyed.

I flew from Geneva to London, then traveled by train to Church Stretton, the village in Shropshire on the Welsh Marches where my mother had retired from her work as an occupational therapist earlier that year in order to pursue her passion for hill-walking. She was waiting for me on the platform. A cold wind blasted me as I stepped off the train, causing my red robes to billow and flap. Although we had written to each other and spoken by phone, this was the first time she had set eyes on me since I left for India six years before. She greeted me with a mother's love that immediately erased my anxieties about how she might think of me after such a long and tense separation. She was clearly relieved that I now lived in nice, clean Switzerland rather than India, but was incapable of understanding what I was doing or why. Her main concern was still that of how I would be able to support myself, particularly as I grew older, if I persisted in this marginal and bizarre vocation as a Buddhist monk in Europe. I remember her saying: "You cannot stay in nirvana forever, dear."

While walking with her through this small English market town, exchanging nods and greetings with her neighbors and fellow dog walkers, I was able to see myself through her eyes. Despite that well-honed British social skill of maintaining a veneer of polite and affable civility, I could sense the agonies of inward embarrassment she was obliged to endure on my behalf. In Switzerland I could always take refuge in the privilege of distance accorded to the foreigner; here, among my own people, I was exposed and had nowhere to hide. At the same time, I took a perverse delight in how my appearance upset the complacency and conceits of middle-class England. My Buddhist monasticism still had its roots in my youthful rebellion against the terror of not fitting in that characterized my mother's generation. On balance, though, this heightened sense of social alienation only further exacerbated my private crisis of faith, which, of course, I never once mentioned to Mum.

Manjushri Institute was located near the Cumbrian town of Ulverston in a vast, dilapidated Victorian folly called Conishead Priory. Deserted for years, it had been purchased in 1975 by English disciples of Lama Yeshe, who were now working around the clock to purge the building of the dry rot that infested its woodwork. Although I had spent less than a week with my mother, I was relieved to return to the comforting familiarity of another Buddhist ghetto. I quickly settled into my cold, damp room and spent most of each day alone with Geshe Kelsang Gyatso, slowly going through the transcripts, correcting and revising them where necessary. It was painstaking but satisfying work. "Geshe Kelsang," I noted in my journal shortly after my arrival, "strikes me as a very fine and exceptional lama. He overflows with joy and optimism beneath his humble and mouselike demeanor." He was also a perceptive scholar, who interpreted Shantideva's text with insight and precision. At the end of the first week, I wrote: "I feel a strong relationship with him, he is extremely endearing."

One of the wealthier students had left a white Alfa Romeo at the center and had offered exclusive use of it to Geshe Kelsang (who couldn't drive). On weekends I would take him for excursions through the Lake District, weaving along the shore of Windermere up to Ambleside, where we would stop for tea and buttered scones. Or we would drive into the depressed, ship-building town of Barrow-in-Furness on the coast, where the two of us in our red robes would walk through somber streets peopled with men in cloth caps and raincoats, who appeared to pay us no attention.

The weeks in Cumbria gave me the opportunity to step back and re-examine my vocation as a monk and my commitment to the Tibetan tradition of Buddhism. My journal entries show me vacillating wildly, pushed and pulled by conflicting desires, unable to make up my mind about what I was looking for. At times I wondered whether I should not consider becoming a Christian monk. At times I worried that monasticism was causing me to be sexually attracted to men. Some evenings I would stay up late talking to the other residents, which made me yearn to live in England again. On others, I would avoid everyone and retire to my room to read *Iron in the Soul* by Jean-Paul Sartre, *The Plague* by Albert Camus, and *Existentialism* by John Macquarrie. Then I was asked to give a series of talks to the community on Buddhist logic and epistemology, which reactivated all my longings for recognition and praise.

I returned to Church Stretton to spend Christmas with my mother and brother, David, who was studying fine art at Trent Polytechnic in Nottingham. "Art," as David practiced it then, had nothing to do with such bourgeois preoccupations as drawing and painting. He and his fellow art students seemed to spend most of their time composing subversive political tracts inciting revolution. He listened to my clumsy attempts to expound the Buddhist vision of a life animated by universal compassion and the wisdom of emptiness with barely disguised scorn. Our respective views of the world were so far apart that we soon lapsed into a sullen, awkward silence. In retrospect, we probably had more in common than we realized: both of us were committed to high-minded ideals but had no clue how to realize them. My mother sought to instill a spirit of Christmas cheer by decorating the house with sprigs of holly and strands of tinsel. That evening we gathered before the television to watch *Eric and Ernie's Xmas Show*, a Yuletide extravaganza with her favorite comedians, which that year featured Harold Wilson, the pipe-smoking former prime minister, allowing himself to be the butt of Eric and Ernie's droll asides. By the end of my stay in England, my inner turmoil was no more resolved than when I arrived. If anything, it had increased.

# 5

# BEING-IN-THE-WORLD

I WAS BEING indoctrinated. Despite a veneer of open, critical inquiry, Geshe Rabten did not seriously expect his students to adopt a view of Buddhism that differed in any significant respect from that of Geluk orthodoxy. I realized that to continue my training under his guidance entailed an obligation to toe the party line. This felt like a straitjacket. I could not accept that one view of Buddhism formulated by Tsongkhapa in fourteenth-century Tibet could be the definitive interpretation of the Dharma, valid in all places for all time. Moreover, to arrive at conclusions that contradicted orthodoxy was, for Geshe, not only anathema but *immoral*. To believe there is no rebirth and no law of moral causation is an evil mental act that will lead to confusion and anguish in this life and hellfire in the world to come. And you did not need to say or do anything to commit it. All I had to do was hold an incorrect opinion in the privacy of my own mind. Such "wrong view" is a thought crime, listed in the classical texts alongside murder, robbery, and rape. Indeed, it is often said to be the heaviest of all evil actions, since it establishes the viewpoint from which every other misdeed stems.

On June 9, 1978—I was twenty-five—I had written in my diary: "Crisis point again as the frailty and turmoil in this community manifests itself [*sic*]. I have to face the fact that my confidence in the Geshes is waning rapidly—my eyes are open to much contradiction. I am here to pursue a genuine spiritual inquiry but, to be honest, that is far from what is being encouraged. The lack of an alternative and my continuing involvement here are worrying. I have to stand on my own feet." Nor was I alone in having doubts about this attempt to transplant a branch of Sera Je Monastery to the Swiss canton of Vaud. The strain of studying logic and epistemology in Tibetan, reciting hours of tantric rituals and memorized texts, while running a growing Buddhist center was proving hard for many of us. On September 12, I wrote: "I am at a point where my decision now will affect my role in future years: either to develop a position of relative independence and try to act as a 'synthesizer' based on more retreat; or to help develop this place into the finest center in Europe—the potential that it certainly has. Intuitively, I feel more value in the former; the attraction of security draws me to the latter."

All of this came to a head in 1979. On my return from Cumbria at the beginning of the year, Geshe Rabten asked me to help organize the visit of the Dalai Lama to the French-speaking part of Switzerland, scheduled for July. Tharpa Choeling was to be the first stop on His Holiness's historic first visit to Europe. My sole qualifications for this complex administrative task were my language skills (English, French, and Tibetan) and ability to drive a car. The amount of work was daunting and my Buddhist studies were effectively suspended. In some ways this was a relief. For a number of months I would be spared the daily struggle to come to terms with the minutiae of Buddhist metaphysics. I also looked forward, as many of us did, to having the opportunity to discuss with the Dalai Lama our difficulties with the traditional and (for many of us) inflexible way in which we were being taught.

In some ways, I had already taken matters into my own hands. Within a few months of arriving in Switzerland I had begun a Jungian analysis with Dora Kalff, a psychotherapist in Zollikon, near Zurich. Frau Kalff had been trained by Emma Jung—Carl Jung's wife—and had gone on to develop her own distinctive method of analysis called "sandplay." This entailed the playful creation of imaginary scenes in a sandbox that were then analyzed in much the same way as dreams. Despite Carl Jung's reservations about Westerners practicing Eastern religions, Dora Kalff was a Buddhist. She had met the Japanese Zen scholar D. T. Suzuki at one of the Jungian-inspired Eranos conferences in Ascona, and while on a visit with Suzuki in Japan in the 1960s, Suzuki encouraged her to go and see the Dalai Lama in India. The Dalai Lama had, in turn, advised her to study with Geshe Rabten, thus making her the first Westerner to receive instruction from him in his hut in Dharamsala.

Dora Kalff believed that Jungian psychology could serve as a vital bridge between Western culture and Buddhism and was eager to introduce Tibetan lamas and their Western students to sandplay therapy. My own interest in psychotherapy, however, had more to do with the need to find ways of addressing some of my own inner struggles.

In particular, I was troubled by how my monastic training provided no effective guidance in dealing with sexuality. When I raised this issue with Geshe Rabten, he would encourage me to meditate on the foulness of the human body by visualizing it as composed of blood, organs, pus, excrement, and viscera. This traditional Buddhist meditation was supposed to generate a sense of revulsion that would overcome any feelings of sexual attraction. Not only did this strike me as crudely reductive, in practice I found that it did not work for more than short periods of time. Just because an exquisite painting may be composed of slimy oil paints, to consider it solely in terms of these elements in no way affects its overall beauty. Likewise, no matter how much I practiced this meditation, it failed to undermine my tendency to fall wretchedly in love with beautiful young women who attended the classes at Tharpa Choeling.

Dora Kalff suggested that the root of this dilemma lay not in unfulfilled sexual longing, but in my failure to integrate my own feminine side into my psychic life. This led me to romantically project my sense of incompleteness onto flesh-and-blood members of the opposite sex, in the futile belief that union with them would result in the sense of completeness I craved. For Frau Kalff, this "sickness" was a symptom of the excessively rational, abstract, and technological culture of the West that was founded on a collective repression of the feminine: i.e., the intuitive, feeling-based, nurturing and creative dimension of human existence. By contrast, she believed that the tantric practices of Tibetan Buddhism, in which monks visualized themselves as sensuous, dancing female deities called "dakinis," addressed this imbalance and produced a more whole and fulfilled person. For her, the psychologically integrated Tibetan lamas she had met over the years were ample confirmation of this theory. In my case, even though I daily visualized myself as Vajrayogini—a bright red, menstruating, sixteen-year-old dakini—the practice did not seem to be working. She proposed that psychotherapy could help heal the dysfunction of my Western psyche, thus enabling me to practice these tantric meditations effectively.

For the rest of my time in Switzerland, I would visit Frau Kalff in Zollikon to do sandplay therapy as regularly as my studies and other duties allowed. I enjoyed the childlike spontaneity of creating scenes in the sandbox out of the hundreds of toys and other objects that lined the shelves of her therapy room, then sitting down to analyze them with her. She was very non-directive in her approach and sought to enable me to arrive at my own insights into the symbolism of the sand-scene rather than impose a formal Jungian interpretation. More than anything, I came to value the "free and sheltered space" she created that allowed me to explore issues in my life that I would have found difficult if not impossible to discuss with Geshe Rabten. I greatly appreciated her maternal acceptance and intelligent sympathy for my plight.

Whether these hours of therapy succeeded in integrating the repressed feminine dimension of my psyche, I honestly cannot say. After four years of sandplay, I still had crushes on women, and imagining myself as a dakini every morning did not seem to make any difference. In the end, the most important idea I gained from Jungian psychology was the concept of "individuation." For Jung, once one has dealt with the neuroses of one's personal unconscious, the psychotherapeutic task becomes that of differentiating one's sense of "I" from its dominance by what he calls the "archetypes" of the collective unconscious of humanity. Rather than being possessed by the idea that one is a "mother," "sage," "child," or, in my case, "monk," one seeks to evolve into the unique and complex individual that one has the capacity to become. Superficially, this might seem to conflict with the Buddhist idea of the "emptiness of self." Yet I found that the concept of individuation enriched and elaborated the central Geluk notion of a fluid, moral, and contingent self. As Geshe Rabten repeatedly told us, to say the self is "empty" does not mean that it is non-existent. I am empty only in the sense that there is nothing fixed or intrinsically real at the core of my identity as a person. Recognition of such emptiness therefore liberates one to change and transform oneself. And this, it seems, is precisely what the Jungian theory of individuation describes, yet in a language that is affirmative rather than negative.

Around the same time as I began to do therapy, I also started exploring Western philosophy and theology. A mixture of frustration and curiosity led me to seek thinkers in my own culture who addressed the questions that were most urgent for me—exemplified by that startling experience of radical astonishment I'd had in the forest in Dharamsala shortly before I left India—but which my Buddhist teachers did not seem to acknowledge as important. *Why is there anything at all, rather than nothing?* Just to pose this question, which, I discovered, had its origins in Plato and has resurfaced in the Western tradition ever since, sent tingles down my spine. The question was far more interesting to me than any of the traditional religious answers, such as "God," in the monotheistic faiths, or, in the case of Buddhism, "the actions (karma) of sentient beings." I was first drawn to existentialism, which led me to the phenomenological writings of the German philosopher Martin Heidegger and, in particular, his book *Being and Time*.

Heidegger's ideas, I wrote on April 27, 1979, "have the thrill of a voyage into unexplored regions; often the steps to be taken produce a fear and sense of danger, at other times his words break through like an opening into a valley." Heidegger had entirely abandoned any dualistic assumption of a separation between mind and matter. In *Being and Time,* he speaks of the primary human experience as one of "being-in-the-world." This is the foundation upon which all distinctions such as "subject" and "object," "mind" and "matter" are subsequently imposed. Because we have become so familiar with such distinctions, we assume them to inhere within the structure of being itself. Yet, for Heidegger, our condition is fundamentally not divided along these or any such lines at all.

This resonated with my own experience of practicing mindfulness. I had noticed that when listening to the song of a bird, it was impossible to differentiate between the cooing of the wood pigeon, on the one hand, and my hearing of it, on the other. Conceptually, the two were clearly different, but, in immediate experience, I could not have one without the other, I could not draw a line between them, I could not say where the birdsong stopped and my hearing of it began. There was just a single, primary, undifferentiated me-hearing-the-birdsong. The same was true for me-sitting-cross-legged-on-a-cushion: I could not tell where my bottom ended and the cushion began. They weirdly blurred into one another. (Sit still for a few minutes, close your eyes, and check for yourself.) Such experiences made it all the more difficult for me to accept that mind and matter were two separate things. The idea that mind existed independently of matter as a kind of formless, ghostly "knowing" made no sense.

Being-in-the-world means that I am inextricably knit into the fabric of this fluid, indivisible, and contingent reality I share with others. There is no room for a disembodied mind or soul, however subtle, to float free from this condition, to contemplate it from a hypothetical Archimedean point outside. Without such a mind or soul, it is hard to conceive of anything that will go on into another life once this one comes to an end. My actions, like the words of dead philosophers, may continue to reverberate and bear fruits long after my death, but I will not be around to witness them.

50

Heidegger describes how being-in-the-world is permeated by the "mood" of anxiety that prompts one to "flee" and attach oneself to particular things in the world in a desperate attempt to find something stable and secure to hold on to. For Heidegger, being-in-the-world is constantly slipping away. He recounts in detail how one's life is invariably a being-toward-death. Death is not an event among other events, something that will just happen one day like anything else, but an ever-present possibility that quivers inside us each moment. Such ideas confirmed what Buddhism taught, but in a language that spoke to me more vividly. Heidegger probed relentlessly into the uncanniness of simply being here at all, without ever appealing to the familiar but misleading dichotomies of reality and appearance, subject and object, mind and matter. His language was often obscure and cumbersome, but that seemed entirely appropriate given the radical nature of what he was trying to do. Heidegger believed that the entire project of Western thought that began with Plato had come to an end. It was necessary to start all over again, to embark on a new way of thinking, which he called *besinnliches Denken:* contemplative thinking.

The works of Heidegger and other Western thinkers soon engaged my interest more than the Buddhist texts we were studying in the monastery. Geshe Rabten did not discourage me in these interests, but it was difficult to discuss them with him in any depth. As I gained greater fluency in Tibetan, I became aware of the language's limitations. It was ideal for studying classical Indian Buddhism (the task for which the written form of Tibetan had been invented), but lacked the vocabulary, context, and range to talk about existential alienation or the significance of Kafka and Beckett.

Despite all the preparations for the Dalai Lama's visit, which were beginning to consume my every waking hour, I nonetheless found the time to go to Fribourg with my friend Charles Genoud—a lay student at Tharpa Choeling—to hear Emmanuel Levinas lecture on Edmund Husserl, the teacher of Heidegger and founder of phenomenology.

Levinas himself had studied with Heidegger in the 1920s and was now one of the leading thinkers in the field of "continental" (as opposed to Anglo-American analytical) philosophy. I was eager to meet a representative of this school, to encounter a living "lineage holder," as the Tibetans would have called him. I wanted to see how a person trained in this way of thinking embodied it in his life.

"For the first time in years," I wrote on May 8, "I sat at a school desk" and found the atmosphere of the classroom "overpoweringly intellectual." Emmanuel Levinas was a short man in a dark suit and tie, with a severe demeanor, who spoke in a self-assured, emphatic manner. He explained how Husserl had developed a way of recovering a sense of the "lifeworld" (*Lebenswelt*) by systematically bracketing concepts and opinions until one encountered the raw immediacy of life itself. The crisis humanity now faces, according to Husserl, is that we have taken this living world for granted and unthinkingly erected upon it the conceptual edifices of logic, mathematics, and science. As science and technology have advanced, human beings have lost touch with the foundations of the lifeworld and become enthralled by technical achievements alone. As Heidegger said in his later writings, this has led to a situation where technology is no longer a tool in the hands of people, but a relentless power that is driving humanity toward the brink of its own destruction. "Only a god," Heidegger famously remarked in an interview published in the magazine *Der Spiegel* after his death in 1976, "can save us now."

The "lifeworld" had the same appeal to me as Heidegger's "being-in-the-world," but I failed to see how, in practice, Husserl and his followers achieved the "bracketing" of concepts that allowed the lifeworld to reappear. M. Levinas shed no light on this question. When pressed, he seemed puzzled. This apparent lack of a method did not seem to be a problem for him. The notion that one might require a rigorous meditative discipline to achieve such a "bracketing" was an entirely alien idea.

After the lecture, I joined a group of students for dinner with M. Levinas. He seemed wary of Buddhism—and being confronted by a shaven-headed man with wire-rimmed glasses in a long red skirt probably did little to mitigate that wariness. He appeared to have made up his mind about Eastern religions in general and showed no interest in exploring the subject further. I found his attitude dismissive and haughty. In his manner too he struck me as guarded. He rarely smiled. He spent most of the evening discoursing to the cluster of awestruck undergraduates around him who hung on his every word. Since much of the discussion (in French) concerned technical issues in phenomenology, I had difficulty following. Then at one point, after praising a point in Heidegger's philosophy, he suddenly stood up and declared: *"Mais je détestais Heidegger. C'était un nazi!"* (Levinas, like Husserl, was Jewish.)

When at last M. Levinas did address the subject of Buddhism, it turned out that his main reservation was that it denied the finality of death, which he regarded as axiomatic for a Western thinker. I have often thought about this remark. I cannot be entirely sure what he meant, but it cast another light on my own inability to accept the doctrine of rebirth. It made me realize that belief in rebirth was a denial of death. And by removing death's finality, you deprive it of its greatest power to affect your life here and now.

I was disappointed by my meeting with Professeur Levinas; whatever thoughts I may have had of returning to university to study for a degree evaporated. It brought back everything I had rejected at school in Britain: an overriding emphasis on the acquisition of information, the purely cerebral approach to learning, that same unwillingness to confront felt experience. This was all the more ironic given that the subject of the lecture had been the lifeworld itself, in contrast to the alienating concepts we lay upon it. No matter how much I was drawn to M. Levinas's ideas, I recognized that I had a far closer kinship with a Buddhist sensibility.

The Dalai Lama's visit was fast approaching. I returned to the complex tasks of hiring a large tent, organizing a shuttle service by bus from

Vevey, providing toilet and eating facilities, drawing up a guest list for the private reception, liaising with the local mayor and police, and fending off demands by people who insisted on having a personal audience with His Holiness. Two days before the Dalai Lama was due to arrive, Geshe Rabten summoned us all to his room. He demanded that any questions we wished to raise with His Holiness must be first submitted to him (Geshe) for approval. He did not want any of us to go over his head by appealing to a higher authority to solve our problems. Nor did he wish for his monastery and its training program to be presented to the spiritual and temporal leader of Tibet in anything but the most glowing terms. In hindsight, it was unrealistic of me to have imagined that the Dalai Lama would have been either willing or able to resolve any of our issues.

The visit was a great success. For three days, several hundred people listened to the Dalai Lama lecture on *The Eight Verses of Training the Mind* in a splendid tent erected near the monastery. When the teachings were over, I was invited to join the small group that accompanied His Holiness for a day's sightseeing in Zermatt. After a sumptuous lunch of veal in cream sauce, we took the little mountain railway up to Gornergrat, where we sat on a terrace for coffee overlooking a rather muddy glacier. The Dalai Lama particularly enjoyed watching marmots appear and disappear from their holes in the ground.

"For the first time," I wrote in my diary that night, "I was able to get a glimpse of him as a person, free from the institution in which he is encapsulated. He is simple but incredibly lucid. There appear to be few knots in his mind. His humility is so overpowering that it constitutes a charisma. It was striking to see him among people in the street unaccompanied by any subservience or pomp." Yet however much I admired him, the Dalai Lama still remained an iconic figure for me rather than someone with whom I could share intimate concerns. Unlike some of my peers, I did not formally request that he be my "teacher." Partly this had to do with my shyness and lack of self-esteem, but, realistically, given his other commitments, I suspected that such a relationship would never be much more than symbolic.

Two days later (July 18), my diary entry reads: "Firmly decided to leave at the year's end. First to India to study Dzogchen and slowly to Japan." Dzogchen (Great Perfection) is an awareness practice, in some respects similar to Vipassana, taught in the Nyingma school of Tibetan Buddhism. My wish to travel on to Japan was likewise motivated by my interest in pursuing the less elaborate and more direct kinds of meditation found in Zen Buddhism. In both cases, I was drawn to Buddhist practices that did not require the visualization of complex deities and mandalas and the endless recitation of mantras. I was finding the daily obligation of chanting devotional *pujas* and reciting the tantric *sadhanas* of Yamantaka and Vajrayogini increasingly meaningless. I continued to do them out of loyalty rather than conviction. They had no discernible effect on the quality of my lived experience.

The next day, July 19, I drove up the winding road to Saanen, a village in the mountains above Lake Geneva, on the back of a motor scooter, to hear the Indian anti-guru Jiddu Krishnamurti speak to an even larger gathering in another tent. As a boy Krishnamurti had been declared the new "World Teacher" by Madame Blavatsky's Theosophical Society and was duly groomed for this role. In 1929, at the age of thirty-four, he formally severed his ties with the Society by announcing that "Truth is a pathless land," which, by its very nature, cannot be organized into a system or controlled by a church. Since then he had tirelessly traveled around the world, preaching this message with the sole concern "to set man free. I desire to free him from all cages, from all fears, and not to found religions, new sects, nor to establish new theories and new philosophies."

Krishnamurti was now a frail old man of eighty-four, impeccably attired, seated on a plain wooden chair, who spoke passionately and uninterruptedly for two hours. I had never before been in the presence of someone with such an ability to keep his audience entranced for so long. I wrote in my diary: "[He said,] 'People adopt robes in order to lead a simple life, but the noise of their simplicity prevents them from being simple.' His talk was thoroughly thought-provoking and immersed me in questioning." I sympathized with Krishnamurti's prophetic vision of the end of all creeds and religious institutions, but, at the same time, something about his approach seemed to contradict the central message of his teaching. "This is not a dogmatic statement," he said at one point, "it is a *fact*." When a man in the audience quoted something a guru had told him, Krishnamurti raised a trembling hand and berated him with the words: "Sir. You must never, ever, submit to the authority of another person." Unless, it would appear, that authority happened to be Krishnamurti.

On August 8 I received the first copy of my translation of Shantideva's *A Guide to the Bodhisattva's Way of Life,* published in Dharamsala by the Library of Tibetan Works and Archives. It was deeply gratifying to hold in my hands the fruit of five years' work and to see my name in print for the first time. Despite all the emphasis Buddhism gave to the importance of cultivating inner qualities of mind as the only genuine source of well-being, this outward recognition of my worth—in the form of a flimsily bound Indian paperback—gave me a sense of self-worth and fulfillment that meditation alone had so far failed to provide.

By the end of the summer, I realized that I stood in a no-man's-land, with Geshe Rabten and the Dalai Lama on one side, Heidegger and Levinas on the other. "I have my feet in both camps," I wrote, "and at times this is extremely uncomfortable." Despite my resolve, I did not leave the monastery at the end of the year. (Nor did I ever study Dzogchen in any depth or spend much time in Japan.) I had told Geshe Rabten of my interest in returning to Asia to further my study and practice of Buddhism. "Needless to say," I noted on August 20, "he didn't jump at the idea but then he didn't dismiss it—it's a matter of time. I felt more confident than before—the reasons were on my side, not his—and I managed to push my point." This was almost certainly wishful thinking. Geshe Rabten would have had little sympathy for either Dzogchen or Zen, both of which, from an orthodox Geluk perspective, were considered heretical.

In the end, I stayed in Europe for another year and a half, as the translator for Geshe Rabten's disciple Geshe Thubten Ngawang, who had recently come from India to teach in Geshe's fledgling center in Hamburg.

I arrived at the Tibetisches Zentrum, located in the genteel suburb of Blankenese, on the banks of the Elbe, on August 25. It was a compromise solution to my dilemma. I only had to translate two evenings a week; Geshe Thubten would tutor me each afternoon in Madhyamaka philosophy; and the rest of the time I could pursue my own studies and meditation. Thus I would continue to serve Geshe Rabten, while also creating a distance between myself and the monastery in Switzerland. Perhaps Geshe Rabten hoped that a spell of isolation in a distant German city under the watchful eye of his disciple would cool my rebellious ardor.

It didn't. I suddenly had a great deal of free time in which to read more widely than ever, reflect more critically on what I was doing, and start organizing my own ideas. On October 22, I wrote: "Just before going to bed last night, the absurdity of mindlessly reciting all these prayers and mantras struck me with its full force. I stopped immediately. Today I haven't said them. I feel no guilt. In spirit I had stopped reciting them long ago; the last vestige of mechanical vocalization just dropped off. I don't believe that a horrible hellfire is awaiting me either. I cannot justify the pursuit of a routine that does not assist in the production of more abundant life. Religion is life living itself: not a mechanical repetition of dogmas motivated by threats and fear." Thus I abandoned all the solemn commitments I had made upon receiving tantric initiations over the past seven years. Never again would I visualize myself as the bull-headed Yamantaka or the blood-drinking Vajrayogini in their celestial mansions of light. By acting solely on my own conviction, I broke with the authority of Tibetan Buddhist tradition.

On December 12, I began writing. I have not stopped since. What started out as notes for a course I was invited to give in Holland the following January turned into an essay entitled "The Existential Foundations of Buddhism." This was my first attempt to articulate my understanding of Buddhism in the language of modern Western thought. "Whenever a religion that is embodied in a culturally and historically alien form attempts to find its footing in a new culture and time," I wrote, "it is necessary that its concepts and symbols undergo a radical restructuring in order to attune with the prevailing 'spirit of the times.'" I sought in this essay to uncover the common ground upon which both Buddhism and existentialism were founded. "What," I asked, "within the very depths of us, moves us to religion? It is because life presents itself as an unresolved question. Existence strikes us as a mystery, as a riddle. This experience reverberates through us, issuing in the sounds 'Why?' and 'What?' The various religions of the world are systematic formulations of the answers to these questions."

I was inspired by the example of several modern theologians who had likewise attempted to interpret their faith through the lens of phenomenological and existentialist thought. In particular, I was influenced by the work of Martin Buber, Gabriel Marcel, Paul Tillich, and John Macquarrie. I was also attracted to Rudolf Bultmann's idea of "demythologizing" Christian tradition, stripping it of mythic and supernatural elements in order to gain a clearer sense of what the original teachings meant in the context of Jesus's time. On reading these authors, I realized that a similar method might be fruitfully applied to Buddhism. Rather than preserving unchanged what had been taught for centuries in the monasteries of Asia, one could rearticulate the core Buddhist ideas in a contemporary language that spoke directly to the concerns of men and women living in twentieth-century Europe and America.

"The Existential Foundations of Buddhism" provided the basis for a book-length study of the same topic, called *Alone With Others: An Existential Approach to Buddhism*, which I completed in Hamburg the following August (1980). I immensely enjoyed the experience of writing. It both clarified and stimulated my thoughts, while providing me with an unfamiliar sense of flourishing as a person. I no longer felt so isolated and alone. I saw myself, arrogantly perhaps, as a participant in a groundbreaking experiment to redefine traditional religious thinking in a way that transcended sectarian identities. This experiment was neither Christian, Jewish, nor Buddhist: it was an attempt to humanize and secularize religion, to free it from the prison of metaphysics and supernatural beliefs, to allow it to speak out in a lucid, impassioned, and committed voice. By the time I finished writing *Alone With Others*, it was inconceivable that I could ever return to my studies of Tibetan Buddhist orthodoxy in Switzerland.

Sometime in the summer of 1980 (my diary entries are sporadic for this period), I told Geshe Rabten of my plans to leave Hamburg at the end of the year and go to a monastery in South Korea to train in Zen. He looked at me sternly and said: *"Dé Hoshang gi tawa, ma réwa?"*—"That's the view of Hoshang, isn't it?" Why, he must have wondered, would I abandon my training with him in order to practice in a school that had been outlawed in Tibet ever since the Indian pandit Kamalashila had roundly defeated in debate the Chinese Zen teacher Hoshang Mahayana? This debate had taken place in Samye Monastery, south of Lhasa, at the end of the eighth century, but, as far as Geshe was concerned, it could have happened a week ago. He slowly raised both his forearms, his hands clenched into fists. "You and Jhampa Kelsang," he said, "are like my two arms." Since Jhampa Kelsang had already left the monastery some months before, the implication was clear. One arm had already been severed. Was I now going to cut off the other? I stared at the floor in silence. I had no answer to this. In an agony of guilt and remorse, I mumbled something about only staying for a year or so before returning, but I suspect that we both knew that this was not going to happen. Finally he said: *"Drig gi maré zer gi maré"*—"I am not saying it's not okay."

# 6

# GREAT DOUBT

I AM AWOKEN—as I will be every morning for the next three and a half years—by the *Dok! Dok! Dok!* of a *moktak* struck by a monk with a stick. In syncopation with his beat, the monk chants a liturgy in a deep, mournful voice that fades and grows louder as he makes his way around the pitch-black courtyard outside. I fumble for the light, grab my glasses, then stand with bare feet on the still-warm paper-covered floor as I hastily put on my gray trousers and jacket. I go out onto the wooden *maru,* step down into my rubber slip-on shoes, and hurry to the stone tank, where I splash bitingly cold water onto my face. Two minutes later, as rapid metallic chimes sound from the courtyard, I am walking blearily with nine other gray-clad, shaven-headed monks counter-clockwise around the hall, waiting for the Ibseung Sunim to strike the *djukpi* to announce the start of our first meditation session of the day, from three to five a.m.

We sit for fifty minutes, then walk briskly around the hall for ten, until the sharp clap of the *djukpi* instructs us to sit down again. Apart from a small shrine to Munsu Bosal (Manjushri—the bodhisattva of wisdom) in a niche to one side, the room is bare, with white walls and a dull yellow-ocher floor on which ten square cushions are arranged in two rows. Suspended from the ceiling is a bamboo pole on which hang our gray, butterfly-sleeved, pleated gowns and brown ceremonial *kesas* (monk's robes). The latticed doors (there are no windows) are pasted over with white rice paper. If I open my eyes, I see only a uniform wall of white before me. And all I do, hour after hour, is ask myself the question: *"What is this?"*

I had long been attracted to Zen and its impossible questions. The very first book I read on Buddhism was *The Way of Zen* by Alan Watts, which I had struggled to make sense of when I was eighteen, shortly after I left grammar school in Watford. I was drawn to Zen's pithy, enigmatic sayings, its down-to-earth simplicity, its stark aesthetic, its ruthless honesty. Throughout my time as a scholar monk in Switzerland, I would occasionally pick up a book of Zen poems by Ryokan or Basho and be struck anew by the crystalline imagery of mountain paths, blades of grass, and bowls of tea. Of all the schools of Buddhism, it seemed the only one that embraced the arts—poetry, painting, calligraphy, landscaping—as integral features of its practice rather than decorative adornments of its rituals and beliefs.

As I started to become disaffected with the forms of meditation taught in the Geluk school of Tibetan Buddhism, I began looking elsewhere for a practice that would better fit my needs and a place where I might eventually pursue an intensive retreat. In the summer of 1976, six months after arriving in Switzerland, I visited the Château de Plaige near Autun in Burgundy, where the eminent lama Kalu Rinpoche of the Tibetan Kagyu school was preparing a small group of Westerners for an intensive three-year, three-month Vajrayana retreat, the first of its kind to be held outside Asia. But when I learned that much of this retreat would consist of acquiring an encyclopedic knowledge of tantric rituals, devotional and purification practices, mantra recitation, and so on, I quickly lost interest.

In 1979 Charles Genoud returned from a visit to East Asia and told me of a Zen monastery in South Korea called Songgwangsa, where a small group of Western monks and nuns were studying under the guidance of a Zen master called Kusan Sunim. Unlike in Japanese Zen "monasteries," which were essentially training seminars for married priests, in Korea the monks still adhered to the celibate monastic rule laid down by the Buddha, which was much the same as that observed in Tibet and Southeast Asia. Moreover, while Zen training in Japan was concentrated into intense weeklong *sesshins,* in Korea the monks sat in uninterrupted meditation retreats for three months each summer and three months each winter. Charles gave me a copy of Kusan Sunim's book *Nine Mountains,* which consisted of transcripts of his lectures on Zen. Although it was largely incomprehensible, I was intrigued by the main practice taught by Kusan Sunim: to ask oneself again and again the koan "What is this?" as a means to cultivate what he called "great doubt." Such an exercise seemed tailor-made for my perplexed and doubt-riddled mind.

From the Tibetisches Zentrum in Hamburg I wrote to Songgwangsa and made tentative inquiries about joining the community. A few weeks later I received a reply from a French nun called Songil, who served as Kusan Sunim's translator. She told me that there were currently no Western monks training in the monastery but I would nonetheless be welcome. She also confirmed that the monastery would accept my Tibetan monastic ordination. I would thus be exempted from the usual six-month probationary period, which entailed working from dawn to dusk in the monastery kitchen and fields.

The following spring, after completing my term as translator in the Hamburg center, I returned to Switzerland, took my formal leave of Geshe Rabten, then boarded a flight from Zurich to Seoul. I flew across the arctic wastes racked by feelings of betrayal and trepidation. I had severed my links to the Tibetan Buddhist world in which I had spent most of my adult life and was now on my way to an unknown monastery in a distant country, to train with a teacher I had never met in a language that I could neither read nor speak.

Songil, the French nun with whom I had been corresponding, met me at Kimpo Airport in Seoul. She was a brisk and efficient woman of my own age, who was fluent in Korean. Like myself, she had traveled overland to Asia on a vaguely spiritual quest but disliked India and kept on going until she reached Korea, where she had now lived for six years as a nun. It was raining as we drove through long, drab streets that were lined with modern concrete buildings until we reached Pomyong-sa, a small temple in a traditional town house, where we lodged overnight. The following day we took a six-hour bus journey to Kwangju, the capital city of Cholla-namdo Province in the far southwest corner of the peninsula. A rattling country bus filled with farmers and schoolchildren deposited us at the village nearest the monastery. Weighed down by a backpack filled with books, I walked into the courtyard of Songgwangsa on the evening of May 13, 1981, five days before the start of that year's three-month summer Zen retreat.

Songgwangsa—"Vast Pines Temple"—was a collection of colorful wooden buildings tucked away inside a circle of steep forested hills, beside a clear, fast-flowing mountain river. It was founded in 1205 by the monk Chinul, one of the seminal figures of Korean Buddhism. Each summer and winter, forty or so monks from all over South Korea would gather to train in meditation for three months under the guidance of Kusan Sunim. In spring and autumn, it was largely empty. Only the abbot, administrative staff, novices, and *Ko Jaengi* ("Nose People," as the Koreans called us) remained there. At the time, Songgwangsa was the only monastery in the country where the facially challenged could stay.

Songil lived with two other Western nuns in a small room in a separate compound across the river from the main monastery complex. As a monk, I was housed in Munsu Jon, a walled compound with its own Sonpang (meditation hall) within the monastery grounds. Songil presented me with a set of gray and brown Korean robes to replace my red Tibetan ones, told me how to bow in the "right" way, instructed me in the use of the four bowls used for meals in the dining hall, and gave me a crash course in how not to offend Koreans with my insensitive Western manner. She then took me—newly attired in uncreasable polyester—to see Kusan Sunim, the Zen master, in his quarters above the courtyard. I wrote: "He is a tiny, radiant man of about seventy with a shining, freshly shaven head. He smiled with much kindness, but I sensed a glint of anarchy in his eyes. He was dressed in loose gray cotton clothing and sat cross-legged behind a low, gnarled table, which had been painstakingly carved from the base of a large tree. He listened with patient bemusement as I nervously explained why I had come to Korea and expressed my wish to study with him. He confidently told me just to look into the nature of my mind and ask myself: 'What is this?' ' "

When the retreat began and I started meditating in earnest on the question "What is this?" my mind insisted on coming up with clever answers. Each time I tried to discuss my latest theory with Kusan Sunim, he would listen patiently for a while, then give a short laugh and say: "Bopchon [my Korean name]. Do you know what it is? No? Then go back and sit." Irrespective of how suitably enigmatic they seemed, my answers were either trite or predictable. After a while, I simply gave up trying to find an answer. "What is this?" is an impossible question: it is designed to short-circuit the brain's answer-giving habit and leave you in a state of serene puzzlement. This doubt, or "perplexity" as I preferred to call it, then slowly starts to infuse one's consciousness as a whole. Rather than struggling with the words of the question, one settles into a mood of quiet focused astonishment, in which one simply waits and listens in the pregnant silence that follows the fading of the words.

All I did for ten hours a day for the next three months was ask myself this question. The first two weeks, when my back hurt and my mind swung between febrile daydreams and lethargy, and the last few days, when I strove unsuccessfully not to look forward to the retreat ending, were the hardest. Throughout the long middle period, I experienced an unprecedented contentment. Rather than meditation being an activity that would take up an hour or so of my day, my daily life now became subsumed within the meditation. The practice of meditation was no longer a matter of becoming proficient in a technique. It was about sustaining a sensibility that encompassed everything I did. After a month or so, I reached a point where the meditation became completely unremarkable, nothing special at all.

By the time I left Switzerland, questions had become far more interesting to me than answers. For eight years, my Tibetan teachers had sought to convince me that the answers to the great questions of life were enshrined in their hermetic system of beliefs. The aim of their training had been to arrive at certainty: to reach a place where all questions had finally been resolved and all doubt vanquished. From their point of view, I had failed. While I valued the rich framework of Buddhist ideas they had given me, I could neither submit myself unquestioningly to the authority of the lamas nor uncritically accept their view of the world and the place of humans within it. The problem with certainty is that it is static; it can do little but endlessly reassert itself. Uncertainty, by contrast, is full of unknowns, possibilities, and risks. The certainties of Tibetan Buddhism had had a suffocating effect upon me, while the uncertainty celebrated in Korean Zen brought me vividly, if anxiously, to life.

"When there is great doubt," says a Zen aphorism that Kusan Sunim kept repeating, "then there is great awakening." This is the key. The depth of any understanding is intimately correlated with the depth of one's confusion. Great awakening resonates at the same "pitch" as great doubt. So rather than negate such doubt by replacing it with belief, which is the standard religious procedure, Zen encourages you to cultivate that doubt until it "coagulates" into a vivid mass of perplexity. This, I suspected, is what had happened to me in Dharamsala when walking back to Elysium House carrying that blue plastic bucket of water. Great doubt is not a purely mental or spiritual state: it reverberates throughout your body and your world. It throws *everything* into question. In developing such doubt, you are told to question "with the marrow of your bones and the pores of your skin." You are exhorted to "be totally without knowledge and understanding, like a three-year-old child."

To pose a question entails that you do not know something. To ask "Who is the abbot?" means that you do not know who the abbot is. To ask "What is this?" means that you do not know what *this* is. To cultivate doubt, therefore, is to value unknowing. To say "I don't know" is not an admission of weakness or ignorance, but an act of truthfulness: an honest acceptance of the limits of the human condition when faced with "the great matter of birth and death." This deep agnosticism is more than the refusal of conventional agnosticism to take a stand on whether God exists or whether the mind survives bodily death. It is the willingness to embrace the fundamental bewilderment of a finite, fallible creature as the basis for leading a life that no longer clings to the superficial consolations of certainty.

By the time I reached Korea, I realized that no single Asian form of Buddhism was likely to be effective as a treatment for the peculiar maladies of a late-twentieth-century post-Christian secular existentialist like myself. Having learned this lesson through my painful disillusion with Tibetan Buddhism, I was careful not to repeat the same mistakes with Korean Zen. I attended to what I was taught without the literalist fervor that marked my initial embrace of the Tibetan tradition. I maintained an ironic but respectful distance from Korean Zen orthodoxy. I put Kusan Sunim's instructions into practice, but in a way that corresponded with my own interests and needs.

To my surprise, Kusan Sunim was just like Geshe Rabten. Despite their largely incompatible versions of Buddhism, they were otherwise very similar. Both men came from humble rural backgrounds and had risen through their own efforts to become the equivalent of bishops; they were conservative, committed to upholding and transmitting what they had been taught by their teachers and lineage; they were convinced of the unique validity of their approach and had no interest in any other; and they embodied a constancy, moral integrity, and nobility that humbled me. I may have had my disagreements with Geshe Rabten, but they had little effect on my respect for him. And when I could not accept something Kusan Sunim taught, that too did not diminish the esteem in which I held him.

In October 1980, I had written to my friend Alan Wallace, a fellow monk from Tharpa Choeling: "If all goes according to plan and the world doesn't blow up before next spring, I shall be going to Korea to further sharpen my confusion by trying to answer some highly illogical questions. I see the whole venture as a bit of a koan sometimes; I have the haunting suspicion that I might just get incredibly bored. Well, we'll see; in any case I will satisfy my curiosity." But I wasn't bored at all and my curiosity, instead of being satisfied, was becoming weirdly enhanced. I felt much at home on this distant peninsula.

My "Zen," I confess, was a rather mixed bag. It was grounded on mindfulness of the breath and body, a practice that Kusan Sunim dismissed as no more meaningful than watching a corpse exhale. The question "What is this?" reminded me very much of Heidegger's *Seinsfrage*—the forgotten "question of being"—as well as the poignant comment at the end of his essay on technology that "questioning is the piety of thought." Nor did I forget what I had learned in Madhyamaka philosophy from my Tibetan teachers: that emptiness is the unfindability of things, which is reached by pursuing an "ultimate inquiry" into their nature. So each time I asked "What is this?" it echoed with these other associations. Nor, in the course of seven three-month retreats, did I have any of the shattering insights or breakthroughs for which Zen is renowned. By the time I went to Korea, I had little interest in such things. I was more concerned with refining my sense of the sheer mysteriousness of life so that it infused each moment of my waking existence, thereby serving as a ground from which to respond more openly and vitally to whatever occurred.

I had difficulties with much of the underlying philosophy of Kusan Sunim's teaching. I struggled with his view that the "this" of "What is this?" denoted a transcendent Mind, which he also called the "Master of the body." When I consulted the Chinese text where the question "What is this?" first appears, it made no mention of Mind or a Master of the body, but simply said: "What is this *thing*, and how did it get here?" I liked the blunt earthiness of "thing," since it offered little scope for metaphysical elaboration. But this is how Kusan Sunim explained what we were doing: "The purpose of Zen meditation is to awaken to the Mind. . . . There is a Master who rules this body who is neither the label 'mind,' the Buddha, a material thing, nor empty space. Having negated these four possibilities, a question will arise as to what this Master really is. If you continue inquiring in this way, the questioning will become more intense. Finally, when this mass of questioning enlarges to a critical point, it will suddenly burst. The entire universe will be shattered and only your original nature will appear before you. In this way you will awaken."

Once again, I found myself confronted by the specter of a disembodied spirit. The logic of Kusan Sunim's argument failed to convince me. It rested on the assumption that there was "something" (i.e., Mind) that rules the body, which was beyond the reach of concepts and language. At the same time, this "something" was also my true original nature, my face before I was born, which somehow animated me. This sounded suspiciously like the Atman (Self/God) of Indian tradition that the Buddha had rejected. I could not reconcile the Zen Buddhist love of snow on bamboo, cypress trees in the courtyard, or the *plop!* of a frog jumping into a pond with the mystical experience of a transcendent Mind revealed once the universe of bamboo, cypresses, and frogs was "shattered." Since Mind was inconceivable, Kusan Sunim told us to abandon any notion of what we were inquiring about when we asked "What is this?" For, as unawakened beings, we could not have the remotest idea of what it was. In which case, I wondered, what difference would it make to ask: "What is ksldkfja?"

Despite the constant emphasis on questioning and doubt, I was again being primed to arrive at an insight that would confirm the foregone conclusions of an orthodoxy. Ironically, the orthodox views of Korean Zen traced themselves back to the idealist Mind Only school of Indian Buddhism, which my Tibetan teachers had been at pains to re-

fute with their Middle Way doctrine of emptiness. I now found myself
in the curious position of practicing meditation in a school whose philosophy I rejected, while adhering to the philosophy of a school whose
meditation practices I had rejected.

Buddhism had arrived in Korea from China in the fourth century CE.
Living in Songgwangsa made me aware, for the first time, of what it
was like to practice the Dharma in a country where Buddhism had had
a long-established presence. Until then, I had lived either in Tibetan
refugee communities in India, a country where Buddhism had not existed for a thousand years, or Switzerland and Germany, where Buddhism had barely been introduced.

Koreans ordained as Buddhist monks for all sorts of reasons. Many
were either unwilling or unable to conform to the demands of a conservative Confucian society with growing materialistic aspirations. But
only a minority of these were drawn to the rigor of the twice-yearly intensive Zen retreats. Most either performed administrative and ceremonial duties, tended the monastery fields, oversaw building projects,
undertook pastoral work, managed small temples, or became entan-
gled in the Byzantine machinations of the Chogye order's headquarters
in Seoul. The community was a cross section of Korean society: from
young orphans to frail old monks of ninety, from intellectuals to former
shopkeepers, from disaffected adolescents to career clerics. For one
who had only known Buddhism among exiled Tibetans and white,
middle-class, twenty-something dropouts, I now saw how the Dharma,
when removed from its lofty spiritual pedestal, impacted the lives of
people from widely diverse backgrounds with very different needs.

Life in a Korean Zen monastery was centered around the notion of
"group spirit." There was no place here for the prissy demands of Western individualism, such as the "need" to have one's own room. "If the
group decides to go to hell," one monk gravely told me, "then you must
go to hell too." Irrespective of your position in the monastery, you lived,
ate, and worked together. At any time, the monks could be summoned

to work. Everyone, from Kusan Sunim to the youngest novice, would be issued a hand scythe to harvest the barley crop or a hoe to weed between the soybean plants. We would unload piles of curved terra-cotta roof tiles from the backs of trucks or form into a chain gang with buckets to dredge the riverbed after a typhoon. At the first frost, we would spend two days bringing cartloads of Chinese cabbages from the fields down to the kitchen area, cleaning them, salting them, leaving them overnight in the communal bathtub, rinsing them in the icy river the next morning, before handing them over to the laywomen to prepare the pickled kimchi for winter. And in autumn, against a brilliant cerulean sky, we would climb trees to gather deep red persimmons and then spear them on bamboo splints to dry.

Korea was a Confucian society and the Zen monastery was a Confucian society in miniature. Each individual had to accept his assigned role, which would change over time, and fulfill it dutifully in order to maintain the harmony of the greater whole. This contrasted with the feudal structure of Tibetan Buddhism, where the lamas formed a privileged spiritual aristocracy who lived and ate separately from the ordinary monks, while possessing an almost absolute authority over their disciples. It became clear to me that Buddhism, as it moved from one country to another in Asia, had adapted itself not only to different intellectual cultures, but also to different social norms.

During the three-month "free" periods in spring and autumn when we were not on retreat, I divided my time between studying the classic texts of Zen Buddhism and traveling to monasteries and hermitages, often with Songil as my guide and translator, to explore the country and visit renowned teachers. I also started taking photographs again. In Korea it was not considered at all unusual or inappropriate for a monk or nun to practice a form of art. Some of the most gifted painters, poets, and calligraphers in the country were monastics, who spent as much time refining their brushwork and writing style as they did sitting in meditation. Rather than considering art as a distraction from the path to awakening—as is the case in some Buddhist schools—in Zen it was seen as a discipline that was entirely compatible with contemplative practice.

When I look now at the hundreds of photographs I took in Korea, they strike me as competent but rather conventional studies of predictable "Zen" subjects: bamboo and pine trees in the snow, monks tilling the fields, Buddha images glowing in the evening sunlight. The importance for me of returning to photography lay less in the quality of the pictures I took and more in the reawakening of an aesthetic sensibility that had lain dormant throughout my years as a Geluk monk. I now found myself in a Buddhist culture that valued the integration of creative expression into the practice of the Dharma.

Under the influence of Zen, my writing took on a more experimental and playful quality. In the pieces I wrote in the monastery, which were eventually published as *The Faith to Doubt,* instead of presenting a carefully constructed linear argument, I addressed my themes in an oblique, impressionistic manner by interweaving personal anecdotes with reflection on texts, widely disparate quotes with fictionalized dialogue, Zen stories with journal entries. By emphasizing doubt rather than belief, perplexity rather than certainty, and questions rather than answers, Zen practice granted me the freedom to imagine.

Over time a trickle of other foreigners arrived at the monastery: a handful of American and European Zen students, two Chinese monks from Singapore, a pair of *bhikkhus* (monks) from Sri Lanka. We became a close-knit group of ten or so monks in our compound in Munsu Jon, with four nuns across the river in their one cramped room. These years at Songgwangsa were the happiest that I spent as a monk. I enjoyed the contemplative rhythm of the three-month retreats twice a year, and the cultural refinement and emotional warmth of the Koreans, who embraced us as part of their community. I enjoyed hiking through the forested mountains, catching sight of golden orioles and delighting in the wild azaleas each spring, then returning at dusk as the smoke from the wood fires of the *ondol*—an underfloor heating system—curled into the air.

In 1983 Songil and I began work on a book of Kusan Sunim's teachings. Songil translated his lectures, then I edited her drafts. We spent many hours together, working and reworking these texts until we arrived at a version that both captured our teacher's voice and read fluently in English. In the course of this labor, we also grew closer together as friends, and I came to look forward to these sessions in a way that raised questions about my continuing vocation as a monk.

Sometimes, even in the midst of a three-month retreat, the younger Korean monks would exchange their robes for camouflaged fatigues, climb onto the back of a truck, and depart for a day of military training. (South Korea was—and still is—technically at war with the North.) Despite their vow not to kill, Buddhist monks are not exempt from this duty. I met one monk who had bound his trigger finger with surgical gauze, dipped it in oil, set it alight, then offered it as a candle to the Buddha. I knew another who had chopped off all the fingers of his right hand with an ax. But these were exceptions. Most monks accepted their position in the reserve army, which recalled for them, perhaps, the monastic militias raised by Zen Master Sosan that played a crucial role in the defeat of the Japanese army that invaded Korea in 1592.

When I queried my Korean friend "Strongman" (among ourselves we foreigners gave the Korean monks nicknames since their real ones sounded so similar to us) about the morals of participating in the state killing machine, he looked at me and asked with disbelief: "Then you would not fight for your country?" No one had challenged my knee-jerk pacifism quite so bluntly before. Even as a child, I had found the thought of killing any living creature, let alone a fellow human, repugnant. I had always assumed that Buddhists, in particular, would feel this way too. "To be honest, Strongman," I said, "no. I would not." He shook his head in amazement, then marched off with his fellow monk-soldiers for target practice and combat drill, leaving the unpatriotic Nose People to stew on their cushions.

In the early 1980s South Korea was beginning to emerge from the catastrophe of thirty-five years of Japanese colonial occupation, followed shortly after by the devastating civil war with the Communist North. The country was ruled by the military dictator Chun Doo-hwan, who had seized control in December 1979 during the turmoil that followed the assassination of Park Chung-hee, another military dictator, who had ruled since 1961. (Park was felled during a cabinet meeting in a volley of bullets fired by the head of the Korean CIA.) Both Chun and Park were Buddhists. In May 1980, one year before I arrived, Chun had dispatched paratroopers to suppress a popular uprising in Kwangju, the city nearest our monastery, in which at least two hundred civilians were killed (the figures are still disputed) and three thousand wounded.

Although the memory of this recent failed uprising must have weighed heavily on the minds of the monks at Songgwangsa, it was not a subject that was mentioned in our presence. They jokingly called Chun "Octopus" (he was bald and had his hands in everything) and his wife "Spatula" (because of the prominent—for Koreans—thrust of her chin), but they were reluctant to discuss their deeper views and feelings about the state of their country. Only the presence of Bop Jong Sunim, a well-known writer and dissident, who throughout my stay lived under house arrest in a hermitage in the forest above the monastery, made us aware of the repressive political climate in which we were living.

As a Western convert, I saw Buddhism as a set of philosophical doctrines, ethical precepts, and meditation practices. For me, to be a Buddhist simply meant to accord one's life with the core values of the tradition: wisdom, compassion, nonviolence, tolerance, calm, and so on. Living in Korea made me realize how naïve I was. By my narrow criteria, a military dictator who violently suppressed a popular uprising could not possibly be a Buddhist. But why not? Is Buddhism reserved only for the morally upright and doctrinally correct, who piously sit in meditation every day? I began to see it as a broad cultural and religious identity, one that provides a framework for fallible humans to make complex decisions in a precarious and unpredictable world. In 1988, as a public gesture of repentance for the worst excesses of his regime, Chun Doo-hwan went into a two-year retreat at Baekdamsa, a monastery in Gangwon Province. While this does not absolve him for the crimes he committed (for which he was later sentenced to death, then pardoned by the Catholic president Kim Dae-jung, whom he had earlier condemned to death), it shows how he drew on the resources of his religion to help him come to terms with the suffering he had caused.

In September 1983, Kusan Sunim fell ill and was confined to his quarters. None of us was told what was wrong or allowed to see him. It was a troubled time. On the first of the month, a civilian Korean airliner (KAL 007) on a flight from New York had been shot down by Soviet jet interceptors just west of Sakhalin Island, near Japan, on its way to Seoul. All 269 people on board, including the U.S. congressman Larry McDonald, were killed. Korea was in a state of national mourning. People wore little black ribbons and shopfronts displayed large wreaths, while Octopus used the occasion to ratchet up anti-Communist feeling to a hysterical pitch.

The three-month winter retreat started on November 19. That evening, I noted: "[Kusan Sunim] is very sick and it is questionable how long he will be able to keep going. It looks as though he has suffered from a stroke. The whole of his left side is paralyzed. He sometimes gets stronger only to relapse again. His weakness is a shadow cast over the retreat." On December 4, we were instructed to do a week of chanting "Kwan Seum Bosal"—the name of the bodhisattva of compassion—in unison in the hope that this might succeed, where medicine had failed, in restoring his health. On December 10, I went to see him in his room. "He is hardly recognizable," I wrote in my diary. "He lies on the floor, all the luster has gone out of his skin, his cheeks are sunken, he cannot walk, talk, or swallow. The only movements I saw him make were fingering his rosary with his right hand and trying to pull his blanket up for warmth. I was very moved by seeing him for what might be the last time. I realized how valuable he has been for me. In a sense, he was the most valuable teacher in that he embodied so forcefully the qualities in which I am lacking." I suspect the qualities I had in mind were his earthy, non-intellectual rigor and simplicity, his moral constancy, and his total confidence in what he was doing.

Kusan Sunim died at 6:20 p.m. on December 16. He was seventy-four. "Since then," I wrote two weeks later, "my life has been turned inside out in a way in which I would never have foreseen." I had never mourned anyone that completely before. I stayed awake for days on end in a state of fragile lucidity, interrupted by bouts of sobbing, as the monastery went through the rituals of bereavement. For the first three days his coffin (L-shaped to accommodate the cross-legged sitting posture in which he had been placed to die) stood on dry ice and the monks sat silently before it in a rota day and night. The funeral took place on December 20. Thousands of people, their breath condensing in the bitterly cold air, packed the main courtyard to pay their last respects. Then the body in its coffin was carried on an elaborate bier studded with chrysanthemums to a terraced field above the monastery, where it was cremated on a bed of charcoal beneath a huge pyre of wood, which burned steadily until dawn the next day.

When the embers had cooled, the ash and fragments of bone were collected and taken to Kusan Sunim's room, where we meticulously sifted through them in search of *sarira*—little crystalline droplets believed to be a sign of spiritual attainment, but probably just a natural consequence of a human body being burned at a sufficiently high temperature for a long enough time. We found fifty-two *sarira*, of different sizes and colors, which were reverently placed on red velvet inside a glass dish. Then we crushed the pieces of bone between roof tiles and poured the coarse, white powder into a celadon vase. The next day, we walked in single file up to Mount Chogye and scattered these remains at the site of his former hermitage. "The crushed bones," I wrote, "dispersed in a tiny cloud as they were released from my outstretched fingers. A puff of white dust lingered for a moment before it was snatched away forever by the wind."

After Kusan Sunim's death it felt as though a light had gone out at Songgwangsa. No one seemed to realize what a somber, disorienting effect his absence would have on the place. He had failed to appoint a successor, and none of the monks seemed to know who would assume his position as Zen master. At the conclusion of the winter retreat, it was announced that he would be replaced by Il Gak Sunim, an elderly monk whose sole qualification was his being the most senior member in the monastic "family." Since Il Gak had spent the last years as abbot of a small temple in Mokpo on the south coast and rarely set foot in Songgwangsa, none of the foreign monks or nuns knew him. When we went for instruction to the Zen master's quarters, this kind, considerate stranger would be seated behind Kusan Sunim's table. He was not a bad teacher, but he wasn't Kusan. Some of the Korean monks we knew from the "old days" began to drift away from the monastery. Our small group of foreigners likewise began to unravel. To preserve some continuity from the past, Songil and I were asked to remain for another year to help oversee the transition to the new regime.

We both knew that we were staying on in Songgwangsa out of a sense of gratitude and duty rather than any wish to train in Zen under the guidance of Il Gak Sunim. We also knew that at some point we would have to decide whether to act on our love for each other and return to lay life together, or remain committed to our vows and part in order to pursue further monastic training. The decision to stay on for another year provided us with the breathing space to ponder and resolve this dilemma. After a month or two of anguished indecision we made up our minds to leave the monastery the following winter and get married. This, of course, raised other unsettling questions: where would we live and how on earth would we support ourselves?

Later that spring, I received a letter from my friend Roger Wheeler, an American former monk whom I knew from Tharpa Choeling in Switzerland. Roger told me that he had recently joined a lay Buddhist community in Devon, England, that had been founded the previous year by a group of Vipassana meditators. Though Roger had no inkling that I was intending to disrobe, I was intrigued by the notion of Songil and me joining such a community. Then I received another letter, this time from Le Mont-Pèlerin, which informed me that Geshe Rabten had been diagnosed with cancer and was seriously ill. I decided to make a hasty visit to Europe, then return to Korea in time for the summer retreat.

I flew to London, spent a few days with my mother in Shropshire, then took a train down to Devon. The community in which Roger was living was located on the upper floor of Sharpham House, a Palladian mansion overlooking the River Dart near the town of Totnes, a well-known center in England for "alternative" living. At the time only five people belonged to the community and they were looking for others to join. I met with Maurice Ash, the owner of the house and co-founder, with his wife, Ruth, of the Sharpham Trust, the educational charity that supported the community. I was enthusiastic about Maurice's Zen-inspired vision of a rural way of life founded on simplicity and meditation, which provided a program of lectures, workshops, and short retreats for those living in the surrounding town and villages. Nothing was decided, but I left Sharpham confident that should we apply to join the community there we would be welcome.

I returned to Switzerland via Bordeaux, where I visited Songil's mother and family, then took an overnight train to Geneva. I made my way up to Le Mont-Pèlerin filled with foreboding. I had had little contact with Tharpa Choeling in the three years since I had left for Korea. Many of the monks and lay students with whom I had studied with Geshe Rabten had left. A few, like myself, had gone to practice more intensive meditation; others had returned to university to study for degrees; some of the monks had disrobed and were working in ordinary jobs. The monastery was populated with new, eager faces. I felt like a ghostly intruder from a former time.

Ven. Helmut took me upstairs to see Geshe Rabten, and I was told not to spend too long with him since he tired easily. Geshe was seated immobile on the bed in his room. He did not seem to be in pain but he exuded a terrible sadness, which resurrected all the guilt I still felt on having deserted him. He appeared to be neither particularly pleased nor displeased to see me. He was curious to know how well the monastery in Korea adhered to the Vinaya—the monastic vows and training rules laid down by the Buddha—and which sutras were studied, but pointedly avoided asking me anything about the kind of meditation practice taught by Kusan Sunim. His face was sunken and weary. As I stood up to go, he told me to wait, and took a small loose-leafed text from a drawer in his desk. He explained that it was a series of twelve verses he had composed while on retreat in his hut in Dharamsala, to which he had later added a prose commentary. It was called *The Song of the Profound View.* He asked me to translate it into English. As I knelt down to take it from him, he laid his hand on my head as a blessing. "Ah, Jampa Tabke [my Tibetan name]," he sighed. I left the room not expecting ever to see him again.

I spent my final months in Korea completing work on the book of Kusan Sunim's teachings. Songil had unearthed some old tape-recorded lectures he had given on the Ten Oxherding Pictures—a classic series of images describing Zen practice—and was busy transcribing them. Weatherhill, a respected Tokyo-based publisher of books on East Asian culture and religion, had agreed to publish the book under the title *The Way of Korean Zen.* I had also been asked by a publisher in Seoul to write a short book on Tibetan Buddhism for translation into Korean, which I managed to finish that autumn. After the ceremony marking the first anniversary of Kusan Sunim's death on December 16, Songil and I left Korea. I was thirty-one and had been a monk for just over ten years. That phase in my life was now over.

*part two*

# LAYMAN

# 7

# A BUDDHIST FAILURE

# (II)

JANUARY 4, 1985. I still have the dog-eared passport with the photograph of myself as a smiling monk and the dated exit stamp from the British Crown territory of Hong Kong. The wood-paneled train strained and clanked as it made its way out of the station at Kowloon toward the border of the People's Republic of China. When I was not peering out of the windows at the shabby, trackside buildings that were barely visible through the mist, I turned my gaze to Songil—or "Martine" as she now insisted on being called—who was seated across from me, our knees bumping together each time the train lurched through another set of switches.

After leaving Songgwangsa, we had flown from Seoul to Hong Kong. Before returning to Europe, we both wanted to visit the monasteries in southern China where the Chan (Zen) tradition had first flowered during the Tang dynasty (618–907 CE). Given what we had heard of the ravages of the Cultural Revolution, we were curious to know whether these places had survived. While waiting for our visas in a drafty corridor in the Chinese Embassy, we heard a rumor that Lhasa had recently been classified as an "open city" by the authorities, which meant that it might now be possible to go there as an independent traveler. When we asked the officials at the embassy if we could go to Tibet, they shook their heads and told us to make inquiries when we arrived in

China. We posted banns to be married at Hong Kong City Hall, then boarded the train to Guangzhou (Canton).

Guangzhou was grim. The paint on the once proud buildings of the pre-Communist period was peeling and blistered, streaked with black lines of filth. It was cold and damp in early January. People shuffled through the streets wrapped in dark coats and hats with earflaps, appearing out of, then vanishing back into, the ground mist with its pervasive smell of coal dust. The locals seemed constantly to be smoking roll-ups or chewing an endless succession of sunflower seeds. They also took a peculiar delight in hawking loudly and then dribbling long drools of spit onto the ground. China was like India in black-and-white. The poverty and squalor were unrelieved by any bursts of color, squalls of laughter, or chimes of temple bells. Yet there were no beggars. The few shops we passed were largely empty of goods, but people appeared well fed and clothed.

We first went to Nan-hua-ssu, the temple of the sixth Chan patriarch, Hui-neng, from whom all the lineages of Zen come down to us today. It was here that Hui-neng asked the young monk Huai-jang: "What is this thing and how did it get here?" thus giving rise to the question "What is this?" which I had spent nearly four years asking myself in Korea. Nan-hua-ssu was shabby but in surprisingly good repair. Around fifty or so monks in long, tattered black robes were living there. A steady stream of laypeople chanted prayers and offered incense at the shrines. The seated body of Hui-neng, embalmed in shiny, black lacquer, with one bulging eye squinting down at us, was still intact in the Hall of the Patriarchs at the rear of the temple.

We took a bus to the nearby monastery of one of the last great Tang dynasty Chan masters, Yun-men. Yun-men was known for his pithy "one word" Zen. When asked "What is the highest teaching of the Buddha?" he replied: "An appropriate statement." On another occasion, he answered: "Cake." I admired his directness. The monastery was largely in ruins. As we picked our way over fallen masonry, it was clear that it had been ransacked and demolished. A broken bell and fragments of a large metal Buddha had been placed respectfully in a small clearing, but otherwise the place seemed abandoned. Then an elderly monk appeared from a splintered doorway. He introduced himself as the abbot Venerable Fo-yuan. He was serenely unperturbed by the devastation and took us on a tour of the rubble, pointing out where shrines, the meditation hall, and monks' cells once stood, as though their physical absence was just a temporary inconvenience.

Ven. Fo-yuan told us to visit Chen-ju-ssu, a monastery on Mount Yün-chü in Kiangsi Province, not far from the city of Nanchang. A bus deposited us in a remote village. The local people pointed to a mist-draped mountain and told us that was where the monks lived. As we climbed the bamboo-lined road that wound up the hillside, it began to snow. A van drew up beside us, full of smiling monks, who offered us a lift to the top of the mountain where the monastery lay surrounded by plowed fields. Having been razed to the ground in the 1960s, Chen-ju-ssu was now a brand-new complex of ornate buildings and temples, some of which were still under construction.

We were taken to the Chan master, Ven. Lang-yao, a tall, dignified figure, who impishly beckoned us to follow him. He took us through a low doorway into a darkened room. As our eyes grew accustomed to the light, we saw forty or so monks seated in meditation on a raised platform of rough wood that lined the walls. They were old men, unshaven, wizened, and stooped, clad in patched gowns and robes. Some were sipping tea from bowls. After a lunch of coarse rice and mushroom broth, we were whisked away in the van, back to the nearest railhead, with a brief explanatory stop at the police station. The monks were nervous. They would have faced criticism or worse had they allowed the two of us to stay any longer.

In 1985 China was just starting to emerge from the bad old days of the Red Guards and the dictatorship of Mao Zedong. We went north to Loyang, where we saw the monumental Buddhas and hundreds of cave temples and shrines, which had been carved over centuries out of the cliffs of the Longmen Gorge. They were essentially undamaged.

On Mount Sung, we visited Shao-lin-ssu, the monastery associated with the first Chan patriarch: the uncouth and enigmatic Bodhidharma. This too had been restored and was slowly resuming its dual role as a center of Buddhist pilgrimage and a shrine for aficionados of Chinese martial arts. (A Hong Kong film studio had recently built a replica film set of the temple next door.)

On returning to the city of Loyang we went to the Public Security Bureau and inquired if it would be possible to visit Lhasa. Without batting an eyelid, the courteous woman official issued each of us a travel permit, and stamped it for Lhasa. We scrapped our plans to explore the ancient city of Xian and traveled by train for two days until we reached Chengdu, the capital of the western province of Sichuan. From there we took the first available flight to Tibet.

As we stood on the tarmac of the Lhasa "airport"—at the time it was no more than a landing strip with a few drab, military-style huts—I was struck by the shocking contrast between the dusty, barren hills all around and the radiant blue sky behind them. The sun shone with a crystalline intensity that did little to diminish the biting chill of the breeze on my cheeks. When I spoke, I found that the air in my lungs was insufficient to allow me to complete my sentences. The final words were lost in a wheeze as I gasped for more oxygen.

Martine and I were the only foreigners—or "aliens" as our internal travel permits described us—on the half-empty Ilyushin. The other passengers were Chinese officials, all dressed in identical olive-green "Mao" suits and caps, none of whom seemed to share our excitement at setting foot on the fabled Roof of the World. Lhasa had been declared an "open" city three months earlier. Until then you could only visit as part of a strictly controlled and overpriced tour group. Now, for some reason, the authorities had decided to allow unmonitored individuals to travel to Lhasa, lodge in the cheap local inns, and—although technically not permitted—explore the surrounding countryside, which the local Tibetans were only too keen to show them.

The paved road from the airport to Lhasa was still under construction. Our bus bucked and swayed across fields, forded rivers, and lurched along rutted farm tracks until it shuddered up onto the bridge that crossed the Kyichu River. The first sight of the golden roofs of the Potala Palace, glistening in the distance, still evoked the thrill and mystique reported by those who had succeeded in reaching Lhasa in the days of old Tibet. As we approached the outskirts of the city, the harsh reality of the modern Chinese frontier town became apparent. We drove along snow-whipped boulevards lined with functional concrete office and apartment buildings. On the way to the bus station, we saw not a single temple or burgundy-robed monk. Only the ubiquitous strings of wind-shredded prayer flags showed that Buddhism still played a role in the life of the modern city and its people.

As in China, the pattern of destruction of monasteries and temples in and around Lhasa was uneven. Zhou Enlai had ordered the army to protect certain buildings of historical and architectural importance, such as the Potala Palace, against the fury of the Red Guards, while other key symbols of the former regime, such as Ganden Monastery, were completely dismantled. In some cases, temple buildings would be emptied of all religious objects and turned into granaries, storehouses, or living quarters. The main cathedral in Lhasa, the Jokhang, was savagely desecrated and used—so I was told—for slaughtering pigs, but the structure remained intact. When I persuaded the Tibetan concierge to let me into Ramoche, Lhasa's second cathedral, I found its religious paintwork undamaged but all the statuary removed and replaced by a large portrait of Mao Zedong. It seemed to have been used as a center for Communist indoctrination and criticism sessions.

Once Tibetans realized, to their astonishment, that I spoke their language and had lived in Dharamsala with the Dalai Lama, they took me aside and vented their rage and pain against the cruelty of the Chinese, who had entered their country uninvited only to attack every aspect of Tibetan culture, while imprisoning or executing anyone who resisted being "liberated" from "feudal slavery." There were other voices too. One man, on overhearing me criticize the Chinese, said calmly: "It was not only the Chinese who destroyed things, you know. Tibetans did that too."

Since it was winter and there was no work to be done on the land, rural people were flocking into Lhasa from all over the country in preparation for Losar, the new year festival. As we circumambulated the Barkor—the quadrangle of streets in the old city around the Jokhang—we found ourselves in a slowly moving crowd of simple but devout men and women dressed in traditional clothes, which at times amounted to no more than a single yak fleece secured with a cord around the waist, spinning prayer wheels, muttering mantras, prostrating full length on the ground, as though the Chinese occupation had somehow passed them by.

Staying in Lhasa brought me full circle in my encounter with Tibet. I was acquiring a tactile intimacy with the places from where the Dalai Lama and Geshe Rabten had fled into exile. Tibet was no longer just my (romantic) impression of their (nostalgic) memories. Here, on the roof of the Potala Palace—now a museum—were the rooms of the young Dalai Lama, where he spent the cold winter months. This is where he would have studied with his tutors. This was his bed, this was his altar, and here was where he held his audiences. The apartments were, to my mind, overdecorated with fussy and garish brocade, but they brought me that much closer to the boyish, bespectacled monk, who, in his free time, would walk out onto the flat roof and observe his people on the streets of the village below through a telescope.

You can see Sera Monastery from the Potala: a dense cluster of whitewashed buildings at the base of the bare, rocky hills that rise on the north side of the Lhasa Valley. When Geshe Rabten fled Sera in March 1959, it was home to around three thousand monks. Now there were no more than a hundred or so, most of whom were boisterous children and adolescents. They were managed by a handful of elderly lamas, who had recently returned to the monastery, having survived twenty or more years of prison camps and forced labor. The entire middle generation, those who normally would have served as teachers and administrators, was missing. One old monk, on learning that I had studied with Geshe Rabten, entreated me to stay there and teach the kids. I found Tehor Khangtsen, the residential compound where Geshe had lived from the age of twenty. Its sole inhabitant was one rather traumatized monk, who, brushing aside tears, said that he remembered my teacher fondly.

The day before our return flight to Chengdu, we rose at four a.m. and joined a huddle of shivering Tibetans on a nearby street corner, which, I had been assured, was the stop for the daily bus to Ganden Monastery, some twenty miles east of the city. The "bus" turned out to be an open-back truck. We clambered aboard and clung to the sides of the throbbing vehicle as the wind bit into our flesh, and our toes and fingers grew numb. Ganden was founded in the fourteenth century by Tsongkhapa, the founder of the Geluk school. Unlike Sera, it was built in a natural amphitheater on the upper slopes of a mountainside, some several hundred feet above the Kyichu Valley. The truck strained and groaned as it zigzagged up the hairpins to the monastery. As dawn rose over the hills, the snow-trimmed remains of Ganden appeared before us like stands of rotted teeth. The Tibetans explained that the local people had been ordered by the Red Guards to demolish the monastery stone by stone. Only ten buildings had since been restored. And instead of the estimated five thousand monks who formerly lived in this bustling monastic township, we met only a handful of elderly men, who somehow managed to survive amid the wreckage.

The enormity of the Tibetans' loss was overwhelming. The Dalai Lama and his retinue were men who had formed the inner circle of power in Tibet. Their rule and influence extended over an area as large as Europe. As senior prelates of the Geluk church, they saw themselves as representatives of a regime that had governed Tibet as a compassionate Buddhist state since the seventeenth century. Suddenly, in the wake of distant political upheavals that seemed to have little bearing on their lives, they found themselves on the wrong side of history.

The time-honored rituals and supplications to the deities who had safeguarded Tibet for so long did not work anymore. The Protectors seemed to have abandoned them. Many assumed that some deeply heinous karma was coming to fruition. As the rest of the world looked on with indifference, the Dalai Lama and his followers were forced to abandon their precious land and trek over the snow peaks into exile.

Martine and I were married in a brief civil ceremony on our return to Hong Kong, witnessed by our friends Peter and Nicole, another former monk and nun who had also married, and now worked in Kowloon. Two days later, we flew to England.

As we headed down to Devon by train, we had no idea whether life in an experimental, consensus-based community of young Europeans and Americans would suit us. We both realized how accustomed we had become to the hierarchy and ordered simplicity of monastic life. By comparison, the situation we were about to enter seemed rather anarchic. We found that we were part of a small migration of Western Buddhists to Devon, many of whom had been drawn to the Totnes area by the presence of Gaia House, a Vipassana retreat center in the village of Denbury. Gaia House had been founded in 1983 by Christopher Titmuss and Christina Feldman, both of whom I had known many years before in Dharamsala when I was studying with Mr. Goenka. Christopher had trained as a monk in Thailand during the 1960s before disrobing in 1975. Christina had been one of the first students of Geshe Rabten in India and then subsequently devoted herself to the practice of Vipassana.

We moved into a single room on the upper floor of Sharpham House where we were to spend the first six years of our married life. Apart from a few books, we had virtually no possessions. Since my visit the previous year, the Sharpham North Community had grown from five to eight members. With the addition of Martine and me, we were now ten. Our community life involved meditating together morning and evening, sharing in a cooking, cleaning, and shopping rota, tending the walled vegetable garden in the grounds, spending hours at weekly meetings in exhausting attempts to resolve our conflicts in a compassionate and non-aggressive manner, and running a program of weekly talks, meditation days, and weekend workshops.

Maurice and Ruth Ash, the owners of Sharpham House and founders of the Sharpham Trust, lived downstairs. Maurice had recently retired as chairman of the nearby Dartington Hall Trust and was keen to transform the estate at Sharpham into an example of a more spiritually aware and environmentally sustainable way of living. Yet neither Maurice nor Ruth were Buddhists. Inspired by a visit some years before to Green Gulch Farm, a rural Zen center in California, they had come to believe that Buddhism, of all the world's religions, would be best suited to help them realize the goals of the Sharpham Trust. One of these goals was to "re-enspirit" the English countryside. The farmers on the estate, who had been tending their cattle and sheep in the rolling hills around the house for years, were skeptical of the endeavor. They called us "the spirits."

I arrived in Mrs. Thatcher's Britain without any money or qualifications, my sole work experience having been the six-month stint as a cleaner in an asbestos factory thirteen years previously. Having left the monastic order, I could no longer expect to be sponsored by other Buddhists. And having practiced in different Buddhist traditions, I no longer identified myself with any one school and had no natural "home" in the Buddhist world. Despite many years of studying and writing about Buddhism, I had no academic degree in the subject that would have enabled me to teach in a school or university. Since a condition for living at Sharpham was that one did not receive state benefits, I survived by giving occasional lectures, conducting meditation workshops and retreats, performing writing assignments for Buddhist publishers, serving as a chaplain in the local jail, and doing manual work on the surrounding farm. Martine was in a similar position. Having spent ten years as a nun, she too lacked any formal qualifications or work skills. To supplement the meager income we earned from teaching together, she worked as Maurice and Ruth's housekeeper.

I did not once regret my decision to disrobe and return to the anonymity of lay life. It was a relief. No longer would I have to stand out in such a public way. To be a shaven-headed man in exotic robes, especially in a secular, non-Buddhist culture like Switzerland, had come to feel like the visual equivalent of screaming. I recognized that my decision to become a monk had been largely a pragmatic one; it had enabled me to study and practice Buddhism in depth. As hard as I had tried to convince myself to the contrary, I do not think I ever really had a monastic vocation. Throughout my years as a monk, I had often suffered the disquieting suspicion that I was an imposter. Moreover, the life of rural simplicity and voluntary poverty in the community at Sharpham allowed both Martine and me to concentrate on our studies and meditation in much the same way as if we had remained as celibate monastics.

Since the time of the Buddha, celibacy has been mandatory for every Buddhist monk and nun. The solitude of monastic life was regarded as a necessary condition for anyone who sought to accomplish the arduous task of realizing nirvana. If one intended to devote oneself wholeheartedly to Buddhist practice, one had to follow the Buddha's example and renounce the householder's life so that nothing could distract one from realizing one's higher goals. Throughout the history of Buddhism, only in Japan and some of the Tibetan tantric orders has such monasticism been replaced by a married priesthood. A celibate monastic order remains the norm throughout the rest of the Buddhist world in Southeast Asia, China, Korea, and Tibet.

Yet long before I disrobed, I had asked myself whether the rule of celibacy had not been required by the social and economic circumstances of the Buddha's time as much as for "spiritual" reasons. The early Buddhist community was dependent for its survival on limited alms and donations and could not realistically expect its supporters to provide for the upkeep of children as well. In the culture of that time, it was expected that anyone who chose to pursue a life of the mind would naturally relinquish the joys of married life. But in a modern society, where one has access to greater leisure, education, financial provision, and—crucially for women—the means of controlling one's fertility, does such a rule of sexual abstinence still make sense? Is someone in a stable and loving sexual relationship, who is capable of supporting him- or herself by leading a life of simplicity, intrinsically less able to realize the fruits of a Buddhist way of life than a celibate monk or nun?

The question of celibacy is as controversial an issue in Buddhism as it is in Christianity. Traditionalists will argue that Buddhism has survived for two and a half thousand years because it has preserved intact a celibate monastic order that has provided each generation since the time of the Buddha with a body of professionals committed to upholding the Dharma. Others will point out that one of the reasons Buddhism failed to survive in India and came close to being wiped out in parts of Asia during the twentieth century was because of the vulnerability of the monastic institutions on which it depended. Since celibate monks tended to live in isolated monasteries that lay outside the protective walls of townships and cities and were forbidden by their vows to bear weapons and engage in combat, they were defenseless against armed force, whether of Muslim armies in India or bands of Red Guards in China. It is too soon to tell whether the pressures of modernity will result in Buddhism moving toward a wider acceptance of a married clergy and granting more authority to the laity, or whether it will resist such developments by strengthening and renewing its communities of celibate monks and nuns.

In traditional Buddhist societies, to become a monk was equivalent to receiving an education. Monasteries like Sera or Songgwangsa were seminaries and training centers rather than closed communities of silent contemplatives. While the monks immersed themselves in the subtleties and complexities of Buddhist theology, the majority of laypeople had to be content with devotional exercises, supplicatory prayer, moral and religious observances, and the provision of dana (donations) to support the monasteries. If they wished to do more, they were encouraged to accumulate "merit" and offer prayers for a better rebirth in their next life. This led to two classes of Buddhists: the professional clergy on the one hand, and the devout but often illiterate laity on the other.

When Martine and I started teaching Buddhism in England, it became clear that such a division between monks and laity no longer seemed relevant. The people who read my books and attended our retreats were well-educated men and women, often with families and careers, who had sufficient leisure time to pursue their religious and philosophical interests, but no wish at all to be ordained as a celibate monk or nun. For many of them, the traditional practices of lay Buddhism appeared uncritically devout, simplistic, and superstitious. They were looking for a coherent and rigorous philosophy of life, coupled with a meditative practice that made an actual difference in their lives here and now, not a set of consoling beliefs and aspirations that promised rewards in a hypothetical future existence. A third way seemed to be called for: one designed for a reflective and educated laity.

In July 1985, four months after returning to England, I traveled to Rikon, in Switzerland, to participate in the Kalachakra initiation, which the Dalai Lama was due to give for the first time in Europe. The Kalachakra (Wheel of Time) tantra is one of the most elaborate of Vajrayana practices, which marked the last flowering of Buddhism in India in the tenth century CE. It is a millennarian doctrine, based on the mythic kingdom of Shambhala, which foretells of a great battle on earth that will be won when the armies of Shambhala defeat the forces of barbarity and inaugurate a new Buddhist golden age. The appeal of such prophecies for a people who had been cast into exile by a "barbarian" Communist power was obvious. Yet rather than alluding to the tragedy of Tibet, the Dalai Lama had started presenting the Kalachakra as a plea for world peace.

I had already received the Kalachakra initiation from the Dalai Lama in 1974 in India, though I had long abandoned any pretense of practicing it. And I had no intention of renewing my commitment to what I now saw as an unnecessarily complex and arcane set of rituals with no discernible relevance to my own life. I had other reasons for coming back to Switzerland, one of which was to see Geshe Rabten.

I had spent my first months at Sharpham translating the text Geshe. had given me on my visit to Tharpa Choeling the previous year. *The Song of the Profound View* turned out to be a dense and—for a Tibetan—surprisingly personal account of his meditations on emptiness during his long retreat in his hut in Dharamsala. At one point, Geshe describes how he came to the conclusion that for something to be empty means that it is "neither existent nor non-existent." Although he had arrived at this insight through his own meditative inquiry, he knew that it contradicted the official view of the Geluk tradition in which he had been trained, which maintains that emptiness is nothing but "the simple absence of inherent existence." After discussing it with his teacher Trijang Rinpoche, the Dalai Lama's junior tutor, he relinquished his own understanding out of respect for his root lama's superior wisdom. It crossed my mind that Geshe may have chosen me to translate this text as a roundabout way of highlighting my own lack of faith in him.

I presented my translation to Geshe Rabten as soon as I met him at Rikon, where he had also come to attend the Kalachakra initiation. Compared to when I had last seen him, he looked much better. The medical treatment he was receiving for his cancer seemed to be working. I had informed him of my decision to disrobe and marry, but this was the first time that he had seen me as a layman accompanied by a wife. He welcomed Martine cordially and made no comment about my change in status, but I could not help but feel that I had again let him down.

My other reason for coming to Switzerland was to ask the Dalai Lama's advice about a controversy that had recently erupted in the pages of *The Middle Way,* the quarterly journal of the Buddhist Society in London, to which I was becoming a regular though unpaid contributor. In the May issue of that year, the journal had published a review of *Kindness, Clarity, and Insight* by the Dalai Lama. The reviewer used the occasion to praise the Dalai Lama for banning the Geluk practice of a protector deity called Dorje Shugden, whose followers, he claimed, had violently persecuted the Nyingma school of Tibetan Buddhism in Eastern Tibet in the early years of the twentieth century, overrunning their monasteries and destroying their religious objects. (The book, however, made no mention of any of these things.) As soon as the review appeared, a furious letter to the editor arrived from the community in Manjushri Institute in Cumbria (where, seven years earlier, I had spent a month working with Geshe Kelsang Gyatso during my first return visit to England), who denounced the reviewer for denigrating their faith and spreading false accusations. John Snelling, the editor of *The Middle Way,* had no idea what was going on. He asked me to consult the Dalai Lama, as patron of the Buddhist Society, for suggestions as to how the journal should proceed in handling this issue.

I had first heard of Dorje Shugden from the rain-stopping Nyingma lama Yeshe Dorje. Shortly before I left Dharamsala, he had taken me aside and whispered urgently into my ear to have nothing to do with this deity. In Switzerland I became aware that Geshe Rabten, following his own teacher Trijang Rinpoche, the junior tutor, was devoted to this practice. Dorje Shugden—a scowling figure with a wide-brimmed hat, seated on a horse—was regarded by his adherents as the one who guards the purity of the teachings of Tsongkhapa, the founder of the Geluk school. It was claimed that this wrathful god would strike down with disease or accident any Geluk practitioner foolhardy enough to receive heretic non-Geluk teachings, particularly that of Dzogchen.

Dzogchen (Great Perfection) is a contemplative practice found in the Nyingma school of Tibetan Buddhism. The Nyingma (Ancient) school traces its origins to the first phase of the dissemination of Buddhism from India to Tibet in the seventh century CE. Dzogchen is founded on the idea of *rigpa,* a Tibetan term that literally means "knowing" but has come to denote a "pristine awareness" that is believed to be the fundamental ground of all experience. *Rigpa* is regarded as the Buddha mind itself, intrinsically pure of imperfection yet immanent in each moment of consciousness. To practice Dzogchen requires that the "empty, radiant, and spontaneously compassionate" nature of *rigpa* be "pointed out" to one by a qualified lama. From then on, one seeks to live every moment from the perspective of *rigpa* rather than that of confused ego-centered consciousness.

Over the centuries, the practice of Dzogchen has led to much controversy in Tibet. Some lamas criticized it as a remnant of the Chan (Zen) doctrine taught by the Chinese teacher Hoshang, which was outlawed in Tibet in the eighth century. Others, particularly those of the Geluk school, saw *rigpa* as a thinly veiled version of the Brahmanic Atman (Self/God), an idea that the Buddha had rejected. The true Dharma, they insisted, was founded on the principles of contingency and emptiness alone and had no place for any quasi-theistic Ground of Being.

From the time I was in Dharamsala, I had been aware that the Dalai Lama himself had been receiving instruction on Dzogchen from the eminent Nyingma lama Dilgo Khyentse Rinpoche. I respected the Dalai Lama's openness in embracing practices from schools of Tibetan Buddhism other than the one in which he had been trained. He sought to develop a synthesis of Tibetan Buddhist teachings in order to overcome the sectarianism that often plagued relations between adherents of the different Tibetan traditions. Indeed, the concluding chapter of his book *Kindness, Clarity, and Insight* was an essay in which he tried to reconcile some of the conflicting views of the Nyingma and Geluk schools. This quest for intersectarian harmony among the exiled Tibetans seems to have been one of the reasons why, since the mid-1970s, he had become increasingly critical of Dorje Shugden. Rather than being a manifestation of the Buddha's wisdom, as adherents of the protector believed, the Dalai Lama now declared that Dorje Shugden was just a mundane spirit and should be accordingly downgraded. If the Dalai Lama was correct, this would imply that some of the most revered teachers of the Geluk tradition—including the saintly and much loved junior tutor—had somehow been hoodwinked by a malefic spook.

I found all of this extremely weird. The same people who expounded a finely reasoned philosophy of emptiness turned out to be fervent believers in what to me was little more than occult mumbo jumbo. I was not granted an audience with the Dalai Lama, but instead was briefed by his private secretary. After being given a short history of the dispute and the Dalai Lama's current position, which confirmed that he indeed sought to forbid the public (but not private) practice of Dorje Shugden, I was asked to tell the editor of the The Middle Way that His Holiness regarded the controversy to be an internal issue within the Tibetan community and that it should not be further discussed in the Western media. As a result, the indignant letter from Cumbria was not published and—for the time being at least—the matter was laid to rest.

Geshe Rabten died on February 27 the following year. He was sixty-six years old. He had suffered enormous hardships during his life: he had fled his home in Eastern Tibet at the age of nineteen to become a monk; he had suffered severe malnutrition at Sera because he had no benefactor; and then he had to cross the Himalayas to arrive as a destitute refugee in India. At the same time he had risen, through his own efforts, from a simple farmboy to become a philosophical assistant to the Dalai Lama. I now realized that his last years were lived in the shadow of the crisis over Dorje Shugden. As a close disciple of the junior tutor, he would have been riven by conflicting loyalties. He would have known that it was only a matter of time before he would have to publicly declare his allegiance either to the junior tutor or to the Dalai Lama.

# 8

# SIDDHATTHA GOTAMA

AT SHARPHAM AND Gaia House, I found myself part of an experimental lay community whose inspiration, ideas, and practices were drawn primarily from the Theravada school, the tradition of Buddhism that prevails in Sri Lanka, Burma, and Thailand. From a Tibetan or Zen Buddhist point of view, for someone like myself, who had taken the bodhisattva vow to save all sentient beings, to embrace these "Hinayana" (Lesser Vehicle) teachings was a backward step. It showed that I was unready for the higher teachings of the Mahayana (Great Vehicle) and needed to accumulate a great deal more "merit" before I could embark on the selfless and compassionate way of the bodhisattva. In addition to my evident spiritual lapse, I had also forsaken my monastic vows and married a former nun. Things did not look good.

I did not see it this way at all. I was beginning to suspect that the Mahayana traditions had, on certain points, lost sight of what the Buddha originally taught. During my years as a monk, I had periodically stumbled upon startling passages in texts from the Pali Canon, which spoke in an entirely different voice and tone from the one I usually associated with the remote and impossibly perfect figure of Shakyamuni Buddha. The Pali Canon is the body of Buddhist literature preserved in the Pali language, which contains hundreds of discourses and detailed instruction on monastic training believed to have been delivered by Siddhattha Gotama, the historical Buddha. Pali is a vernacular form of classical Sanskrit, which originated in the North Indian dialects that Gotama himself would have spoken. The Canon was preserved orally through memorization by monks for about four hundred years before it was written down in Sri Lanka in the first century BCE.*

One of the most striking Pali texts I came across was called the *Kalama Sutta,* a discourse the Buddha gave to the Kalama people, in the town of Kesaputta in the kingdom of Kosala. The Kalama people are confused. They tell Gotama how when different teachers arrive in Kesaputta, they "expound and explain only their own doctrines, the doctrines of others they despise, revile and pull to pieces." They ask his advice on how to distinguish between those who are speaking the truth and those who are not.

And the Buddha replies: "It is proper for you, Kalamas, to doubt, to be uncertain. Come, Kalamas. Do not go upon what has been heard by repeated hearing; nor upon tradition; nor upon rumor; nor upon what is in a sacred teaching; nor upon surmise; nor upon an axiom; nor upon specious reasoning; nor upon a bias toward a notion that has been pondered over; nor upon another's seeming ability; nor upon the consideration, 'this monk is our teacher.' Kalamas, when you know for yourselves: these things are bad, these things are blamable; these things are censured by the wise; undertaken and observed, these things lead to harm and ill: then abandon them."

This unambiguous call for the valuing of uncertainty and the need to establish the truth of things for oneself rather than rely on the authority of others struck a deep chord within me. The Buddha encourages the Kalamas to observe for themselves the consequences of greed, hatred, and stupidity on human beings, so they can judge for themselves what thoughts and acts lead to harm and suffering and which do not. His sole criterion for evaluating a doctrine is whether it causes or mitigates suffering. Even more startling is a statement toward the end of

*See Appendix I for a detailed description of the Pali Canon.

the text, where he tells the Kalamas of the benefits of such an approach: "Suppose there is no hereafter and there is no fruit of deeds done well or ill. Yet in this world, here and now, free from hatred, free from malice, safe and sound, and happy, I keep myself."

The *Kalama Sutta* presents a vision of the Buddha's teaching that goes against the grain of much Buddhist orthodoxy. Rather than deference to tradition and lineage, it celebrates self-reliance; rather than belief in doctrine, it stresses the importance of testing ideas to see if they work; and rather than insisting on a metaphysics of rebirth and karma, it suggests that this world might indeed be the only one there is.

From the texts of the Pali Canon, I also became familiar with the metaphysical questions the Buddha refuses to comment upon. These are some of the "big" questions to which religions claim to provide the answers: Is the universe eternal or not eternal? Is it finite or infinite? Is the mind the same as or different from the body? Does one continue to exist after death or not? The Buddha dismisses such questions, because to pursue them would not contribute to cultivating the kind of path he teaches. He compares a person who is preoccupied with such speculations to a man who has been wounded by a poisoned arrow but refuses to have it removed until he knows "the name and clan of the person who fired it; whether the bow was a longbow or a crossbow; whether the arrow was hoof-tipped, curved or barbed." The only legitimate concern for such a person would be the removal of the arrow. The rest is irrelevant.

In another Pali discourse the Buddha compares people who are obsessed with answering such questions to a group of blind men who are summoned by a king to describe an elephant. Each blind person is invited to touch a different part of the animal. The one holding the trunk declares that the elephant is a tube; the one feeling the side says that the elephant is a wall; while the one holding the tail is convinced that the elephant is a rope. Thus preoccupation with metaphysics not only fails to address the primary issue of suffering, but also leads to a partial and distorted picture of the complex totality of the human situation.

It seemed clear from these texts that the Buddha's original approach was therapeutic and pragmatic rather than speculative and metaphysical. By refusing to address whether mind and body are the same or different or whether one exists after death or not, he undermines the possibility of constructing a theory of reincarnation. For without affirming an immaterial mind and a postmortem existence, it is difficult—if not impossible—to speak coherently about rebirth and karma. Yet contrary to what the Buddha said in these texts, my Tibetan teachers insisted that if one did not accept that mind was different from the body and that one is reborn after death, then one could not even consider oneself a Buddhist. As the words of Siddhattha Gotama metamorphosed into the religion called "Buddhism," I began to suspect that something might have gone awry.

In my quest for a language that would speak to the condition of a contemporary layperson who was comfortable with a secular and scientific worldview and skeptical about traditional religious beliefs, I found myself returning more and more to the texts of the Pali Canon in order to seek out other passages like those in the *Kalama Sutta*. I realized that what I found difficult to accept in Buddhism were precisely those ideas and doctrines that it shared with its Indian sister religion: Hinduism. Rebirth, the law of karma, gods, other realms of existence, freedom from the cycle of birth and death, unconditioned consciousness: these were all ideas that *predated* the Buddha. For many of his contemporaries, such notions would have been uncritically accepted as a description of how the world worked. They were not, therefore, intrinsic to what he taught, but simply a reflection of ancient Indian cosmology and soteriology.

I also came to recognize that what spoke to me most directly in the Buddha's teaching were precisely those ideas that could *not* be derived from the matrix of classical Indian thought. What I needed to do, therefore, was to go carefully through the Pali Canon and extract all those passages that had the stamp of Siddhattha Gotama's own distinctive voice. Anything attributed to him that could just as well have been said in the classical Indian texts of the Upanishads or Vedas, I would bracket off and put to one side. Having done this, I would then have to see whether what I had sifted out as the Buddha's word provided an adequate foundation for formulating a coherent vision for leading a contemporary lay Buddhist life.

This was easier said than done. The Pali Canon is a vast patchwork of thousands of pages of text, woven and sewn together over many generations. It contains different voices and narrative styles, internal contradictions, psychological insights followed by tirades on hellfire and damnation, a hopelessly scrambled chronology of events, and mind-numbing repetitions of stock passages. As a novice in Pali studies, I felt like a child cautiously dipping his toes into an ocean that extends for miles before him. Although I had spent years learning to read Tibetan, it was of no use to me, since the bulk of what is recorded in the Pali Canon had not been translated into Tibetan. Fortunately, over the past 130 years, the entire corpus of Pali canonical texts has been translated and retranslated into English by a small group of dedicated monks and scholars. Without their invaluable help, I would have been seriously hampered in pursuing the task I had set myself.

As my familiarity with the Pali Canon grew, not only did my understanding of Buddhism begin to change but also my understanding of what kind of person Siddhattha Gotama was. While studying with Geshe Rabten in Switzerland in the late 1970s, I had come across a book called *The Life of the Buddha,* written by an English monk called Nanamoli Thera in Ceylon in the 1950s. Nanamoli tells the story of Gotama and his teaching entirely through passages selected from the Pali Canon, in the form of a series of radio broadcasts. While I was familiar with the core doctrines of early Buddhism from my Tibetan teachers, I had never before encountered them in their original context. Nanamoli's elegant translations made them come alive in a vivid and compelling way and, for the first time, located them for me within the context of Gotama's life on earth.

Around the same time, I also read *The Buddha: Buddhist Civilization in India and Ceylon* by the British academic Trevor Ling. In contrast to Nanamoli's reverential approach, Ling offers a critical, historical perspective, influenced by Marxist analysis. For Ling, the life of Siddhattha Gotama is unintelligible if one does not have a clear picture of the socioeconomic conditions in which he lived. Buddhism would simply not have arisen in the Gangetic basin had economic conditions in the fifth century BCE not generated a sufficient surplus of wealth to provide for non-productive members of society. Ling describes how this economic growth led to the formation of the first cities in India and the emergence of a powerful middle class of merchants and bankers. The same prosperity allowed rulers to raise standing armies, thereby enabling them to conquer their neighbors by force and secure ever-larger territories over which to rule. This led to the absorption of the small tribal republics (as Gotama's homeland of Sakiya had once been) into an entirely new kind of political state: centralized, autocratic monarchy.

Ling provocatively claimed that Gotama did not intend to found a new religion but a new *civilization*. The various forms of the Buddhist religion, as we know them today, are, he argues, the remnants of a civilization that failed to take root in India. I found this idea compelling. It has remained central to my thinking about the Buddha and Buddhism ever since.

Yet both Nanamoli Théra and Trevor Ling failed to provide a convincing portrait of this person Siddhattha Gotama. There were occasional glimpses of his humanity—such as when he calls his cousin Devadatta a "lick-spittle"—but neither author seemed interested in fleshing out his character more fully. Likewise, while both books helped dispel some of my naïve and romantic ideas about the Buddha, there was little attempt to analyze his relationships with the numerous other characters who appear in the Pali discourses or construct a detailed chronology of the events in his life. As in most books that purport to tell this story, episodes from Gotama's teaching career tended to serve as little more than a series of pegs on which to hang Buddhist doctrines. Thus I was still left in the curious position of regarding myself as a follower of the Buddha with only the vaguest idea of who this man was.

In contrast to the Christian gospels, where the life of Jesus lies at the heart of the Christian message, Buddhist canonical texts tend to treat Siddhattha Gotama's eighty years of life on earth as though they were largely incidental to what he taught. This is particularly true of his life *after* the awakening. What happened to him during his remaining years, once he resolved his existential struggle and became the Buddha, appears to be of little if any consequence. I had the impression that for forty-five years he wandered around North India, teaching and meditating, surrounded by an ever-growing number of devout disciples, until one day he lay down to die in the town of Kusinara. A close reading of the Pali Canon, however, reveals that things were not so simple.

One of the greatest obstacles to understanding the Buddha's life is the story that Buddhism traditionally tells of it. In this well-known version, Prince Siddhattha was born as the son and heir of King Suddhodana and was raised in the luxury of royal palaces in the kingdom of Sakiya. One day, curious to know more about the realm over which he one day would rule, he made an excursion beyond the palace walls and for the first time encountered a sick person, an aging person, a corpse, and a wandering monk. These sights shocked the spoiled young man into an awareness of his own mortality. Unable any longer to lead the idle and sensuous life of a young prince, he fled the palace at night, discarded his luxurious robes and jewels, shaved his head, and became a wandering monk. After six years of strenuous meditation and asceticism, he sat beneath the Bodhi tree and realized Awakening and thus became the Buddha—the Awakened One.

But this account contradicts what we know about Siddhattha Gotama in the Pali Canon. The Buddha's father was not a king but a leading nobleman of the Gotama clan, who would have served as chairman of the Assembly in Sakiya. At most he would have been a sort of regional headman or governor. Sakiya was part of the powerful kingdom of Kosala, ruled by King Pasenadi from the capital city of Savatthi, about eighty miles to the west. "The Sakiyans are vassals of the King of Kosala," acknowledged Siddhattha Gotama. "They offer him humble service and salute him, rise and do him homage and pay him fitting service." And although the story of the four sights is related by Gotama in one of the Pali discourses, it forms part of a mythical tale about another Buddha called Vipassi, who lived in the distant past. The story has nothing to do with Gotama himself.

Nor does the Buddha's first name, "Siddhattha," appear in the Canon. In the discourses and monastic texts he is referred to either as *Gotama*—his family or clan name—or the *Bhagavat,* an honorific term meaning "Lord," often translated as the "Blessed One." When speaking of himself, he tends to use the curious epithet *Tathagata*—the "One Who Is Just So." For simplicity, I will refer to him either as "Gotama" or by the epithet "the Buddha" (Awakened One). In the more intimate settings with his family I will call him "Siddhattha," to distinguish him from the other Gotamas.

The key to unraveling both the character of Siddhattha Gotama and the chronology of his life lies, I believe, in his relationship with King Pasenadi of Kosala. At the time of their first recorded meeting, Gotama would have been about forty years old—the same age as the king. In appearance, he would have looked no different from the many other monks of the time, who wandered along the dusty roads of North India, begging for their sustenance in the villages and towns scattered across the vast, fertile Gangetic Plain. His head would have been shaven, with, at most, a two-week growth of hair and beard. His dress would have consisted of three simple robes, hand-dyed yellow ocher or brown, either stitched together from discarded rags or, given his rising prominence as a teacher, patches of finer cloth donated by an admiring benefactor. His possessions would have amounted to no more than a metal or clay bowl, a needle and thread, a razor, a water strainer, and, if he were unwell, some medicine.

King Pasenadi, on the other hand, would have awoken that morning in his sumptuous apartments in the city of Savatthi. Had he stepped out onto the upper terrace of his palace, he would have beheld, across the rooftops of the mud and wooden dwellings of his capital, the broad sweep of the Aciravati River, the busy fishing villages along its shore, and the fields and forest beyond. As the monarch of the most powerful kingdom north of the Ganges, he could call upon a small army of officials, guards, attendants, and concubines to cater to his every whim. He was a fat man, noted for consuming vast amounts of rice and curry, and a sensualist, who would discuss with his vassals how to achieve the most refined kinds of pleasure. He could be cruel as well. He was known to bind his enemies in ropes and chains, impale rebels and assassins on stakes, and organize bloody sacrifices of cattle, goats, and sheep, prepared by "slaves, servants and workers, spurred on by punishment and fear, wailing with tearful faces." He would go to any lengths to ensure his power was not challenged, even infiltrating the religious communities around Savatthi with his spies, who disguised themselves as monks and ascetics.

Below the king's quarters, in the courtyard of the palace, caparisoned elephants would be waiting to carry the royal party from the bustling city to the monastic retreat of Jeta's Grove a mile away. Sumana, Pasenadi's younger sister, who cared for their elderly grandmother, was one of the group. Since this appears to be the first time that the king was making a formal visit to Siddhattha Gotama, a fellow nobleman from Kosala who had risen to become a renowned teacher, it is likely that Bandhula, the king's close friend and commander of the Kosalan army, and the general's devout wife, Mallika, were also present among the retinue. The procession would have left around midmorning, bearing gifts and ample food to offer the community of monks and nuns for their sole meal at midday.

Once the formalities of the meal were over, King Pasenadi would

have made his way to the Gandhakuti, the "Scented Hut," where Gotama lived and received visitors. The king considered himself to be
an intellectual and a patron of learning. As a young man, together
with Bandhula, he had studied at the renowned university of Takkasila
(Taxila), the capital of the Persian satrapy of Gandhara, where men
throughout India traveled to train in the various arts and sciences of
the day. On becoming king, Pasenadi made a point of visiting the itinerant teachers who came to Savatthi in order to question them about
their doctrines and attainments, ask their advice, and, if pleased, offer
them his protection and support. Now it was Gotama's turn.

The two men exchanged greetings, chatted cordially for a while,
then the king sat down and came straight to the point: "So, Master Gotama, how can you, who are still so young and have only recently left
home, possibly say that you are a sage?"

Gotama, I imagine, would have looked the pompous monarch in the
eye, a faint, ironic smile darting across his face: "There are four things,
Your Majesty, that should not be disparaged on account of their youth:
a fire, a snake, a warrior, and a monk. If a tiny flame gains a stock of
fuel, it becomes a conflagration. A little snake chanced upon in a village or forest may attack and kill the person who does not heed it. A
warrior prince might likewise one day seize your throne and thrash you.
And if you tamper with a virtuous monk, you will risk remaining child-
less and heirless like the stump of a Palmyra tree."

By identifying himself (a monk) with these potentially dangerous
forces, Gotama implied that he and his teaching might also be a threat
to the established order of things. He played on the king's fears and su-
perstitions. Like every monarch of the time, Pasenadi would know that
other members of his family (his brother Jeta, for example) were almost certainly vying for his throne behind his back. Moreover, since
the king had yet to produce an heir, his own lineage was far from secure. Gotama did not beat around the bush. He impressed his authority on the king. And the gambit paid off. Instead of flying into a rage,

Pasenadi was favorably struck by Gotama's reply and asked to be accepted as a follower.

This was a—if not *the*—key moment in Gotama's career. After he had spent five or more years of teaching and building up a following across North India, the supreme ruler of the Kingdom of Kosala, the man to whom Gotama had owed fealty his entire adult life, had finally deigned to come and see him. With the support of Pasenadi, Gotama's tenure at Savatthi was now assured. There, at Jeta's Grove, he would spend every Rains for the next twenty-five years, where he would deliver the majority of his discourses, where he would work out the details of his monastic rule. Pasenadi became a regular visitor at Jeta's Grove. Over time, the monk and the tyrant became friends and, eventually, through marriage, relatives.

Pasenadi's devotion to Siddhattha Gotama and his teaching did not, however, work a miraculous transformation on the royal ego. Among all the many dialogues in the Pali Canon between the two, the king is not once recorded as achieving any insight. The only time he is seen to benefit from Gotama's instruction is when he follows his advice to go on a diet. From "a bucket measure of rice and curries" he reduces his intake to "at most a pint-pot measure of boiled rice," and, as a result, becomes "quite slim." In all other respects, Pasenadi's appetites and paranoid fears seem little affected by anything Gotama tells him.

"I was sitting in the law court," said Pasenadi to Gotama one day, "and what did I see? All these affluent judges telling lies in order to further enrich themselves. Then I thought: 'I've had enough of this. From now on, Handsome's in charge. I'll be able to trust his judgments.'" "Handsome" was the nickname by which Bandhula, Pasenadi's friend and commander of his army, was affectionately known. Yet no sooner had Bandhula been appointed chief justice, than the disgraced judges began circulating a rumor that the general and his sons were planning to assassinate Pasenadi and seize the throne. The king appears to have panicked. He dispatched Bandhula and his sons to quell an uprising on the northern border, then, on their return to Savatthi, had them ambushed and killed.

When Mallika, Bandhula's wife, heard this news, she was in the midst of preparing a midday meal for Gotama and his monks. She kept calm and instructed her daughters-in-law to voice no criticism of Pasenadi, who, she correctly surmised, would soon be overcome with remorse at having murdered his oldest friend and ally. Pasenadi spared the lives of the women and provided them with safe conduct back to Bandhula's estates at Kusinara. As an additional act of atonement, he appointed Digha Karayana, Bandhula's nephew, to replace "Handsome" as head of the army, a move he would later bitterly regret.

Gotama's reaction to this brutal murder committed by his foremost patron is not recorded. Since he could not have afforded to jeopardize his standing in Savatthi, it is unlikely that he would have openly criticized the king for his behavior. Bandhula's death would have been a warning to him. For no matter how high one might be held in Pasenadi's esteem one day, if the tyrant's mood suddenly shifted, the next day one could be dead. We can assume that Gotama knew Bandhula well—they were sons of the governors of neighboring provinces in eastern Kosala: Gotama in Sakiya and Bandhula in Malla, and both had risen to prominence at Savatthi under the patronage of the king. Four decades later, Gotama would lie down to die between two *sal* trees outside the Mallan town of Kusinara, and Mallika, Bandhula's frail old widow, would unfurl her most precious jeweled cloak over his corpse.

This story of intrigue, betrayal, and murder locates Gotama in the midst of a highly volatile world in which he was deeply implicated. He was dependent on Pasenadi. Without the tryant's support, he would be unable to realize his goals. He could not just wander off with his monks en masse into the mountains or forest. Not only would they be subject to attacks from brigands, cannibals, and wild animals, they would have nowhere to go to seek alms and sustenance. Thus he was obliged to base his main centers close to large urban settlements. He had no choice but to find favor with the local rulers, military chiefs, and prosperous merchants. In order to establish his ideas and found a community, he required two things: a guarantee of security and access to wealth.

In my quest for the historical Buddha, I keep having to strip away layer upon layer of myth that has encrusted itself around the human person. In order to arrive at a sense of who this man was, I have had to discard the idealized image of the serene and perfect teacher who is incapable of ever making a wrong move. Gotama, like the rest of us, inhabited an uncertain and unpredictable world. He had no idea what might happen the next day or the next month. He could not foresee what mood or suspicion might seize a patron and lead him suddenly to withdraw his support. He was unable to predict whether a natural calamity might befall Kosala, or whether a war would break out or a coup be mounted, or whether a sickness would suddenly strike him down.

I also have had to be on guard against the widespread image of Gotama as a world-renouncing monk, a contemplative mystic whose sole aim was to show his followers the way to final liberation from the cycle of death and rebirth. This picture obscures his role as a social critic and reformer, as one who rejected key religious and philosophical ideas of his time, who ridiculed the priestly caste and its theistic beliefs, who envisioned an entirely new way in which people could lead their individual and communal lives.

Siddhattha Gotama compared himself to a man who had gone into a forest and discovered "an ancient path traveled upon by people in the past." On following it, the man came to the ruins of "an ancient city, with parks, groves, ponds and ramparts, a delightful place." The man then went to the local king, told him of his discovery, and then encouraged the monarch "to renovate the city so it would become successful, prosperous and filled with people once again." Gotama explained that this "ancient path" is a metaphor for the middle way to which he had awoken. Yet rather than presenting the middle way as a path that leads to nirvana, he presented it as a path that leads to the restoration of a *city*. He saw his teaching—the Dhamma—as the template for a *civilization*. He was fully aware that in order to realize his goal of restoring that ancient city, he would need more than the enthusiastic support of monks and nuns. He would require the cooperation of men such as King Pasenadi of Kosala.

I also have to be alert to the tendency to project onto Gotama all my own preferences and values. I recognize that every Buddhist through history has constructed his or her own Siddhattha Gotama and I am no different. I have to acknowledge that the vast majority of Buddhists have shown little if any interest in the personality of the man who founded their religion; they have been content to revere a remote and idealized figure. I realize that everything I discover about this distant historical person will also reveal something about myself. I cannot claim that my version of the Buddha is somehow more true or correct than yours. All I can say is that the materials buried in the Pali Canon and elsewhere have not yet exhausted their capacity to generate more stories about Gotama and what he taught.

# 9

# THE NORTH ROAD

IN FEBRUARY 2003, my friend Allan Hunt Badiner commissioned me to make a journey through the North Indian states of Bihar and Uttar Pradesh, including a brief excursion into Nepal, to visit the historic sites connected to the Buddha's life and teaching. I was forty-nine. My task was to produce a detailed photographic record of these places for a book Allan was writing on Buddhist pilgrimage in India. This provided an ideal opportunity to undertake a journey that I had long intended to make, but, for one reason or another, had never got round to doing.

Since returning to Europe from Korea I had continued to practice photography. Over time I became more and more interested in taking images of everyday objects in a way that revealed aspects of them that I normally ignored or overlooked. "The pursuit of meditation and photography," I wrote in an essay, "leads away from fascination with the extraordinary and back to a rediscovery of the ordinary. Just as I had once hoped for mystical transcendence through meditation, so I assumed exotic places and unusual things to be ideal subjects for photography." When Martine was commissioned by a publisher in London to write a book on Buddhist meditation, I was asked to provide eighty color and black-and-white photographs to illustrate the text. I produced a series of images that sought to "open up the world in a startling and unexpected way that, like the experience of meditation, was both compelling and unsettling." *Meditation for Life* appeared in 2001. It was on seeing my photos in this book that Allan invited me to go to India to take pictures to illustrate his work in progress on Buddhist pilgrimage.

It is pitch-dark as my driver Mr. Khan and I pull into the Royal Retreat Hotel near the village of Shivpati Nagar, not far from the ruins of Kapilavatthu, where Siddhattha Gotama grew up. The headlights of our car sweep across an impeccable grass lawn, then come to rest on the pillars of a whitewashed colonial bungalow. Liveried servants scurry out to meet us. The hotel was built as a hunting lodge in the eighteenth century by the local maharaja, and faded tiger skins still hang on the walls, leather-bound books crack and crumble inside glass cabinets, the oppressive smell of ancient furnishings and musty carpets penetrates everywhere. After the generator is switched off, I fall asleep to the soaring wail of jackals.

After breakfast I follow a narrow path that disappears into the indigenous forest around the lodge. I sit down cross-legged on a small patch of packed, reddish-gray earth. All around me, skinny trees, vines, and creepers snake upward. Giant leaves, perforated by caterpillars, dangle and sway before my eyes. An occasional bird shrieks from the canopy above. From the distance comes the rhythmic slapping of wet clothes on stone by a pond or stream. Then I hear an animal move through the brush and stop. My heart accelerates. I squint through the dense tangle of undergrowth to find a pair of slit, amber-colored eyes staring at me. It's a jackal. We hold each other's gaze for a while, then it calmly moves on.

At mid-morning I set off with Mr. Khan to discover what remains of Kapilavatthu today. The landscape of North India through which we drive is much the same as that Gotama would have known. If you remove the trucks and bicycles, the industrially dyed saris and cheap radios, little has changed since his time. Gotama once compared his patched monk's robe to a patchwork of fields, which would have been much like the jumbled array of bright green paddies and yellow-flowering mustard fields, separated one from the other by raised earth pathways, that I can see through the window of the Land Cruiser as we bump and shudder along potholed roads. We pass mango groves, the earth beneath their dark canopy of leaves neatly swept by local women, and mighty banyan trees, their aerial roots hanging like fibrous tentacles from their branches, both familiar to me from the Pali texts, but now rendered more vivid and real. And every now and again, looming toward us, come placid, cream-colored bullocks with humps and dewlaps, distant descendants of those Gotama saw, still hauling creaking wooden carts piled high with swaying loads of sugarcane.

But what I see is also *not* what Siddhattha Gotama saw. Everything to the north of the Ganges is an alluvial plain, a flat expanse of slowly shifting earth and water, hundreds of miles wide, formed over millions of years from sediment washed down from the Himalayas. There are no hills or rocky outcrops, no single natural landmark that Gotama too could have seen. As sediment builds up from snowmelt and monsoon rain, the elevation of the plain changes and rivers divert to newer, lower courses. Populations follow, leaving behind their mud, wood, and thatch dwellings to dissolve into the earth and vanish without trace. Then fallen leaves, decaying vegetation, droppings of birds and animals, shells of snails, bones of cattle, particles of human skin all contribute to raising farther the level of the plain. The ground on which I am driving is at least eight feet above the soil on which Gotama and his monks would have trodden two and a half thousand years ago.

There is not a soul in sight when we reach Piprahwa. A warm, lazy breeze wafts across the flat, endless fields. From somewhere in the distance, a muezzin calls the faithful to prayer. Mr. Khan sits on his heels by the roadside, tugging indifferently on a *beedi*. I walk through the open wrought iron gate that leads into the park. A gardener has left a hose running. A puddle, glinting silver in the midday light, stealthily expands on the green lawn. No trace now of the North Road and its steady traffic that once might have run past this garden. No hint of the thriving market town of Kapilavatthu, secure within its mud and wood ramparts. Not the faintest echo of the feuding Gotamas and Koliyas whose ambitions and fears once animated the proud province of Sakiya: only the brick core of a stupa—a domed funerary mound in which the relics of Buddhist monks are enshrined—and, next to it, the foundations of a monastery.

The sun is beating down. Shaded by my safari hat, I self-consciously circumambulate the stupa in the clockwise manner of a pilgrim. Round and round I go. I am still the only person in the park. The puddle on the lawn is spreading. Mr. Khan has returned to the Land Cruiser to listen at speaker-popping volume to the wailing of Bollywood film music.

I run my fingers over the rough brickwork of the stupa. Though suitably old and worn-looking, these flat slabs did not exist at Gotama's time. Kiln-fired bricks were unavailable in India at that period. Nor would these bricks have formed the outer surface of the stupa: that would have been a smooth dome of whitewashed plaster. What I see and touch now is the core of an edifice dating back to the centuries after Gotama's death, which would probably have replaced an earlier, less durable structure of sunbaked mud and wood.

In 1897 William Peppé, a local British estate manager, cleared the earth and vegetation off the stupa in order to undertake the first excavations here. After digging through eighteen feet of this brickwork, he found "a massive sandstone coffer in a state of perfect preservation, hollowed from a solid block of rock." He pried open the lid to discover three small soapstone vases, a soapstone box, and a crystal bowl, inside which were "pieces of bone, which might have been picked up a few days ago." On the smallest urn were inscribed the words "This shrine for the relics of the Buddha is that of the Sakiyas." The coffer and caskets were dispatched to the Indian Museum in Calcutta, while the relics were donated to King Chulalankara of Siam, who reverently distributed them among the Thai, Ceylonese, and Burmese Buddhists.

During further excavations in 1972, Indian archaeologists dug deeper under the core of brick and discovered two more urns containing fragments of bone. But if these were the relics of Gotama, what were the ones that Mr. Peppé found, which are now revered on altars throughout much of Southeast Asia? It is hard to say. Over the next two years, further excavation revealed foundations of houses and wells, shards of pottery, coins, rusted metal implements, beads, bangles, and, crucially, a number of terra-cotta seals of the Kushan dynasty (c. 50–320 CE), bearing the inscription "Community of Buddhist monks of Kapilavastu."

Siddhattha Gotama was born in the Lumbini park, a few miles to the north, now just across the border inside Nepal. An inscribed pillar, erected about a hundred and fifty years later by the Buddhist emperor Ashoka, still marks the spot. His mother died shortly after giving birth. The boy was nursed and raised by her sister Pajapati, who married Suddhodana, Siddhattha's father.

Although born in Sakiya, Gotama always described himself as a citizen of Kosala, the kingdom into which the ancient Sakiyan republic was already incorporated at the time of his birth. Until his death, his loyalty as a subject was to King Pasenadi in Savatthi, who ruled over a territory that extended from the northern banks of the Ganges all the way to the Himalayan foothills. To the west of Kosala lay Gandhara (much of modern Pakistan), which was then a satrapy of the Achaemenid Empire of Persia, the greatest world power of the day. At the time of Gotama's birth (c. 480 BCE), Indian soldiers from this region were fighting in the Persian army against the Greeks at the battle of Thermopylae, a hundred miles northwest of Athens.

The Sakiyans were farmers. They cultivated rice, millet, mustard seed, lentils, and sugarcane, and raised cattle, sheep, and goats for meat and milk. Gotama's destiny was tied to the patchwork of fields and woodland scattered across the plains of his homeland. The buildings, from the hovels of the slaves to the grander edifices of the nobility, would have been constructed of baked mud, wood, and thatch. As the eldest son of a powerful family, Siddhattha would not have toiled daily in the fields—that would have been done by peasants and slaves.

But he would have been brought up with a keen awareness of his father's responsibility to ensure the yearly harvest on which the community's survival depended.

Kapilavatthu may have been a provincial farming town like many others, but it differed in one important respect. It was a staging post on the North Road, the major commercial and cultural artery of the day, which linked the kingdom of Magadha, south of the Ganges, with that of Kosala to the north. From Savatthi the highway continued a further seven hundred miles northwest to Takkasila in Gandhara. Wealthy and privileged Sakiyans such as the Gotamas would have been exposed to the traffic of goods and ideas that moved between the Indian heartlands of Magadha and Kosala and the vast Persian territories to the west.

As the son and heir of a leading nobleman, it is likely that Siddhattha would have accompanied his father to Savatthi, eighty miles to the west of Kapilavatthu, either on official or commercial business. Suddhodana would not have seen his gifted son's prospects of future glory lying in the rural backwater of Sakiya. Any advancement for a young nobleman in the Kosalan state would come from his gaining the attention and patronage of a powerful figure at the royal court in Savatthi. It is possible, therefore, that long before becoming the Buddha, Siddhattha was already moving in the circles of the young Kosalan prince Pasenadi, which would have included such figures as Bandhula, another ambitious son of a headman of an outlying province.

The Pali Canon is curiously silent about Siddhattha Gotama's formative years. Almost nothing is recorded about him until his dramatic departure from Sakiya at the age of twenty-nine in order to become a wandering monk. One of the few events he recounts of his childhood is that he once fell into a meditative state when seated in the shade of a rose-apple tree while his father attended to some business in the fields. Nothing is said about how he was raised, the kind of education he received, the people he knew, his first ambitions and passions, or the activities in which he was engaged. The entire period from his adolescence to the age of twenty-nine is a blank.

Far more, however, is known about some of his peers. Five in particular stand out: Pasenadi, the future king of Kosala; Bandhula, the son of the governor of Malla and later Pasenadi's army chief; Angulimala, the son of a Savatthi brahmin who became a ritual murderer; Mahali, a Licchavi nobleman from the city of Vesali; and Jivaka, a courtesan's son from Rajagaha who rose to become the royal physician of Magadha. All these men were of the same generation as Siddhattha Gotama and all remained close to him throughout their lives, though none of them except Angulimala became a monk. In addition to sharing this famous friend, what also bound them together was that they were fellow students at the university of Takkasila (Taxila).

Takkasila, the capital of Gandhara, was the preeminent center of learning in the region. Young men from the newly emerging cities of North India were sent there to train in the arts of government and war, to become doctors and surgeons, to study religion and philosophy, or to master magic and ritual. Living in a city of the Achaemenid Empire, at the crossroads of major trade routes, they were exposed to a more cosmopolitan culture than they would have known at home in a provincial town on the Gangetic Plain. In Takkasila they would have met Persians and Greeks and other citizens of the far-flung empire. For an Indian nobleman to send his son to Takkasila was the equivalent of a wealthy Indian industrialist sending a gifted son or daughter to Oxford or Harvard today. Given his background, Siddhattha Gotama too may have studied at Takkasila. And even if he did not, he would have come of age in the company of others who had.*

The Canon also tells us that Siddhattha fathered a son, Rahula, in Sakiya when he was twenty-seven or twenty-eight years old. Since it would have been the custom in such societies for members of the nobility to marry in their teens, he was relatively old when he fathered his first child. One explanation for this would be that he had been absent

---

*See Appendix II for further reflections on the possibility that the Buddha studied at Takkasila.

from Sakiya during his formative years, possibly studying in Takkasila or employed in some military or administrative capacity by the Kosalan state. He would then have returned to his homeland in his late twenties in order to marry and fulfill his family responsibilities in producing an heir. His wife is a shadowy figure called Bhaddakaccana, or possibly Bimba, a maternal cousin and the sister of Devadatta, his future rival. It was not long after the birth of Rahula that Siddhattha decided to flee from Kosala.

What drove him to do this? His own account in the Canon sheds little light on this question. He says that he decided to leave home in order to seek the "deathless supreme security from bondage," rather than seek satisfaction in mortal and transient things. But this is simply a restatement of the world-renouncing norms of the Indian ascetic tradition of the day. It seems that he underwent a deep personal crisis of some kind and was seized by "existential" questions: What is this life for? What does it all mean? Why have I been born only to die? He may have realized that everything he had done up until this point had only brought him to a dead end. So he chose to abandon all that was familiar to him: his king and country, his duties as a nobleman, his clan, his wife, his young son. This apparently desperate step could have been the only option left to him for resolving his dilemma. And he would have taken it with no assurance at all of a successful outcome.

"Though my mother and father wished otherwise," he recalled, "and wept with tearful faces, I shaved off my hair and beard, put on the yellow robe, and went forth from the home life into homelessness." Thus with a shaven head, wearing just a robe patched together from rags, a bowl under his arm, probably barefoot, he headed off along the North Road. As I imagine him walking away from Sakiya, I must be careful not to judge his actions by the values of my own time and culture. The abandonment of his wife and son would probably have troubled him less—they would have been well cared for by his extended family—than the rejection of his duties to the Gotama clan and the Sakiyan community. His departure may well have been accompanied by a sense of enormous relief and freedom. He would say later, "In a home, life is stifled in an atmosphere of dust. But life gone forth is open wide."

He would have joined slow-moving caravans of ox-drawn carts, covering about ten miles a day, passing through forests inhabited by rhinoceros, tigers, lions, bears, and bands of indigenous people, and occasional market towns surrounded by villages and fields. During the monsoon rains, from June to September, the roads became muddy quagmires, impassable to traffic. He would have spent that time camped in parks and groves, arguing, thinking, and meditating. This pattern of walking slowly from one place to the next, then settling down for the three months of the rains, would continue until the end of his life.

On leaving the Kosalan province of Malla, he would have entered Vajji, the last of the ancient republics, still governed from the city of Vesali by a parliament rather than a king. When he reached the Ganges, the natural border separating Vajji and Kosala from the powerful kingdom of Magadha, he would have been rowed across by ferry. He would have stepped ashore at the village of Patali on the southern bank and followed the North Road to its terminus at Rajagaha, the Magadhan capital, which lay enclosed within its ring of hills sixty miles farther south.

Today the forests have all but disappeared, the land is intensively cultivated and the roads are cluttered with trucks, buses, carts, oxen, and people. Instead of a ferry, the three-and-a-half-mile-long Mahatma Gandhi bridge takes you across the Ganges into Patna, as Patali is now called. From the elevation of the streamlined, concrete overpass, you can see why this great, broad river formed such a daunting barrier between the rival kingdoms of ancient India. On the north shore, a wide stretch of mud and sandbars separates the dense banana plantations on terra firma from the brown, sluggish body of water. On the southern bank, by contrast, buildings lie packed together along the waterfront.

From the bridge, which—for India—is oddly devoid of traffic, Mr. Khan and I descend into the chaos of the state capital of Bihar, a sprawling, congested city of nearly two million people. A haze of dust and fumes hangs over the dingy concrete buildings, while the streets resound with the shrieking horns of cars and trucks and the incessant ringing of bicycle and rickshaw bells.

We pull up outside Jadu Ghar, the decaying colonial museum the British built here in 1917. I have come to see the casket containing relics of Gotama, which was unearthed during excavations at nearby Vesali in 1958 from a stupa identified with the help of an account written by a seventh-century Chinese pilgrim. An elderly museum official with trembling hands unlocks a door, ushers me into a small circular room with a moldy carpet, and switches on the harsh fluorescent lights. Behind thick glass, standing alone on a red velvet cloth, is a cracked spherical casket, about two inches high, made of cream-colored soapstone. A framed photograph shows the open casket with its contents displayed beside it: a little mound of ash, a copper punch-marked coin, a fragment of gold leaf, a tiny conch shell, and two glass beads.

The curator clears his throat and starts reciting a memorized description of the relics in extremely loud but unintelligible English. As he rattles on, I notice that I have placed my palms together and am bowing deferentially toward these objects. This is just a well-honed Buddhist habit. I don't feel any reverence at all. I'm confused, disheartened, and a little ashamed of myself. What did I expect? Dancing lights? Flowers falling from the heavens? This tawdry secular shrine dispirits me.

Mr. Khan is crouched on the road outside, polishing the hubcaps of the Land Cruiser with a soiled rag. A handful of bored young men has gathered around him. On seeing me approach, with one movement he tosses his *beedi* aside and swings open the driver's door. By the time I am seated beside him, he is carefully combing his hair in the rearview mirror. As we weave through the traffic, the outer shell of the car becomes his own skin. Each time I reflexively raise my hands to guard against an imminent collision, he smiles knowingly to himself as he misses the man/cow/rickshaw/truck by millimeters.

From Patna we follow the Ganges eastward, then turn south at Bakhtiarpur to Rajgir—as Rajagaha is now known. As we approach the ancient capital of Magadha, sheer rocky outcrops rise from the flat landscape. These are the first spurs of the Chota Nagpur Plateau, the hills that form the southern extremity of the Gangetic Valley. Compared to the rich alluvial plain to the north, here the land is parched and dusty. Tracts of barren, stony ground become more frequent. Then the towering hills that form a natural protective circle around Rajagaha come into view. Along their ridge I can make out intact sections of the stone ramparts, dating back to Gotama's time, which would have further shielded the citizens against attack.

It is dusk by the time we pull into the brick-walled compound of the Hokke Hotel, which lies on the outer side of the ring of hills. I am escorted to a Japanese-style tatami room, while Mr. Khan disappears around the back of the complex into the netherworld of drivers, servants, cooks, cleaners, washerwomen, guards, and off-duty policemen. Not only does the Hokke serve passable bento-box cuisine, every evening you can share a luxurious soak in its *onsen* (hot tub) with Japanese pilgrims, most of whom are here to visit the revered Vulture's Peak, where the *Lotus Sutra, Diamond Sutra,* and *Heart Sutra* are said to have been preached by the Buddha.

Before dawn the next morning, we drive out to Vulture's Peak, stopping on the way to pick up a lanky, khaki-uniformed policeman called Gurudev, who has a bolt-action rifle slung over one shoulder. Any foreigner who ventures into the hills at irregular hours has to be accompanied by an armed bodyguard as protection against the *dacoits* who supposedly hide out there. From the cluster of gift stalls and tea shops at the base of the hill, it takes Gurudev and me half an hour to climb up the old stone pathway that leads to the top.

When we arrive, my grandiose Buddhist expectations of Vulture's

Peak are dashed. It's just an outcrop of boulders on one of the lower spurs of a ridge, straddled by Tibetan prayer flags. A number of caves, where Gotama and his monks would have stayed for periods of quiet meditation, are tucked among the confusion of boulders, some of which house impromptu shrines of candles, smudges of gold leaf, and white offering scarves. On the spur itself is a rectangular platform enclosed by a low brick wall, with a makeshift altar operated by a mercenary "priest," where no more than thirty or so pilgrims can be squeezed in at any one time. As the sun rises, it affords an excellent view of the site of the ancient city. Today, nothing remains inside the circle of hills but an open expanse of scrubland and small, stunted trees.

When Gotama arrived here from Kapilavatthu around 450 BCE, he would have found himself in one of the most populous and thriving cities of the day. Rajagaha was a busy commercial center blessed with hot springs that provided a constant source of water. It was an industrial town, with iron and copper mines nearby, and a heavily fortified military base. It was also an important gathering place for monks and ascetics, who debated their doctrines in its parks, retreated to its hills for solitude, and wandered its streets begging for alms. The kingdom of Magadha was ruled from here by Bimbisara, a powerful and—as far as one can make out—respected monarch. As part of an alliance with Kosala, its major political rival, Bimbisara had married King Pasenadi's sister, Princess Devi.

According to the *Sutta Nipata,* one of the oldest sections of the Pali Canon, the king of Magadha saw, from the roof of his palace, Gotama walking calmly through the streets of the city. He ordered his retainers to find out who that person was and where he was staying. He then took a chariot to the Pandava Hill in order to meet him. He said: "You are young and tender, in the prime of your life, a nobleman of good birth who should be adorning an army, at the head of a team of elephants. I would be happy to grant you position and wealth. Tell me: where were you born?" Gotama explained that he was a native of Kosala, of the Solar lineage, from the Sakiyan clan, a people who lived on the flanks of the Himalayas. But he rejected the king's offer. "I am secure in my renunciation of the world," he told Bimbisara. "My mind delights in the struggle to which I am committed."

What did this struggle entail? All we know is that he spent some time in the communities of two teachers: Alara Kalama and Uddaka Ramaputta. Both men taught him exercises in single-minded mental absorption, the former by concentrating on "nothingness," the latter on "neither-perception-nor-non-perception." These were probably yogic exercises designed to suspend all identification with the phenomenal world in order to achieve union with Brahman, the absolute and transcendent reality of God. Gotama gained proficiency in these meditations and each teacher tried to recruit him as a fellow leader of his group. But he found that no matter how long he remained in these deep trancelike states, they failed to provide the kind of insight he sought. "Not being satisfied with those teachings," he concluded, "I left them and went away."

The only other discipline he is recorded as undertaking was that of extreme self-mortification. "I took very little food," he recalled, "a handful each meal, whether of bean soup or lentil soup or vetch soup or pea soup. Because of eating so little, my body reached a state of extreme emaciation. My limbs became like the jointed segments of bamboo; my backside became like a camel's hoof; my ribs jutted out as gaunt as the crazy rafters on an old roofless barn; the gleam of my eyes sank far down in their sockets; my scalp shriveled and withered; my belly adhered to the backbone; if I defecated or urinated, I fell over on my face; if I tried to ease my body by rubbing my limbs with my hands, the hair, rotted at the roots, fell out."

This overwrought account of self-abuse describes a man at his wit's end, locked in conflict with the demands of his body, in search of a desperate transcendence. "By this racking practice of austerities," he realized, "I have not attained any higher state of mind or any distinction in knowledge and vision. Could there be another way?" He then remembered the time when he was sitting beneath a rose-apple tree as a child and "entered upon and abided in a focused state of mind accompanied by applied and sustained thought, with rapture and pleasure born from seclusion." Such pleasure, he realized, is not something to be afraid of. It might even enable him to resolve his dilemma. But "with a body so excessively emaciated, it is not easy to attain that pleasure. Suppose I ate some boiled rice and bread." Which he then proceeded to do.

This account serves the interests of those who are intent on portraying Gotama as a world-renouncing monk, who mastered then rejected the normative spiritual practices of the day. It shows that he had acquired sufficient yogic kudos to start a religious movement, but gives no sense at all of the development of his ideas. One has the impression that during these six years Gotama did nothing but experiment with forms of trance and self-punishment. There is no mention of the discussions and arguments he would have had with his fellow wanderers, no mention of the philosophical and religious topics of the moment, no mention of what hopes and anxieties animated him. It fails to explain how, when he starts teaching, his discourses have such a distinctive style, tone, and content. Gotama's voice is confident, ironic, at times playful, anti-metaphysical, and pragmatic. Over the course of his formative years, he had achieved an articulate and self-assured distance from the doctrines and values of Brahmanic tradition. But exactly how he did this, we don't know.

# 10

# AGAINST THE STREAM

ON EXTRICATING OURSELVES from the narrow, dilapidated streets of Gaya, Mr. Khan and I join the road that runs beside the great sandy riverbed of the Neranjara into Bodh Gaya, the present name of Uruvela, the site of Siddhattha Gotama's awakening. We wind our way into an acquisitive pilgrimage town that is bustling, noisy, and polluted and sprawls for miles. A jet roars overhead, delivering pilgrims direct from either Colombo or Bangkok to the local airport. Luxury hotels compete with shabby guesthouses; temples of every Buddhist hue can be glimpsed behind high walls and through wrought iron gates. Monks, nuns, and lay pilgrims from all over Asia, as well as Westerners sporting telltale Buddhist insignia, throng the streets, trailed by beggars, lepers, and cripples rattling coins in tin cans. And at the far edge of the conurbation, fields have already given way to yet more building sites. Buddhism is booming in this little pocket of Bihar.

I have not set foot in Bodh Gaya for nearly thirty years. In December 1974, I traveled by overnight train from Pathankot to Gaya, squeezed into a rope luggage rack in a packed third-class compartment. I covered the remaining ten miles from Gaya in the relative luxury of a bicycle rickshaw. I was twenty-one and still living in Dharamsala. In June of that year I had become a novice monk.

I was there to receive the Kalachakra initiation from the Dalai Lama.

At the same time an estimated hundred thousand Tibetans, Bhutanese, Ladhakis, and Sikkimese also descended from the Himalayas onto the sleepy Indian village. They had established a vast, unsanitary tent-camp in the surrounding fields and among the trees along the bank of the Neranjara River. Rumor had it that this would be the last time His Holiness would confer the Kalachakra initiation. It was also the first time that a significant number of Western Buddhists would receive it.

Apart from the towering Mahabodhi temple beside the famous pipal tree, Bodh Gaya then consisted of a single dirt road, a scattering of other temples and viharas that catered to pilgrims from Thailand, Burma, and Japan, and a handful of shops selling Buddhist religious paraphernalia. The main form of transport was the bicycle. Occasionally a jeep or Ambassador car would drive through in a cloud of dust, startling the chickens and causing sleeping mongrels to open an eyelid. Together with some other *Injis*, I lodged at a nearby farm and slept on bundles of straw in a brick outbuilding that smelled of cattle.

The initiation took several days and there was no translation. I tried to follow the complicated proceedings as Geshe Dhargyey had described them before we left Dharamsala but was more interested in observing the Bhutanese family around me in their purply-striped *kiras* and *ghos,* felt boots and exotic headgear, who spent more time chatting, arguing, laughing, playing with their children, and picnicking than listening to what the Dalai Lama was saying from atop his brocade-draped throne. For them it was a carnival, a rare opportunity to relax and have fun together, rather than a dour religious event. Only the burgundy-robed monks at the front and the grim Western converts, seated motionless, their eyes tightly closed, at the back, seemed to be taking it very seriously. In conclusion, we formed an immensely long line (another occasion for lots of jostling and merriment) that passed in front of His Holiness so that each person could offer him a *katag* (ceremonial scarf), receive a blessing on the head, and a red string to tie around their wrist.

When it was all over, the crowds evaporated and Bodh Gaya reverted to its usual languid serenity. I went to the Burmese vihara on the edge of the village, where I spent three weeks in silence practicing mindfulness of body and feelings under the guidance of Mr. Goenka.

I am glad I belong to a religion that worships a tree. The magnificent pipal, whose outspread branches offer shade to those who walk below on white marble flagstones as they circumambulate the Mahabodhi temple, is indifferent to the pilgrimage industry that has surged around it in recent years. It does not mind that its great trunk is wrapped with garish satin cloths, that its limbs are strung with prayer flags or its fallen leaves collected by the children of the devout. This tree, a distant descendant of the one beneath which Gotama sat, has seen many tides of human beings come and go: Hindu priests who used the adjoining temple as a shrine to Shiva; archaeologists of the Raj, who rediscovered the temple in the nineteenth century; Anagarika Dharmapala, the Ceylonese reformer, who vowed to return the tree, temple, and surrounding monuments to Buddhist control; the thousands of Tibetans who fled with the Dalai Lama across the mountains in 1959; the millions of Indian ex-untouchables, who have recently embraced Buddhism to escape the indignity of caste; as well as occasional pale-faced converts like myself.

"This Dhamma I have reached," said Gotama in describing what he discovered that night under the branches of the original tree,

is deep, hard to see, difficult to awaken to, quiet and excellent, not confined by thought, subtle, sensed by the wise. But people love their place: they delight and revel in their place. It is hard for people who love, delight and revel in their place to see this ground: this-conditionality, conditioned arising.

This is the account of a man who set out on a journey and reached his destination. What he found there was deeply strange and unfamiliar, difficult to conceptualize or put into words. At the same time, he realized that others must have experienced it too. For what he had woken up to, "this-conditionality"—that specific things give rise to other specific things—was, in one sense, rather obvious. Everyone knows that seeds give rise to plants and eggs give rise to chickens. Yet, he insisted, this "conditioned arising" is extremely hard to see.

Why? Because people are blinded to the fundamental contingency of their existence by attachment to their *place*. One's place is that to which one is most strongly bound. It is the foundation on which the entire edifice of one's identity is built. It is formed through identification with a physical location and social position, by one's religious and political beliefs, through that instinctive conviction of being a solitary ego. One's place is where one stands, and whence one takes a stand against everything that seems to challenge what is "mine." This stance is your posture vis-à-vis the world: it encompasses everything that lies on this side of the line that separates "you" from "me." Delight in it creates a sense of being fixed and secure in the midst of an existence that is anything but fixed and secure. Loss of it, one fears, would mean that everything one cherishes would be overwhelmed by chaos, meaninglessness, or madness.

Gotama's quest led him to abandon everything to do with his place—his king, his homeland, his social standing, his position in the family, his beliefs, his conviction of being a self in charge of a body and mind—but it did not result in psychotic collapse. For in relinquishing his place (*ālaya*), he arrived at a ground (*ṭṭhāna*). But this ground is quite unlike the seemingly solid ground of a place. It is the contingent, transient, ambiguous, unpredictable, fascinating, and terrifying ground called "life." Life is a groundless ground: no sooner does it appear, than it disappears, only to renew itself, then immediately break up and vanish again. It pours forth endlessly, like the river of Heraclitus into which one cannot step twice. If you try to grasp it, it slips away between your fingers.

This groundless ground is not the absence of support. It supports you in a different way. Whereas a place can tie you down and close you off, this ground lets you go and opens you up. It does not stand still for a moment. To be supported by it, you have to be with it in a different way. Instead of standing firmly on your feet and holding on tight with both hands in order to feel secure in your place, here you have to dart across its liquid, shimmering surface like a long-legged fly, swim with its current like a fast-moving fish. Gotama compared the experience to "entering a stream."

Gotama's awakening involved a radical shift of perspective rather than the gaining of privileged knowledge into some higher truth. He did not use the words *know* and *truth* to describe it. He spoke only of waking up to a contingent ground—"this-conditionality, conditioned arising"—that until then had been obscured by his attachment to a fixed position. While such an awakening is bound to lead to a reconsideration of what one "knows," the awakening itself is not primarily a cognitive act. It is an existential readjustment, a seismic shift in the core of oneself and one's relation to others and the world. Rather than providing Gotama with a set of ready-made answers to life's big questions, it allowed him to respond to those questions from an entirely new perspective.

To live on this shifting ground, one first needs to stop obsessing about what has happened before and what might happen later. One needs to be more vitally conscious of what is happening now. This is not to deny the reality of past and future. It is about embarking on a new relationship with the impermanence and temporality of life. Instead of hankering after the past and speculating about the future, one sees the present as the fruit of what has been and the germ of what will be. Gotama did not encourage withdrawal to a timeless, mystical now, but an unflinching encounter with the contingent world as it unravels moment to moment.

To be conscious of what is happening in the present requires training in mindfulness, which Gotama described as "the one way" to achieve the kind of focused presence and responsiveness needed to function optimally on a groundless ground. Indeed, he spoke of mindfulness (*sati*) as being grounded (*paṭṭhāna*) in whatever occurs in one's body, feelings, and mind as well as in the world about one. Mindfulness is to *be aware* of what is happening, as opposed to either letting things drift by in a semiconscious haze or being assailed by events with such intensity that one reacts before one has even had time to think.

Mindfulness focuses entirely on the specific conditions of one's day-to-day experience. It is not concerned with anything transcendent or divine. It serves as an antidote to theism, a cure for sentimental piety, a scalpel for excising the tumor of metaphysical belief. "When a monk breathes out long," said Gotama, "he knows: 'I am breathing out long.' Breathing in short, he knows: 'I am breathing in short.'" Such a person

acts in full awareness when looking ahead and looking away, when flexing and extending his limbs, when wearing his robes and carrying his bowl, when eating, drinking and tasting, when defecating and urinating, when walking, standing, sitting, falling asleep, waking up, talking and keeping silent.

There is nothing so lowly or mundane that it is unworthy of being embraced by mindful attention. Mindfulness accepts as its focus of inquiry whatever arises in one's field of awareness, no matter how disturbing or painful it might be. One neither seeks nor expects to find some greater truth lurking behind the veil of appearances. What appears and how you respond to it: that alone is what matters.

By paying attention to what was happening within and around him, Gotama woke up to this vast open field of contingently arising events. His awakening was not the result of intellectual theorizing alone but of sustained, focused attention to the texture and fabric of experience. The ground he reached also included the new perspective on life that opened up within him through his exposure to conditioned arising. For those "who delight and revel in their place," he continued, "it is also hard to see this ground: the stilling of compulsions, the fading away of craving, detachment, stopping, nirvana."

Something deep within Gotama seems to have stopped. He was freed not to live in this world from the closed perspective of his place. He could remain fully present to the turbulent cascade of events without being tossed around by the desires and fears it evoked within him. A still calm lay at the heart of this vision, a strange dropping away of familiar habits, the absence, at least momentarily, of anxiety and turmoil. He had found a way of being in this world that was not conditioned by greed, hatred, or confusion. This was nirvana. The way was now open for him to engage with the world from the perspective of detachment, love, and lucidity.

The heart of Gotama's awakening lay in his unequivocal embrace of contingency. "One who sees conditioned arising," he said, "sees the Dhamma; and one who sees the Dhamma, sees conditioned arising." He recognized how both he and the world in which he lived were fluid, contingent events that sprang from other fluid, contingent events, but that *need not have happened.* Had he made other choices, things would have turned out differently. "Let be the past," he said to the wanderer Udayin. "Let be the future. I shall teach you the Dhamma: when this exists, that comes to be; with the arising of this, that arises. When this does not exist, that does not come to be; with the cessation of this, that ceases."

Siddhattha Gotama rejected the idea that freedom or salvation lay in gaining privileged access to an eternal, non-contingent source or ground, whether it be called Atman or God, Pure Consciousness or the Absolute. Freedom, for Gotama, meant freedom from greed, from hatred, and from confusion. Moreover, such freedom (nirvana) was to be found not by turning away from the world but by penetrating deep into its contingent heart.

The brahmins of Gotama's day maintained that a human being was animated by an eternal soul or self (*atman*), whose nature was identical to that of the transcendent, perfect reality of Brahman (God). This belief is deeply alluring because it means that what we *really* are will not die. And it is compelling because it appears to be confirmed by that deeply embedded intuition of being an unchanging witness to the flux of moment-to-moment experience. The sight of a flock of starlings swooping through the sky, the taste of a peach, or the melody of Bach's Sixth Brandenburg Concerto may come and go, but the sense of being the one who knows these things remains the same.

From my earliest childhood until now, I have been intuitively convinced that the very same consciousness has witnessed and continues to witness every event in my life. If I look at a photograph of myself as a baby, or consider how I have grown up and changed over the years, I realize that this timeless witness cannot be the same as the puzzled little boy, the rebellious adolescent, the devout young monk, or the skeptical middle-aged man. All these aspects of myself, it seems, are just different manifestations of my "ego" or "personality," but have nothing to do with the essential, unchanging self who knows and remembers these things.

At the same time, one of the most unsettling memories of my youth is of an occasion when my mother inadvertently challenged my instinctive certainty of being "me." It was Christmas, and I must have been about sixteen. My mother and her sister, my aunt Betty, were leafing through a volume of photographs on the kitchen table. They came to a snapshot of a man in military fatigues—eyes squinting against the desert sun, pipe clenched between teeth. My mother said to me: "If things had worked out differently, he would have been your father." I thought: *But if that man had been my father, would I have been me?* This led me to wonder: If another of my actual father's myriad spermatozoa impregnated my mother's ovum, would the child born from such a mingling of chromosomes have been me? Or had the same spermatozoon burrowed home in her next ovarian cycle, would that baby have been me?

Despite such unnerving glimpses of my own contingency, the conviction of my being a permanent, timeless witness has remained as steady and self-evident to me as the view I have of the sun rising every morning in the east, crossing the sky, then setting in the west. I seem to be hardwired to experience my self and the world in this way. Yet despite the undeniable evidence of my own eyes, I know that the earth sets and rises, not the sun. Gotama did for the self what Copernicus did for the earth: he put it in its rightful place, despite its continuing to appear just as it did before. Gotama no more rejected the existence of the self than Copernicus rejected the existence of the earth. Instead, rather than regarding it as a fixed, non-contingent point around which everything else turned, he recognized that each self was a fluid, contingent process just like everything else.

The view that a human being consists of a pristine spiritual soul temporarily attached to a corrupt and ephemeral body was widespread throughout the ancient world. All the way from Baranasi to Athens, there were sages and philosophers who believed that after physical death the soul would be reborn according to its good or evil deeds, either as a human, an animal, or some other form of life. Salvation, therefore, entailed the systematic disassociation of the soul from the body, which was achieved through austere living, philosophical reflection, and contemplative practice. Such disciplines led one to realize that the true nature of one's soul has nothing to do with the body but is identical to the transcendent reality of God. The goal, therefore, is to achieve mystical union of the individual soul with the Absolute.

"The ignorant go after outward pleasures," said the Indian *Katha Upanishad,* "and fall into the snare of widespread death. Wise men only, knowing the nature of what is deathless, look not for anything stable here among things unstable. . . . When all the ties of the heart are severed here on earth, then the mortal becomes immortal." "And therefore while we live," said Gotama's Greek contemporary Socrates in the *Phaedo,* "it would seem that we shall be closest to knowledge in this way—if we consort with the body as little as possible, and do not commune with it, except in so far as we must, and do not infect ourselves with its nature, but remain pure from it, until God himself shall release us."

Gotama declared that his awakening to the contingent ground of life went "against the stream." It was counterintuitive. It went against the instinctive sense of being a timeless witness of one's experience. It contradicted the belief in an eternal soul and, by implication, in the transcendent reality of God. Rather than disassociating oneself from the world in order to achieve union with God, Gotama encouraged his followers to pay close, penetrating attention to the rise and fall of the phenomenal world itself. The way in which he presented the practice of meditation turned the received wisdom of the day on its head. Instead of instructing his students to turn their attention inward to contemplate the nature of their soul, he told them to be acutely aware of their bodies, to be calmly mindful of whatever was impacting one's senses in that very moment, noticing its emergence and disappearance, its ephemerality, its impersonality, its joy and its tragedy, its allure, its terror.

The metaphors he used to describe the practice of mindfulness are earthy and practical. He compared the meditator to a skilled wood-turner and butcher, men who have learned to use their tools with extraordinary precision, who can shape a piece of wood or dissect a carcass with minimal effort and maximum efficiency. Mindful awareness is not presented as a passive concentration on a single, steady object, but as a refined engagement with a shifting, complex world. Mindfulness is a skill that can be developed. It is a choice, an act, a response that springs from a quiet but curious intelligence. And it is empathetic, keenly sensitized to the peculiar texture of one's own and others' suffering.

What Gotama taught flew in the face of the orthodoxies of his time. No wonder he wryly commented after his awakening that it would be "tiring and vexing" for him to teach others. After all, people desire immortality and do not wish to embrace the inescapable reality of death; they long for happiness and shy away from the contemplation of pain; they want to preserve their sense of self, not deconstruct it into its fleeting and impersonal components. It is counterintuitive to accept that deathlessness is experienced each moment we are released from the deathlike grip of greed and hatred; that happiness in this world is only possible for those who realize that this world is incapable of providing happiness; that one becomes a fully individuated person only by relinquishing beliefs in an essential self.

Siddhattha Gotama was a dissenter, a radical, an iconoclast. He wanted nothing to do with the priestly religion of the brahmins. He dismissed its theology as unintelligible, its rituals as pointless, and the social structure it legitimated as unjust. Yet he fully understood its visceral appeal, its addictive hold on the human mind and heart. He refused to play the role of an enlightened guru who demanded uncritical submission before initiating his disciples into doctrines reserved for the spiritual elite. Yet he could not remain silent. There came a point when he had to act. He realized that there must be some people, "those with little dust on their eyes," who would understand him. So he left his tree in Uruvela and went to Baranasi, where he knew that some of his former companions, a group of five brahmins from Sakiya, were staying in a Deer Park near the village of Isipatana.

# 11

## CLEARING THE PATH

IN THE AUTUMN of 1989, during a break in a retreat Martine and I were leading at Gaia House, the meditation center near Sharpham, I was idly perusing the small collection of books that had been donated to the center's library. I came across a clothbound volume of nearly six hundred pages entitled *Clearing the Path,* written by one Nanavira Thera, a man I had never heard of, published by an obscure press in Colombo, Sri Lanka, and printed in Bangkok by the Funny Publishing Limited Partnership.

I opened the thick black tome at random and started reading a letter written to Robert Brady, a young librarian at the British Council in Colombo, on December 3, 1964. "How irritating the Buddha's teaching must sometimes appear!" wrote Nanavira. "Here you are, having been to an ashram and learned or realized the Great Truth that 'reality is consciousness'—and now here I am with the distressing duty of having to inform you that the Buddha says (I simplify slightly): 'Without matter, without feeling, without perception, without determinations, that there should be consciousness—such a thing is not possible.'" Nanavira then backs up these words from the Pali Canon with a quote from Jean-Paul Sartre, who likewise affirms that consciousness is always consciousness *of* something. "From this, again, you will see why I am essentially anti-mystical. And this explains why, from the Western point-of-view I am not a religious person."

I had been coming to similar conclusions myself: that the practice of Buddhist meditation was *not* a quest for mystical experience. I also was aware that I felt less and less like a "religious person." For Gotama rejected any assumption of a transcendent reality—irrespective of whether you call it God, Self, or Consciousness—and encouraged instead a contemplative examination of the complex, fluctuating, and highly specific world that is present to our senses here and now. "I do not *deny* that we may have 'experience of God,' " Nanavira wrote to Brady five days later. "It is a fashionable blunder to hail modern science as vindicating the Buddha's teaching. The assumption is that the Buddha solved the whole question of transcendence (self) or Transcendence (God) by anticipating the impersonal attitude of the scientist. But this is rubbish, and it simply makes the Dhamma a kind of logical positivism and myself a kind of Bertrand Russell in Robes. No—numinous experience is just as real as sex or romantic love or aesthetic experience; and the question that must be answered is whether these things are to be taken at face value as evidence of some kind of transcendent reality or whether the eternity they point to is a delusion."

Whoever Nanavira Thera was, I sensed an immediate affinity with him. I took *Clearing the Path* home and read it from cover to cover. I was captivated by the prose—its playfully sardonic tone, its wide-ranging erudition, the wry-verging-on-black sense of humor—and, above all, by the rebellious candor of the author. I had never before been so powerfully affected by a Buddhist book written in English.

I wanted to know more about Nanavira Thera. I made inquiries to monks in Sri Lanka, explored libraries and archives of Buddhist centers in England, contacted people who might have heard of or known him, and tracked down a great-niece in London. I learned that Nanavira Thera was an Englishman. He was born as Harold Musson in

1920 into an upper-class military family. An only child, prone to moody introspection, he grew up in a graystone mansion in Hampshire. In 1938 he went up to Magdalene College, Cambridge, where he read mathematics and then modern languages. He enlisted in the army at the outbreak of the Second World War and in 1941 was commissioned as an officer in the Intelligence Corps. He initially served in Algiers and later in Italy. His task was to interrogate prisoners of war. In 1945 he was hospitalized in Sorrento and became absorbed in a newly published book on Buddhism called *La dottrina del risveglio* (*The Doctrine of Awakening*) by the Italian Julius Evola.

On the face of it, Julius Evola was a most improbable advocate of Buddhism. As twenty-five-year-old Captain Musson was reading *La dottrina del risveglio* on his hospital bed in Sorrento, unbeknown to him, Evola was in Vienna—he fled Italy after the fall of Mussolini—translating Masonic texts for Himmler's Ahnenerbe, a Nazi think tank devoted to establishing the historical supremacy of the Aryan race. The Ahnenerbe suspected that Siddhattha Gotama might have been of good Aryan stock and in 1938 had sent an expedition to Tibet under the leadership of SS Hauptsturmführer Ernst Schäfer to find further evidence of this. The Germans spent two months in Lhasa in early 1939, measuring Tibetans' skulls and facial features and collecting Buddhist texts. They did not meet the newly discovered four-year-old Dalai Lama, who was still in his parents' village near the Chinese border, preparing to leave for his enthronement in Lhasa. Evola's attraction to Buddhism, however, lay in his conviction that the teachings of the Pali Canon preserved the true Aryan spirit of ascetic self-discipline, which was "essentially aristocratic," "anti-mystical," "anti-evolutionist," and "manly." For Evola, this Aryan tradition had been largely lost in the West through "the influence on European faiths of concepts of Semitic and Asiatic-Mediterranean origin."

After serving as a foot soldier in the First World War, like many of his generation Evola had been overcome with "feelings of the inconsistency and vanity of the aims that usually engage human activities." In reaction, he became an abstract painter within the Dadaist movement and a friend of its founding figure, the Romanian Tristan Tzara. By 1921 he had grown disillusioned with the Dadaist project and rejected the arts as inadequate to the task of resolving his spiritual unrest. He then experimented with drugs through which he attained "states of consciousness partially detached from the physical senses . . . frequently approaching close to the sphere of visionary hallucinations and perhaps also madness." Such experiences only aggravated his dilemma by intensifying his sense of personal disintegration and confusion to the point where he decided, at the age of twenty-three, to commit suicide.

He was dissuaded from carrying this out by reading a passage in the Middle Length Discourses of the Pali Canon where the Buddha says: "Whoever thinks: 'extinction is mine,' and rejoices in extinction, such a person, I declare, does not know extinction." For Evola, this was "like a sudden illumination. I realised that this desire to end it all, to dissolve myself, was a bond—'ignorance' as opposed to true freedom." Evola did not, however, become a Buddhist. He regarded the writing of *La dottrina del risveglio* as repayment of the "debt" he owed to the Buddha for saving him from suicide.

What drew Harold Musson to Evola's book, as he wrote three years later in the foreword to his English translation of the book, was that *La dottrina del risveglio* "recaptured the spirit of Buddhism in its original form," and cleared away "some of the woolly ideas that have gathered round the central figure, Prince Siddhartha, and round the doctrine that he disclosed." Its "real significance," however, was to be found in "its encouragement of a practical application of the doctrine it discusses."

Harold Musson was not alone in his excitement about Evola's book. Osbert "Bertie" Moore, a fellow captain in the Intelligence Corps, fifteen years his senior, was likewise entranced by the work. In a letter written at the time to a friend at home, Bertie described *La dottrina del risveglio* as "the best treatise on Buddhism I have so far come across—a remarkably clear, objective and complete exposé of the subject."

Bertie Moore had been born into impoverished gentility on the tiny island of Tresco, one of the Scilly Isles, off the coast of Cornwall, in 1905. He had little formal education as a child, but showed remarkable linguistic abilities, on the strength of which he won a scholarship to Exeter College, Oxford, where he read modern languages. His fluency in Italian led to his being inducted into military intelligence, which led to his meeting Harold Musson at Caserta, the Allied headquarters near Naples, where they were both engaged in the "absorbingly interesting work" of interrogating high-ranking Italian Fascists. (How, I wonder, would they have reacted had Julius Evola been hauled before one of their tribunals?) Shy, sensitive, and contemplative by nature, as the war progressed, Bertie had become increasingly drawn to philosophy and meditation while experiencing a growing disgust for what he called "the stinking mass of corruption, exploitation and hatred that seems to be in prospect for Europe for the next fifty years."

The impact of Buddhist ideas also led Bertie to question the morality of his work in military intelligence. Interrogations of spies would sometimes lead to executions; morally unable to engage in any further acts that would cause death, he asked his senior officers to relieve him of counterespionage duties and told them that henceforth he would not divulge information in cases already known to him. This could have led to charges of insubordination and a court-martial, but his superiors agreed to release him from military service instead.

After the war, the two men remained close friends and moved into a flat together in Primrose Hill, London. Harold, thanks to a private income, passed his days translating Evola's book into English, while the impecunious Bertie worked in the Italian section at the BBC. As their shared disillusion with and distaste for postwar Britain grew, they began to think seriously of taking their interest in Buddhism to its logical conclusion. They learned of the existence of a small community of European Buddhist monks in Ceylon. With hardly any warning to their friends, parents, and colleagues, Harold and Bertie abruptly fled England in November 1948.

Nanavira Thera would later write that what impelled him to leave England for the East was "the desire for some definite non-mystical form of practice." Western thought, he had concluded, "seemed . . . to oscillate between the extremes of mysticism and rationalism, both of which were distasteful to me, and the yoga practices—in a general sense—of India offered themselves as a possible solution." As his understanding of Buddhism grew, this anti-Western stance became more pronounced. Toward the end of his life, he wrote: "The Buddha's Teaching is quite alien to the European tradition, and a European who adopts it is a rebel."

The two men were ordained as novice Buddhist monks in an open glade at the Island Hermitage in Dodanduwa, Ceylon, by the German monk Nyanatiloka Mahathera on April 24, 1949. Nyanatiloka (Anton Gueth) was seventy-one and the senior-most Western Buddhist monk in the world. A pioneer in Pali studies, he had been ordained in Burma in 1904 before moving to Ceylon where he founded the Island Hermitage in 1911. Nyanatiloka gave Harold the name "Nanavira" and Bertie the name "Nanamoli."

While Nanamoli began to learn Pali, Nanavira devoted himself to the practice of meditative absorption (jhana). But after a year of intense concentration, he contracted typhoid, which left him with chronic indigestion so severe that at times he would "roll about on [his] bed with the pain." Unable to sit still in meditation, he set about reading the Buddha's discourses and their traditional commentaries. The more he studied the discourses, however, the more he came to doubt the validity of the commentaries.

A turning point in Nanavira's thinking occurred when he came across a dialogue between the Buddha and a wanderer called Sivaka. In that discourse, Sivaka approached Gotama and asked him to comment on the widely held view that whatever a person experiences as pleasure or pain is the result of his or her former actions (karma). This, as Nanavira knew, was the view of orthodox Theravada Buddhism in Ceylon. (It was also what I had been taught by my teachers in the Tibetan tradition.) Yet in reply to Sivaka's question, the Buddha said that people who hold such a view "go beyond what is known by themselves and what is reckoned to be true by the world" and are therefore "in the wrong." He pointed out how the experience of pleasure or pain may simply be the result of ill health, inclement weather, carelessness, or assault. Even on such occasions when it is the result of former actions, that should be something you should be able to understand for yourself or with the help of others. The Buddha thus categorically rejected one of the central dogmas of orthodox Buddhism and, in its place, presented an entirely empirical view of the sources of human experience.

For Nanavira, that "came as a bit of a shock (though also as a bit of relief)." In the end, he came to view only two of the three "baskets" (*Pitaka*) of the Pali Canon as authentic: those containing the Buddha's discourses (*Sutta*) and the monastic training (*Vinaya*). "No other Pali books whatsoever," he insisted, "should be taken as authoritative; and ignorance of them (and particularly of the traditional Commentaries) may be counted a positive advantage, as leaving less to be unlearned." Nanamoli, by contrast, embarked on the translation of the greatest commentary of them all: Buddhaghosa's "The Path of Purity" (*Visuddhimagga*).

In 1954 Nanavira left his friend and the monastic community of the Island Hermitage in order to become a hermit. He eventually settled in a solitary hut in the jungle near Bundala, a village near Galle in the far south of Ceylon. Despite persistent ill health, he continued his study of the Pali Canon and the practice of mindfulness. Then, on the evening of June 27, 1959, something happened that radically changed the course of his life. He recorded the event in Pali in a private journal:

HOMAGE TO THE AUSPICIOUS ONE, WORTHY, FULLY AWAK-
ENED. At one time the monk Nanavira was staying in a forest hut near
Bundala village. It was during that time, as he was walking up and down
in the first watch of the night, that the monk Nanavira made his mind
quite pure of constraining things, and kept thinking and pondering and
reflexively observing the Dhamma as he had heard and learnt it, the
clear and stainless Eye of the Dhamma arose in him: "Whatever has the
nature of arising, all that has the nature of ceasing." Having been a
teaching-follower for a month, he became one attained to right view.

In other words, Nanavira was convinced that he had become a
"stream entrant" and thereby become "independent of the opinions of
others regarding the Buddha's teaching." He believed that he had
ceased to be a *puthujjana* (an ordinary, unawakened person) and become an *ariya,* a "noble one," whose final liberation from the cycle of
birth and death was assured. This led him to cease his correspondence
with his friend Nanamoli, because "there was no longer anything for
me to discuss with him, since the former relationship of parity between us regarding the Dhamma had suddenly come to an end."

What drew me to Nanavira Thera was that he had no interest in writing *about* Buddhism or promoting the Buddhist religion. The terms
*Buddhism* and *Buddhist* had for him "a slightly displeasing air about
them—they are too much like labels one sticks on the outside of packages regardless of what the packages contain." *Clearing the Path* is simply an articulation of where his own life had led him. He insisted his
analyses of key Pali technical terms, entitled *Notes on Dhamma,* which
form the core of *Clearing the Path,* "were not written to pander to people's tastes" and were made "as unattractive, academically speaking, as
possible." He said that he would be satisfied if only one person were
ever to benefit from them.

I too found myself in this no-man's-land that lies between the academic study of Buddhism and the dogmas of Buddhist orthodoxy. Nei-

ther approach is satisfying. The Dhamma demands of its practitioners a personal commitment to ethical integrity, meditation, and self-analysis as a response to the questions of human existence, whereas a scholar of Buddhism, commented Nanavira, can only feel safe as long as the texts he is studying "are not one day going to get up and look him between the eyes. . . . (Quite the last thing that a professor of Buddhism would dream of doing is to profess Buddhism—*that* is left to mere amateurs like myself.)" At the same time, Nanavira's writings were intended as an explicit critique of orthodox Theravada Buddhism, "with the purpose of clearing away a mass of dead matter which is choking the *suttas* (discourses)."

On returning to England, I could have enrolled in a university, gained a degree in religious studies, and then pursued an academic career. Indeed, many of my peers, who had also trained with Tibetan lamas or Zen masters in Asia, chose this option after disrobing and returning to the West. But I found the entire academic approach to Buddhism chilling. Much as I valued the meticulous work of scholars in dissecting and analyzing Buddhist texts, I could not bring myself to adopt the clinical distance required for achieving such "objectivity." To have done so would have felt like a betrayal. Nanavira said that there was nothing in his writings "to interest the professional scholar, for whom the question of personal existence does not arise; for the scholar's whole concern is to eliminate or ignore the individual point of view in an effort to establish the objective truth—a would-be impersonal synthesis of public facts."

Nanavira had also been drawn to existentialism and phenomenology as found in the writings of Kierkegaard, Husserl, Sartre, and, in particular, Martin Heidegger's *Being and Time*. He appreciated how these writers had discarded the detached, rationalist approach to philosophy and gave priority to the questions posed by concrete personal existence. He recognized how someone "would never reach the point of listening to the Buddha's teaching had he not first been disquieted by existential questions about himself and the world." To this end, the existentialist philosophers can provide a helpful bridge, especially to a modern reader puzzled by the jargon of Buddhism, to understanding the relevance of Gotama's discourses in the Pali Canon to their own lives.

I also shared Nanavira's wariness of the pious dogmas of Buddhist orthodoxy, which he compared to "a mass of dead matter." While the professor of Buddhism may suffer from an excess of objective disinterest, the devout Buddhist tends to suffer from an excess of subjective conviction. As I had discovered with my Tibetan and Zen teachers, the body of opinion that constitutes their respective orthodoxies is neither flexible nor negotiable. If you cannot accept its primary tenets, there is no place for you in their tradition. In reading Nanavira, I became aware that the situation was no different among Theravada Buddhists, who insist that their orthodoxy (founded on the work of the fifth-century CE commentator Buddhaghosa) is the final and definitive interpretation of what the Buddha taught.

Nanavira wrote in 1963: "I am quite unable to identify myself with any organised body or cause (even if it is a body of opposition or a lost cause). I am a born blackleg." I have the same problem (if a problem it be). For the more I pursue my study and practice of the Dhamma, the more distant I feel from Buddhism as an institutional religion. And the closer I get to the life and teaching of Gotama, the further I find myself from the complacent certainties of any Buddhist orthodoxy.

Although I had not heard of Nanavira until I came across a copy of *Clearing the Path*, I had long been familiar with the work of his friend Bertie—that is, Nanamoli Thera—in particular his posthumously published *The Life of the Buddha*, which I had read when I was a monk in Switzerland. After spending eleven years in the Island Hermitage, Nanamoli Thera died of a heart attack while on a walking tour in rural Ceylon on March 8, 1960. He was fifty-five years old. Nanamoli left behind some of the most highly regarded translations of classical Pali texts into English, most of which are still in print today.

Ill health was also taking its toll on Nanavira, still living alone in his hut in the jungle. He succumbed to an endless succession of tropical diseases. One of the most severe and persistent was amoebiasis, a parasitic infection of the intestine, which made it impossible for him to sit for any length of time in meditation. In the summer of 1962, he began to be overwhelmed by incapacitating erotic fantasies. He regarded this as a disease: satyriasis (nowadays called "hypersexuality"), the uncontrollable desire to engage in sexual activity. "Under the pressure of this affliction," he noted on December 11 of that year, "I am oscillating between two poles. If I indulge the sensual images that offer themselves, my thought turns towards the state of a layman; if I resist them, my thought turns towards suicide. Wife or knife, one might say." By November 1963, he had "given up all hope of making any further progress for myself in this life" and had also resolved not to disrobe. It was simply a question of how long he could "stand the strain."

While Buddhism usually considers suicide as ethically equivalent to murder, for one who has become a stream entrant it is acceptable under circumstances that prevent further practice. There are a number of instances in the Pali Canon where Gotama condones the suicides of accomplished monks who, like Nanavira, had contracted incurable diseases. The traditional rationale for this is that once one has "entered the stream," one can be assured of only having to take a maximum of further seven births before escaping the round of rebirth forever.

Nanavira's critical attitude toward Buddhist orthodoxy did not lead him to query the traditional doctrines of rebirth, non-human realms of existence, and the moral law of karma. Although he rejected mysticism, he accepted that meditation could grant one "powers" such as levitation, clairvoyance, and recollection of past lives. Once he had cleared away the "dead matter" of the commentaries, he refused to question the authority of the Buddha's discourses themselves. "It was, and is, my attitude towards the *suttas* that, if I find anything in them that is against my own view, *they are right*, and I am *wrong*." Such fundamentalism sits uneasily with the skeptical rigor that characterizes so much of his writing. It does not seem to occur to Nanavira that the discourses themselves might also be riddled with dead matter inherited from the Indian ascetic tradition. He unquestioningly accepted that the sole aim of the Buddha's teaching was to free oneself from the cycle of repeated rebirth. He expressed a loathing for life itself. "There is a way out," he insisted, "there is a way to put a stop to existence, if only we have the courage to let go of our cherished humanity."

I found this fundamentalist and ascetic streak in Nanavira's writings disturbing and repellent. Yet it forced me to recognize how deeply Buddhism was tied to the world-renouncing norms of much Indian religion. Even the Mahayana Buddhism propounded by the Dalai Lama and other Tibetan and Zen teachers, with all its talk of compassion and love, still has as its ultimate goal the ending of rebirth and thus of life as we know it. The only difference is that for the bodhisattva—one who has vowed to attain awakening for the sake of others—the aspiration to end the cycle of repeated birth and death extends to all sentient beings rather than him- or herself alone. Mahayana Buddhism is no more a life-affirming creed than the "Hinayana" doctrine it claims to supersede. By reflecting on Nanavira's dilemma, I came to realize how little my own sense of the intrinsic value of life had been affected by my years of exposure to Buddhist thought. Whether I liked it or not, I was a secular, post-Christian European. Unlike Nanavira, I had no wish to let go of my cherished humanity.

Nanavira might well have been fooling himself. He could have been attracted to suicide by unconscious fears and desires over which he had no awareness or control. In a letter of May 16, 1963, he confessed: "Do not think that I regard suicide as praiseworthy—that there can easily be an element of weakness in it, I am the first to admit . . . but I certainly regard it as preferable to a number of other possibilities. (I would a hundred times rather have it said of the *Notes* that the author killed himself as a *bhikkhu* (monk) than that he disrobed; for *bhikkhus* have become *arhants* (i.e., liberated from rebirth) in the act of suicide, but it is not recorded that anyone became *arhant* in the act of disrobing.)"

He spent most of 1963 preparing his *Notes on Dhamma* for publication, which he would have considered "an intolerable disturbance" had it not been for his ill health. With the help of the Ceylonese judge Lionel Samaratunga a limited edition of 250 cyclostyled copies was produced toward the end of the year and distributed to leading Buddhist figures of the time and various libraries and institutions. The response was largely one of polite incomprehension. For the next two years, he continued to revise the *Notes,* while maintaining his simple routine of meditation, correspondence, and daily chores.

On January 8, 1965, Nanavira received a visit from Robin Maugham—the nephew of W. Somerset Maugham—a novelist and journalist who was wintering that year in Ceylon. Lord Maugham was accompanied by Peter Maddock, his eighteen-year-old assistant and amanuensis. Maddock's impression of Nanavira in his primitive hut in Bundala was that of "an emaciated Edwardian gentleman in a *dhoti,* but still exactly who he was before. I don't think there had been a change in personality, like some people who become British gurus and set up ashrams." He recalled that Nanavira's tone of voice "was very much that of the English oblique, that is to say he was not earnest in any way, and saw things through the prism of the English upper classes. He was very calm, but not happy. Happiness was not an element there. Nor was there any despair—I suspect it was probably boredom that killed him, and illness. . . . He spoke obliquely, with a sense of humor, but had a totally different way of seeing things."

On the afternoon of July 7, 1965, Nanavira Thera ended his life by putting his head into a cellophane bag containing ethyl chloride, tied in such a way that he could not undo the knot. Only a month earlier his letters had been exploring the meaning of humor. He was forty-five years old. On November 11, his young correspondent Robert Brady wrote a letter in which he struggled as a Christian to come to terms with Nanavira's death: "Man must never cease to transcend himself," he declared. "My self is a poor pathetic trivial thing but it has a little spark of the divine. We must never forget that. But Nanavira's theory denied it and he took his interpretation as the Buddha's real meaning. But the corpse of a suicide is no recommendation for any theory, is it?"

In 1972 Julius Evola completed his autobiography *Il cammino del cinabro* (*The Path of Cinnabar*), where he explains how he wrote *La dottrina del risveglio,* the book that led Harold and Bertie to become monks, to repay the debt he felt to the Buddha for having saved him from suicide. Evola, however, saw Buddhism as the "'dry' and intellectual path of pure detachment" as opposed to that of the Indian tantras which taught "affirmation, engagement, the utilisation and transformation of immanent forces liberated through the awakening of the Shakti, i.e., the root power of all vital energy, particularly that of sex." He added: "The person who translated the work, a certain Musson, found in it an incitant to leave Europe and withdraw to the Orient in the hope of finding there a centre where one still cultivated the disciplines that I recommended; unfortunately, I have had no further news of him."

It was not until 1987 that Nanavira's *Notes on Dhamma,* together with his letters from 1960 until his death, were published together as *Clearing the Path.*

# 12

# EMBRACE SUFFERING

WHEREVER I LOOKED—in India, China, Southeast Asia, or Tibet—it was always the serene, world-renouncing, contemplative monk who represented the ideal of a Buddhist life. Laypeople tended to be seen as second-rate Buddhists, whose duties in the world prevented them from pursuing a high-octane spiritual career. And those exceptional lay figures who did achieve prominence in their traditions are presented as having done so *in spite of* their lay status.

The unstated presumption is this: what really matters is inner spiritual experience, which, by definition, consists of irreducibly private states of mind. Today, Buddhist meditation practices are widely promoted as techniques, which, if correctly applied, will lead one to greater inner happiness, peace, and contentment. No matter what is going on in the world around him, the good Buddhist is depicted as an unflappable beacon of smiling calm, ready to respond at any moment with a kind gesture or some choice words of wisdom. As a way of coping with the hectic pace and stress of modern life, the housewife or business executive alike is encouraged to become a monk in lay clothing.

But as a culture and civilization, Buddhism consists of far more than inner experiences. It is known through buildings, gardens, sculptures, paintings, calligraphy, poetry, and craftwork. It is present in each mark made by artists and artisans on rocks, clay votive tablets, fragile palm leaves, primed canvases, hand-pressed paper, wooden printing blocks, raked gravel, and paper lanterns. On my visits to monasteries in Tibet, the polished furrows in the rock, worn into the mountain by centuries of passing feet, moved me far more than the shrines to which they led. Who were the men and women who made them? Who were the people who constructed the intricately carved stone gateways at Sanchi, chipped out the black basalt temples at Ajanta, erected the giant stupa at Borobodur, built the Kumbum at Gyantse, designed the soaring cathedrals at Pagan, laid out the rock gardens at Ryoanji, or sculpted the standing Buddhas at Bamiyan? We don't know.

These forgotten people are my fellows. They are the silent ones on whose behalf I want to speak. I know nothing of their religious beliefs or spiritual attainments. Their understanding of the subtleties of Buddhist doctrine is irrelevant. They left behind visible and tangible objects created by their own hands: dumb things that speak to me across the centuries in a language that no text can reproduce. Irrespective of what Buddhist icon a painted scroll may depict, it embodies the intelligence and imagination, the passion and care of its creator. I feel an affinity with the makers of these things. A Zen garden can say as much about what the Buddha taught as the most erudite treatise on emptiness.

"Just as a farmer irrigates his fields," said Gotama in the *Dhammapada,* "just as a fletcher fashions an arrow, just as a carpenter shapes a block of wood, so does the sage tame the self." This is an odd statement. Rather than encouraging the renunciation of self, here, if we follow these metaphors, the Buddha seemed to be encouraging the *creation* of a self. To "tame" in this context means to pacify the selfish and unruly aspects of oneself in order to begin forging a more caring, focused, and integrated character. The examples he used are of working people: farmers, fletchers, carpenters. Just as he compared the practice of mindfulness to the way a skilled woodturner uses his tools, here he admired the work of those who till the soil, make arrows, and carve wood. Their handicrafts serve to illustrate how to nurture, fashion, and direct the raw materials—sensations, feelings, emotions, perceptions, intentions—of one's self.

Rather than dismiss the self as a fiction, Gotama presented it as a project to be realized. By "self" he referred not to the transcendent Self of the brahmins, which, by definition, cannot be anything other than what it eternally *Is,* but the functional, moral self that breathes and acts in this world. He compared this self to a *field:* a potentially fertile ground that, when irrigated and tended, enables plants to flourish. He compared it to an *arrow:* a wooden shaft, metal head, and feather fletching, which, when assembled, can be projected on an unerring course to its target. And he compared the self to a *block of wood,* something one can fashion and shape into a utensil or roof beam. In each case, simple things are worked and transformed to achieve human ends.

Such a model of self is more pertinent to a layman or laywoman living in this world than to a monk or nun intent on renouncing it. It presents a very different sort of challenge. Instead of training oneself to achieve a serene detachment from the turbulent events of this life, it encourages one to grapple with these events in order to imbue them with meaning and purpose. The emphasis is on action rather than inaction, on engagement rather than disengagement. And there are social implications too. If a person is the result of what he or she *does* rather than what he or she *is,* then any notion of a divinely ordained system of social identity breaks down. Gotama said, "By action is one a farmer, by action a craftsman,

> "By action is one a merchant, by action a servant,
> By action is one a thief, by action a soldier,
> By action is one a priest, by action a ruler.
> In this way the sage sees action as it operates,
> Seeing conditioned arising, understanding the effects of acts."

Gotama started teaching his ideas in the Deer Park at Isipatana— the modern town of Sarnath—just outside Baranasi (Varanasi), the holy city of the brahmins on the northern shore of the Ganges. He had to find a way of translating his insight into "this-conditionality, conditioned arising" into a practice and way of life. He resolved this in *Turning the Wheel of Dhamma,* the first discourse he gave in the Deer Park, in which he presented his seminal teaching of the Four Noble Truths.*

In that discourse he unambiguously described his awakening as the result of having recognized, performed, and completed four tasks:

1. fully knowing suffering
2. letting go of craving
3. experiencing cessation [of craving]
4. cultivating an eightfold path

These "Four Noble Truths" are, as Nanavira put it, "the ultimate tasks for a man's performance." Nanavira illustrated this with an episode from *Alice's Adventures in Wonderland.* After Alice has fallen down a rabbit hole, she enters a room where she finds a bottle labeled "Drink Me." Instead of describing what the bottle contains, the label tells Alice what to do with the bottle. In the same way, the Four Truths are injunctions to do something rather than claims to be believed or disbelieved.

Gotama described how each truth presents its own challenge: suffering is to be *fully known;* craving is to be *let go of;* cessation is to be *experienced;* and the path is to be *cultivated.* The Four Truths are suggestions to act in certain ways under particular circumstances. Just as Alice saw the label "Drink Me" on the bottle and so proceeded to drink its contents, when encountering pain, one can see it labeled "Know Me" and then embrace that pain instead of shying away from it. Or instead of automatically following the promptings of craving to grab hold

*See Appendix III for a translation of *Turning the Wheel of Dhamma.*

or get rid of something, one can imagine it whispering: "Let Go of Me," thus encouraging one to relax one's grip and rest in equanimity.

The Four Noble Truths are pragmatic rather than dogmatic. They suggest a course of action to be followed rather than a set of dogmas to be believed. The four truths are prescriptions for behavior rather than descriptions of reality. The Buddha compared himself to a doctor who offers a course of therapeutic treatment to heal one's ills. To embark on such therapy is not designed to bring one any closer to "the Truth" but to enable one's life to flourish here and now, hopefully leaving a legacy that will continue to have beneficial repercussions after one's death. Whether one embarks on such a path is entirely one's own choice.

By practicing the truths in this way, the "sage" is able to "tame" the fickle and restless self just as a farmer works a field, a fletcher makes an arrow, and a carpenter shapes a piece of wood. The aim is not the attainment of nirvana but cultivation of a way of life that allows every aspect of one's humanity to flourish. Gotama called this way of life an "eightfold" path: i.e., appropriate vision, thought, speech, action, livelihood, effort, mindfulness, and concentration. Such a path embraces how we see and think about ourselves and the world, how we respond to others through our words and deeds, how we provide for ourselves and others through our work, and how we focus our attention through the practice of mindfulness and concentration.

Gotama began and ended his teaching career by stressing the importance of this eightfold path. It is the first thing he spoke of in his first discourse *Turning the Wheel of Dhamma* and it was the last thing he spoke of to his final disciple, Subhadda, while lying on his deathbed in Kusinara forty-five years later. If conditioned arising was the $e = mc^2$ of Gotama's vision, the eightfold path was his first move in translating that axiom from an abstract principle into a civilizing force.

He presented the eightfold path as a middle way that avoids the dead ends of infatuation and mortification, both of which he dismissed as "uncivilized." A dead end is a path that goes nowhere; to pursue one is to keep banging my head against a wall. No matter how much energy

I devote to indulging my appetites or punishing myself for my excesses, I keep coming back to the same place I started. One minute I am thrilled and excited by something, but in the next I am in a funk of self-doubt and boredom where nothing interests me. I veer between these two poles, going around and around in circles. Indulgence and mortification are dead ends in that they lead to an inner paralysis, which blocks the capacity to live abundantly.

For Siddhattha Gotama, life in Kosala had become a dead end. His experiments in meditation and asceticism had turned out to be dead ends. Beneath the Bodhi tree he realized that attachment to *any* place was a dead end. Even monasticism and religious behavior can become dead ends. "Those who hold training as the essence," he would say later,

> or who hold virtue-and-vow, pure livelihood, celibacy, and service as the essence—this is one dead end. And those with such theories and such views as "there is no fault in sensual desires"—this is another dead end. . . . By not penetrating these two dead ends, some hold back and some go too far.

In a shifting, contingent, and unpredictable world, the practice of such a middle path is a juggling act. There is no guarantee that having found it, one will not lose it again. This way of life that might once have been liberating can turn into another dead end if one clings to it too tightly. As a way of life, a middle path is an ongoing task of responsiveness and risk, grounded on a groundless ground. Its twists and turns are as turbulent and unpredictable as life itself.

How do you find this middle path? Do you have to wait until you stumble across it one day by chance? Do you need to join a religious organization and be initiated into it by an enlightened monk? Is it revealed to you in a moment of mystical rapture? Or do you force yourself onto it by an immense act of will? In *Turning the Wheel of Dhamma*, Gotama showed how one enters the stream of the middle path through the practice of the Four Noble Truths. In keeping with the principle of conditioned arising, each truth is the condition that gives rise to the next: fully knowing suffering leads to letting go of craving; letting go of craving leads to experiencing its cessation; and those moments of cessation open up the free and purposive space of the eightfold path itself.

Rather than seek God—the goal of the brahmins—Gotama suggested that you turn your attention to what is most far from God: the anguish and pain of life on this earth. In a contingent world, change and suffering are inevitable. Just look at what happens here: creatures are constantly being born, falling ill, growing old, and dying. These are the unavoidable facts of our existence. As contingent beings, we do not survive. And when I am honest with myself, when I drop all my stoic conceits, this is unbearable.

To embrace the contingency of one's life is to embrace one's fate as an ephemeral but sentient being. As Nietzsche claimed, one can come to love that fate. But to do so one must first embrace it, though one instinctively recoils at such a prospect. To steady one's gaze on the finitude, contingency, and anguish of one's existence is not easy; it requires mindfulness and concentration. One needs to make a conscious shift from delight in a fixed place to awareness of a contingent ground. Places to which I am instinctively attracted are places where I imagine suffering to be absent. "There," I think, "if only I could get there, then I would suffer no more." The groundless ground of contingency, however, holds out no such hope. For this is the ground where you are born and die, get sick and grow old, are disappointed and frustrated.

To fully know suffering goes against the grain of what I am primed to desire. Yet a contingent, impermanent world does not exist in order to gratify my desires. It cannot provide the non-contingent, permanent well-being I crave. A place where things happen that I do not want to happen is not a place where everything is likely to turn out all right in the end. I struggle to order my life in accord with my longings and fears, but have little if any control over what will befall me even in the next moment.

The aim of mindfulness is to know suffering fully. It entails paying calm, unflinching attention to whatever impacts the organism, be it the song of a lark or the scream of a child, the bubbling of a playful idea or a twinge in the lower back. You attend not just to the outward stimuli themselves, but equally to your inward reactions to them. You do not condemn what you see as your failings or applaud what you regard as success. You notice things come, you notice them go. Over time, the practice becomes less a self-conscious exercise in meditation done at fixed periods each day and more a sensibility that infuses one's awareness at all times.

Mindfulness can have a sobering effect on the restless, jittery psyche. The stiller and more focused it becomes, the more I am able to peer into the sources of my febrile reactivity, to catch the first stirring of hatred before it overwhelms me with loathing and spite, to observe with ironic detachment the conceited babbling of the ego, to notice at its inception the self-demeaning story that could tip me into depression.

And I am not the only one who suffers. You suffer too. Every sentient creature suffers. When my self is no longer the all-consuming preoccupation it once was, when I see it as one narrative thread among myriad others, when I understand it to be as contingent and transient as anything else, then the barrier that separates "me" from "not me" begins to crumble. The conviction of being a closed cell of self is not only delusive but anesthetic. It numbs me to the suffering of the world. To embrace suffering culminates in greater empathy, the capacity to feel what it is like for the other to suffer, which is the ground for unsentimental compassion and love.

On one occasion, the Buddha and his attendant Ananda visited a monastery and discovered a sick monk lying uncared for in his own excrement and urine. They fetched some water, washed the monk, lifted him up, and settled him on a bed. Then Gotama berated the other monks in the community for not caring for their fellow. "When you have neither father nor mother to care for you," he said, "you need to care for one another. Whoever would tend to me, should tend to the sick." In identifying himself with those in pain, he affirmed that the key to awakening lies in one's embrace of and response to the suffering of others.

Mindfulness of suffering does not, however, lead to morbidity and despair. The more one internalizes a sense of the contingency of things, the less one is depressed and irked by pain (for it will pass) and the more one is awestruck by the presence of the simplest joys: to see a bud unfold, hear a wave rush over a beach, touch another person's hand (these too will pass). As in great music, theater, and literature, the tragic sense of life evokes a strange, disquieting beauty. A self-portrait of Rembrandt, an adagio from a late Beethoven quartet, the agonies of King Lear do not depress but elevate me. They move me in my depths, arouse a keen perception of what it means to be alive rather than dead.

To know, deep in your bones, how everything you experience is fleeting, poignant, and unreliable undermines the rationale for trying to grasp hold of, possess, and control it. To fully know suffering begins to affect how you relate to the world, how you respond to others, how you manage your own life. For how can I seek lasting solace in something that I know is incapable of providing it? Why would I stake all my hopes for happiness on something that I know will finally let me down? To embrace this suffering world challenges my innate tendency to see everything from the perspective of self-centered craving.

Craving is not something I can willfully discard, no matter how hard I tell myself to stop. In keeping with the principle of conditioned arising, to be free from craving requires the removal of the conditions that produce it. In the Buddha's analysis, the root of craving lies in the misconception that lasting, non-contingent happiness is to be found in a fleeting, contingent world. As you come to realize how impossible this is, craving starts to subside and fall away of its own accord.

Like the child who one year returns to the seaside to find he is no longer interested in building sand castles, so, over time, by coming to see the world in a more penetrating and honest way, I may start to lose interest in what previously obsessed me. As with outgrowing the making of sand castles, letting go of craving may not entail any great epiphany. To the one undergoing it, the change may be fairly imperceptible. As my perspective on life shifts from delight in places to an encounter with a contingent ground, I realize how grasping at things makes less and less sense. And when I catch myself doing it—for these habits die hard—I can do so with the ironic self-regard of "heigh-ho, here we go again."

Just as embracing suffering may lead to the letting go of craving, so the letting go of craving can lead to moments of quiet repose when the craving stops. (Or if it doesn't actually stop, you realize that you are no longer beholden to it, which, in practice, amounts to the same thing.) Thus the second truth, letting go of craving, leads to the third truth, experiencing cessation. You come to a point when you know for yourself, without a flicker of doubt, that your response to life need not be driven by your craving for things to be the way you want them to be. You realize that you are free *not* to act on the prompts of craving. This is the freedom of which Gotama spoke: the freedom from the imperatives of desire and hate.

An experience of such stopping may last only a few moments. It might just be a flash of conviction that I do not have to lead my life from the familiar standpoint of grasping and rejecting. Or it could be an experience of deep inner repose and clarity achieved through sustained meditation. Or it might be a lucid calm that suddenly overcomes me in the midst of turmoil and stress, enabling me to respond to others in ways that surprise me. Instead of fearing an encounter with a person I dislike, I find myself reaching out to him or her. Instead of consoling someone in pain by reciting some received wisdom, I find myself addressing the person's condition in my own distinct voice.

The decline of craving can result in greater freedom and autonomy, as well as in the potential for greater wisdom and love. One is released, at least momentarily, from fixed conceptions of who you are as a person, from attachment to socially sanctioned norms and rules of behavior, from uncertainty about the validity of what one is doing, from the sense that in matters of greatest importance one has to defer to the authority of others. One is freed to set off by oneself along a path, trusting one's own judgment, willing to take risks. One's life becomes oriented around ways to realize one's deepest values in each situation rather than around the fulfillment of egoistic desires or slavish conformity with a set of religious beliefs. In Buddhist technical language, one "enters the stream of the eightfold path" and becomes "independent of the opinions of others in regard to the Buddha's teaching."

The fourth truth is the eightfold path itself: appropriate vision, thought, speech, action, livelihood, effort, mindfulness, and concentration. When craving subsides, a space opens up in one's life where new possibilities can be realized. This space is where the eightfold path itself unfolds. To experience the cessation of craving, even momentarily, is to gain a glimpse of what the Buddha called "nirvana." In this sense, nirvana is not the goal of the eightfold path, but its starting point. The person who enters such a path is one who aspires to a life no longer conditioned and dictated by the narrow demands of craving. The possibility of a more honest and empathetic engagement with the world emerges, which serves as the basis for how one then thinks, speaks, acts, and works, and how one thinks, speaks, acts, and works provides the philosophical and moral foundations for mindfulness and concentration.

In practice, the eightfold path is not a linear trajectory from A to Z, but a complex feedback loop that constantly needs to be renewed and restored. For when you reach mindfulness and concentration (i.e., steps seven and eight), this does not mean you have come to the end of the path. For what are you mindful of? What do you concentrate on? You focus this mindful concentration on the task of fully knowing suffering (the first truth), which leads to letting go of craving (the second truth), and so on. The path itself does not lie there waiting for you to walk along it. It needs to be cultivated, nurtured—literally, "brought into being." Such a path might open up in a revealing moment of insight, only to be lost again through subsequent neglect. To believe in a path is not enough. One has to create and maintain it. The practice of the eightfold path is a creative act.

*Turning the Wheel of Dhamma,* the discourse Gotama delivered in the Deer Park in which he outlined his understanding of the Four Noble Truths, boils down to this:

> *Embrace,* with self-compassionate mindfulness
> *Let go,* relax your grip
> *Stop:* and stay calm
> *Act!* in an empathetic, self-compassionate, imaginative way

This template can be applied to every situation in life. Rather than shying away from or ignoring what is happening, embrace it with mindful attention; rather than craving to seize it or get rid of it, relax one's grip; rather than getting caught up in a cascade of reactivity, stop and stay calm; rather than repeat what you have said and done a thousand times before, act in an empathetic and imaginative way.

Siddhattha Gotama compared himself to a man who has wandered into a forest and found an ancient path hidden beneath the undergrowth. On following the path, the man arrived at the ruins of an ancient city. He then told the king and his ministers of what he had discovered and urged them to rebuild the city so that it may flourish once again. The Buddha then explained the meaning of this metaphor. The "ancient path" refers to the eightfold noble path, while the "ancient city" refers to the realization of the Four Noble Truths. He thus recognized that the tasks entailed by the Four Truths are those required to build the kind of civilization he envisioned. Since this is not something a person can accomplish on his or her own, it implies that the practice of the Four Truths is a communal undertaking, which requires the support of "the king and his ministers," i.e., those who have the resources and power to realize such a grand project.

# 13

# IN JETA'S GROVE

IT IS DIFFICULT to photograph the places where the Buddha lived and taught because today they all look much the same. Apart from Rajagaha with its dramatic ring of hills, the other sites lie on a featureless rural plain and consist of the brick foundations of monastic buildings and stupas, most of which were not constructed until several hundred years after the Buddha's time. Most of these places were only rediscovered in the nineteenth century by English civil servants and employees of the East India Company, who pursued amateur archaeology in their spare time. The sites had ceased to serve as living centers of pilgrimage since Buddhism became extinct in India eight hundred years ago. Now they are the property of the Archaeological Survey of India, a secular institution that maintains them as public parks and tolerates rather than welcomes Buddhist pilgrims.

The Deer Park in Isipatana (Sarnath), where the Buddha delivered *Turning the Wheel of Dhamma,* is now a well-tended park of lawns, flower beds, and trees, sealed off by iron railings from the dust, cripples, hawkers, and beggar women carrying snot-nosed babies on their hips outside. All that remains of the monastic complex that once flourished here are floors, remains of walls, and cores of small stupas, all in monotonous reddish-brown brick.

Dominating the park is the Dhamekh Stupa, a cylindrical tower ninety feet wide and a hundred feet tall, marking the spot, it is assumed, where Gotama taught the Four Noble Truths, thereby setting the Wheel of Dhamma in motion. A group of young Tibetans has gathered on the lawn in front of the stupa. I watch a young man with red braids woven into his hair take a stone and secure it to the end of a long white offering scarf. He hurls it upward with a grunt, aiming for one of the ornate niches in the upper brickwork. It arcs away from him like a silk comet and lodges in the niche. His friends whoop with glee and slap him on the back. I wonder how the minions of the Archaeological Survey of India are going to get the scarf down.

Instead of providing me with an opportunity to take exquisite photographs, my journey to these places was making me aware of the geography of the Buddha's world. I had read about Savatthi, Rajagaha, and Vesali many times but had no idea where they were located or how far they were from one another. Though I was familiar with the Buddha's ideas, I lacked any sense of the physical world in which he lived. As this physical world became more real for me, I grew more conscious of the social and political world in which he moved. The towns and cities ceased to be just dots on a map and became centers of power and conflict, inhabited by people with ambitions and fears, who married and fought each other, bore children, and grew feeble with age. My quest for photos was turning into a quest for the historical Buddha. The man Siddhattha Gotama started slowly coming into focus.

The Buddha stayed with his five companions in the Deer Park at Isipatana near Baranasi for the three months of the Rains. Much of this time would have been spent discussing the implications of the ideas he was teaching. He attracted a small number of followers, most of whom were the family and friends of a young brahmin merchant called Yasa. Now that he had disciples, he was faced with the question of how to establish a community. He had to address the practical issues of livelihood and survival. How could he create the conditions that would enable his ideas to take root in the competitively charged atmosphere of the time and survive his death? He would need benefactors: people powerful enough to protect his community and wealthy enough to provide for its needs.

As soon as the monsoon was over, Gotama and his band of followers left the Deer Park, crossed the Ganges, and headed back east via Uruvela (Bodh Gaya) to Rajagaha, the capital of Magadha, enclosed by its ring of hills, the seat of King Bimbisara. On learning of Gotama's return, Bimbisara went to hear him speak. By the end of the discourse, the king had "gone beyond doubt, gained intrepidity and become independent" in his understanding of what the Buddha taught, thus entering the stream of the middle path. Bimbisara declared that his ambitions in life had now been fulfilled. He offered Gotama a disused park called Bamboo Grove near the hot springs on the edge of Rajagaha, where he could base his community. Shortly after, Sariputta and Moggallana, the leading disciples of the prominent local guru Sanjaya, became followers on hearing a summary of the teaching on conditioned arising. The rest of Sanjaya's students followed suit, leaving Sanjaya "spitting hot blood."

This was an extraordinary achievement for a thirty-five-year-old man from a rural province in the rival kingdom of Kosala. Not only was Gotama sponsored by one of the most powerful kings of the day, his disciples included converted brahmin priests, some of whom had been respected teachers in their own right. Then one day Anathapindika, a wealthy banker from Savatthi, came to Rajagaha on business. He was immediately impressed with what Gotama was saying and became a follower. Before returning to Kosala, he asked Gotama whether he could offer him a residence in Savatthi where he and his monks could spend the Rains. By accepting this offer, Gotama agreed to return to his homeland and establish a base for his community in King Pasenadi's capital.

Despite Anathapindika's enthusiasm and wealth, years elapsed before the banker was able to provide a grove that would supply a suitable base for the Buddha. In the meantime, Gotama returned to

Kapilavatthu and reconciled himself with his family. His father, Suddhodana, was converted to his ideas. His eight-year-old son, Rahula, became a novice. The following year, several Sakiyan noblemen—including his cousins Ananda, Anuruddha, and Devadatta—joined the order of monks. On a subsequent visit home, he settled a dispute over access to water from the Rohini River, thereby preventing an outbreak of hostilities between the Gotamas and the Koliyas, the clan of his cousin Devadatta. From this point on, it seems, he could do no wrong.

Numerous Sakiyans asked to join the community, including his stepmother and aunt, Pajapati. He refused her request but she persisted. She shaved her head, donned yellow robes, and together with several other women from Sakiya, followed him to Vesali, where she once more pleaded with him to ordain her. This time he accepted and agreed to establish an order of *bhikkhuni* (nuns). This was the first time in India that women were received into an order of wandering mendicants as spiritual equals with monks. It was a hazardous move. Not only did he risk alienating his lay patrons, but also some of his own monks—in particular those from the priestly brahmin caste.

After the death of Suddhodana, the governorship of Sakiya—the role that Siddhattha would probably have assumed had he not left home—passed to Siddhattha Gotama's cousin Mahanama. Little is known about Mahanama. The Canon depicts him as politically and socially ambitious. He appears to have conspired with his mother to persuade his brother Anuruddha and his political rival Bhaddiya to become monks with Siddhattha in Rajagaha, thus leaving the way clear for him, as headman of the Gotama clan, to chair the Kapilavatthu Assembly from the solar seat. My sense is that he was a weak and vain man, who exploited his cousin's prestige for his own ends but was fatally unable to enforce his authority over his extended family.

Anathapindika spared no expense in designing a luxurious park for Siddhattha Gotama in the Kosalan capital of Savatthi. For an exorbitant sum he purchased a wooded grove outside the city from Pasenadi's brother (or cousin) Prince Jeta. Beneath the canopy of trees, he constructed "monks' cells, dormitories, attendance halls, heated halls, storerooms, toilets, outdoor and indoor walking areas, wells, bathrooms, ponds and sheds," at the heart of which stood Gotama's Scented Hut. Inspired by Anathapindika's zeal, Prince Jeta provided timber for the buildings and spent all the money the banker had paid him for the park on an elaborate, multistoried gateway. It is said that the sumptuous festivals to dedicate the buildings went on for months and cost as much as the park itself. In the end, Anathapindika's generosity bankrupted him and he spent the last years of his life in penury.

Jeta's Grove became Gotama's base. Once it was completed, he spent a total of nineteen Rains and delivered 844 discourses there, incomparably more than anywhere else. As his monks grew older and the community expanded, Jeta's Grove became more of a residential monastery and administrative headquarters of the order than merely a shelter for the three months of monsoon. Since the long, stable middle period of Gotama's career coincides with his tenure at Savatthi, Jeta's Grove would have been where Gotama's ideas were refined, organized, memorized, communally recited, and then disseminated. It became the nerve center of Gotama's mission, the hub to which his other groves and projects were connected.

By sponsoring Siddhattha Gotama in such a grand, even ostentatious, way, King Pasenadi, Anathapindika, and other nobles, merchants, and military officers of Savatthi affirmed their support of a teacher who, in many respects, was a rebel. This was a man who rejected all notions of a transcendent God or Self, openly criticized the system of caste, mocked the beliefs of the brahmins and other religious teachers of his day, and accepted nuns into his community as equals with the monks. Partly his sponsors may have given Gotama their backing because he was "one of them," i.e., a Kosalan nobleman in whose achievements they could take a vicarious pride, but their longstanding devotion to him suggests they were sincerely committed to what he taught.

The success of Gotama's work in Savatthi depended on his maintaining cordial relations with the churlish King Pasenadi. If Pasenadi turned against him, his entire project would be jeopardized. The many dialogues recorded between them give the impression that the two men knew each other well. Their exchanges are marked by a frankness and absence of formality. At times, the king seemed to tease or provoke Gotama, as though he wanted to test him. And Gotama's responses often seem guarded and circumspect, as though he was wary of saying anything that might be construed as an attack on the king.

At one point, we find the two of them observing what appears to be a religious gathering. Pasenadi pointed out some of the monks and ascetics present and asked Gotama whether, in his opinion, these men were "enlightened" or not. "It's difficult to say," replied Gotama. "Only by staying with people for a long time and paying close attention to them can you come to know them well enough to answer that. You only find out how strong a man is by observing him under adversity. Just as you can only learn how wise he is by talking with him." His answer was consistent with his understanding that a person is formed from a continuum of words and actions over time and cannot be reduced to a fixed "self" that is either "enlightened" or "unenlightened."

"Those are my spies," said Pasenadi. "I send them all over the place. When they've disclosed their information, I tell them to wash the dust and dirt from their bodies, trim their hair and beards, dress in fine clothes, then go and enjoy themselves. I give them whatever they want in the way of sensual pleasures." Gotama did not criticize the king. He did not intimate that disguising spies as monks might not be a good idea. All he said is "In the guise of disciplined men, undisciplined men wander through the land." The implication is clear. Pasenadi was letting him know that there could be spies among his own monks. The king might be watching him. He should be careful of what he says. He can never be sure who is listening and to whom his words might be reported.

King Pasenadi's most pressing concern was that he needed a son and heir. Although he had married a sister of King Bimbisara of Magadha (possibly as part of a reciprocal alliance with Magadha when his own sister, Devi, was married to Bimbisara), nothing is known either of this queen or any child from the union. Then one day, as Pasenadi was returning from a military expedition, he rode past the garden of the city's garland maker and heard a young woman singing from behind a wall. He went into the courtyard, where Mallika, the garland maker's daughter, interrupted her song, took the reins of the horse, and invited the weary king inside, where he spent the afternoon with his head resting on her lap. He was besotted both by her beauty and intelligence. That evening he sent a chariot to bring her to the palace and installed her as his queen.

Many at court, particularly the brahmin priests, would have been scandalized by the king's union with a low-caste girl. They might have blamed the influence of Gotama's rejection of caste for leading the king into such an inappropriate liaison. Mallika too followed the unorthodox teachings of Gotama. The courtiers would have been even more shocked by reports of the couple's sexual antics. Pasenadi used to spy on Mallika in her bath. One morning he saw her being nuzzled by one of her dogs. But instead of pushing it away, Mallika allowed the animal to mount her from behind. When he challenged her about this, she explained that it was just a trick of the light. "You go to the bathhouse," she said, "and I'll tell you what I see from here." The king did as he was told. "Can you see me?" he shouted. "Yes," she said. "But why are you fucking that nanny goat?"

Gotama too was accused of sexual improprieties. A female renunciant called Sundari was seen entering Jeta's Grove in the evening with perfumes and flowers, then leaving at dawn. After a while, she disappeared. Her fellow renunciants not only accused Gotama of sleeping with her, but of murdering her and then hiding the body beneath a heap of rubbish in Jeta's Grove. King Pasenadi ordered the grounds to be searched and Sundari's corpse was found not far from Gotama's Scented Hut. The body was then paraded around the city as people chanted: "Behold the deeds of the Sakiyan monks!" Ananda, the Buddha's attendant, was so distraught at this that he suggested to Gotama that they leave Savatthi at once. Gotama told him to calm down, that in a few days' time the matter would be resolved.

In the end, it was Ananda's personal avowal to Pasenadi that persuaded the king that Gotama was innocent. Ananda appears to have been the only person Pasenadi was willing to trust. Shortly afterward, the king's spies overheard the murderers quarreling about their deed among themselves while drunk. They were arrested and confessed that the renunciants themselves had employed them to kill Sundari as part of a plot to discredit Gotama.

Eventually, Mallika became pregnant and gave birth to a daughter. Pasenadi heard this news while visiting Gotama in the Scented Hut. He was furious that this woman, whom he had taken from a poor household and made his wife, should fail him in that way. Gotama tried to console him. "A woman may turn out to be better than a man," he said. "She may be wise and virtuous, a devoted wife, revering her mother-in-law." In the end, Pasenadi came to adore his daughter Vajiri. "Should anything happen to her," he later confessed to Mallika, "that would change my life irrevocably. Sorrow, lamentation, grief and despair would overwhelm me." Yet however much he loved his daughter, it did not alter the fact that the king was still without a male heir. Mallika did not conceive again.

King Pasenadi needed another wife. This time, he decided to marry a girl from the province of Sakiya. Perhaps he thought that mixing his seed with the blood of a kinswoman of Siddhattha Gotama would improve his chances of having a son. Whatever the reasons, for the king of Kosala to wed a Sakiyan bride would have been a signal honor for Gotama. And since the woman he chose—Lady Vasabha—was the daughter of Mahanama, the Sakiyan governor and cousin of the Buddha, the marriage would elevate Gotama into a member of the royal family.

Everything turned out well. Lady Vasabha gave birth to a son, Prince

Vidudabha. Now Gotama was both Pasenadi's personal teacher and a blood relation of the heir to the Kosalan throne. But there was a problem. Vasabha was not a "Lady" at all. She was the illegitimate daughter of Mahanama by a slavewoman called Nagamunda. The notoriously proud Sakiyans would have refused to allow any pure-blooded woman to marry outside their clan, even to their overlord in Savatthi. Mahanama had found himself trapped in an impossible situation. He could neither refuse his king's demand for a wife nor grant it without alienating himself from his own community. He had been obliged to send the king a slave girl and pass her off as a noblewoman.

Given Pasenadi's violent mood swings and spy networks, this deception was dangerous and foolhardy. Gotama may not have been privy to the plan, but once it was realized, it is hard to imagine how he could have remained ignorant of what had happened. He too was placed in an impossible situation: to reveal the deception would have put his life's work in jeopardy, whereas not to reveal the deception would have made him appear complicit in it. Through no action of his own, Gotama found his position in Savatthi compromised by the ambitions, lies, and pride of his relatives in Sakiya. Every day he would have been aware of the precarious nature of his tenure in Jeta's Grove. The survival of his community depended on the acting skills of a slave girl.

It is dark by the time I arrive in Sahet-Mahet, the shabby Indian village in Uttar Pradesh closest to the ruins of Savatthi. An armed guard swings open the heavy iron gates of the Lotus Nikko Hotel, a new and, by the look of it, hastily constructed edifice built to cash in on the growing number of Buddhist pilgrims. From the back comes the chugging of a generator to which the lights of the building appear to quiver in sympathy. The dining room is packed with a busload of moonfaced Korean laywomen with tightly curled perms, dressed in uniform gray baggy trousers and jackets, chatting and laughing as they devour kimchi and rice wrapped in squares of pressed laver from plastic boxes spread across the tables. Much sucking of teeth and bowing ensues when I discover that this is a group from Songgwangsa, my former monastery. Ven. Hyon-bong, an old monk friend and fellow disciple of Kusan Sunim, is in charge of taking these *bosalnim* around the "Buddhist circuit" at breakneck Korean speed.

Early next morning, Mr. Khan drives me out to the site of the long-abandoned city. It is quiet and deserted. I climb up the most prominent mound of brickwork, which, conceivably, might mark the spot where King Pasenadi's palace once stood. From there, I can make out a ring of almost continuous mounds, which would once have been the ramparts. Beyond them, fields and occasional trees stretch in all directions to the hazy green horizon. There is no sign of the Aciravati, the great river that, in Gotama's time, made the city into a thriving port. All that remains of the mighty capital of Kosala is an unexcavated expanse of rubble-strewn shrubland, home to the occasional jackal and peacock. Through my telephoto lens I peer at a colony of painted storks roosting in a solitary silk-cotton tree among the ruins. Every couple of minutes, one of them takes off and climbs laboriously into the sky like a little pink and white pterodactyl.

The ruins of Jeta's Grove lie about a mile away. Anathapindika's luxurious park is now a well-excavated archaeological site, laid out around prim lawns and tidy flower beds, cordoned off by iron railings from the throng of whining beggars and purveyors of religious trinkets and soft drinks outside. Pathways meander past piles of bricks, some more extensive than others: the floors, walls, and wells of what once were monasteries and temples. A prominent, raised structure in the middle of the park has been identified as the site of Gotama's Scented Hut. This serves as the focal point for pilgrims, who rub onto the brickwork little squares of gold leaf that shimmer and tremble in the breeze. A group of white-clad Sri Lankans sits cross-legged upon its hallowed surface, their palms placed together, chanting in nasal Pali. They leave in their wake smoldering sticks of sweet Indian incense, flower petals, and candles.

Ignoring the signs that forbid it, I roll out a bamboo mat and sit cross-legged on the lawn in the shade of a neem tree. Within minutes I am joined by a half-dozen emaciated, nearly hairless mongrels, who sit in front of me carefully licking their sores. I close my eyes as much to avoid the sight of these wretched creatures as to concentrate on my inbreath and outbreath. It strikes me that there is no ancient stupa either among the ruins at Savatthi or here at Jeta's Grove. For the place where Gotama delivered the bulk of his teaching and spent the greatest number of monsoons, one would have thought that some of his earthly relics would have been enshrined here. But, strangely, Savatthi is not included as one of the eight places from which Gotama's followers requested a share of the relics after his death. Why? By the end of his life, was Siddhattha Gotama so compromised in the eyes of its citizens that they did not wish even to honor his memory?

# 14

# AN IRONIC ATHEIST

THROUGHOUT MY YEARS in the community at Sharpham, writing continued to be my primary activity. As my articles and books on Buddhism became more widely known, they slowly began to provide a livelihood. In 1986 I was commissioned to write a guidebook to Tibet. This entailed returning to Lhasa for a two-month research trip in order to document and photograph all the major monasteries, shrines, and other sites of historic and religious importance in Central Tibet. I found most of these to have been badly damaged and only just beginning to be restored. *The Tibet Guide* was published in February 1988, with a foreword by the Dalai Lama, and went on to win the Thomas Cook award for that year. Two years later I published *The Faith to Doubt,* a series of essays on Zen, based on my time as a monk in Korea. This was followed by a commission to write a historical survey of the encounter between Buddhism and Western culture, from the ancient Greeks until modern times, which appeared in 1994 as *The Awakening of the West.*

In 1992 I was invited to become a contributing editor to a new Buddhist journal, *Tricycle* magazine, the first issue of which had appeared in New York the previous November. Until then, Buddhist periodicals in English had been little more than newsletters to promote the interests of particular organizations and their teachers. *Tricycle* changed all this. Not only was the editorial policy of the magazine strictly non-sectarian, *Tricycle* was also committed to high literary and aesthetic standards. It became the first Buddhist journal to appear alongside other magazines on newsstands and in bookstores, thus presenting Buddhist ideas and values to a general public rather than committed believers. I very much shared the vision of *Tricycle*'s founders and began writing regularly for the magazine.

In 1995, Helen Tworkov, the editor, asked me whether I would consider writing an introduction to Buddhism as part of a new series of Tricycle Books. She was looking for someone to present the basic ideas and practices of Buddhism to a lay audience without using any foreign words or technical jargon. I agreed. The result was called *Buddhism Without Beliefs,* which was published in March 1997. Instead of being the non-contentious introduction to Buddhism that was initially conceived, *Buddhism Without Beliefs* triggered what *Time* magazine, in its cover issue on Buddhism in America the following October, called "a civil but ferociously felt argument" about whether it was necessary for Buddhists to believe in karma and rebirth. I had proposed in the book that one could hold an agnostic position on these points, i.e., keep an open mind without either affirming or denying them. Naïvely perhaps, I had not anticipated the furor that this suggestion would create.

The ensuing controversy showed that Buddhists could be as fervent and irrational in their views about karma and rebirth as Christians and Muslims could be in their convictions about the existence of God. For some Western converts, Buddhism became a substitute religion every bit as inflexible and intolerant as the religions they rejected before becoming Buddhists. I argued that Buddhism was not so much a creedal religion as a broad culture of awakening that, throughout its history, had showed a remarkable ability to adapt to changing conditions. For a while I hoped that *Buddhism Without Beliefs* might stimulate more public debate and inquiry among Buddhists about these issues, but this did not happen. Instead, it revealed a fault line in the nascent Western Buddhist community between traditionalists, for whom such doctrines are non-negotiable truths, and liberals, like myself, who tend to see them more as contingent products of historical circumstance.

What is it that makes a person insist passionately on the existence of metaphysical realities that can be neither demonstrated nor refuted? I suppose some of it has to do with fear of death, the terror that you and your loved ones will disappear and become nothing. But I suspect that for such people, the world as presented to their senses and reason appears intrinsically inadequate, incapable of fulfilling their deepest longings for meaning, truth, justice, or goodness. Whether one believes in God or karma and rebirth, in both cases one can place one's trust in a higher power or law that appears capable of explaining this fraught and brief life on earth. One assumes the existence of hidden forces that lie deep beneath the surface of the contingent and untrustworthy world of day-to-day experience. Many Buddhists would argue that to jettison belief in the law of karma—a scheme of moral bookkeeping mysteriously inhering within the structure of reality itself— would be tantamount to removing the foundations of ethics. Good acts would not be rewarded and evil deeds not punished. Theists have said exactly the same about the consequences of abandoning belief in God and divine judgment.

Through my writings, I slowly came to be regarded as an "authority" on Buddhism, as a result of which I was frequently invited to interfaith seminars, BBC radio panel discussions, and other media events that sought a Buddhist angle on some pressing issue of the day. Typically, I would find myself sitting around a table with a Christian minister, a Jewish rabbi, a Muslim imam, and a Hindu swami. Once the opening platitudes were out of the way, the discussion would almost invariably shift into God-speak. I would then be faced with a dilemma: Do I politely go along with this kind of language for the sake of interreligious harmony? Or do I put my foot down and say: "Sorry, chaps, I don't have a clue what you're talking about"?

Whenever someone asks me whether I believe in God, I simply have no idea what the question means. Since those who ask tend to be educated and intelligent, I know they are not referring to a bearded old man sitting on a throne in the sky. But what are they referring to? I am just as puzzled by someone who says with equivalent conviction: "No, I do not believe in God." What is it that they so emphatically do not believe in? The word *God* is such an ingrained cultural habit of speech that, as a native English speaker, it is assumed automatically that I know how to use it. "I rather find myself at a loss when a question of God is raised," wrote Nanavira in a letter to Robert Brady. "I feel that I am expected to say something (even if it is only goodbye), and I don't find anything to say."

I have read many theological tomes, which do their best to explain the meaning of God, but I am still not much the wiser. God is presented as the source and ground of everything. For Thomas Aquinas, God is *esse ipsum:* Being itself. But how do you believe *in* "the source and ground of everything" let alone in "Being itself"? The New Testament tells us that God is Love and that He sent his only begotten Son into the world. But how can the ultimate source and ground of everything have an emotion like "love" or an intention to "incarnate"? In what possible sense can Being itself be thought of as a Person? At this point, you learn that God is unknowable and utterly beyond any concept you can have of Him, that all descriptions of God are mere figures of speech, imperfect metaphors required to render intelligible something so mysterious and sublime that the human mind is incapable of ever grasping it. I had the funny feeling that I was being led around in circles.

The same kind of intractable theological problems occur in Indian religious thought too. Learned pandits and mystics have struggled for centuries to explain how the unknowable, unitary, and transcendent Brahman—i.e., God—can give rise to this knowable, highly differentiated, and utterly specific world. They have developed complex cosmogonies and philosophies as well as elaborate systems of yoga and meditation in order to help the frail human mind to understand this.

Instead of speaking of Brahman as a Person, the Upanishads prefer another quintessentially human trait to describe the ultimate source and ground of everything: Consciousness. But the same anthropomorphic error occurs in describing God as Consciousness as it does in thinking of Him as a Person. Both images of God bear the indelible imprint of their creator: the conscious human person.

A young brahmin called Vasettha once went to see Gotama. "This is the only straight path," he declared, "the path of salvation that leads one who follows it to union with Brahma, as is taught by brahmin Pokkharasati!" Gotama asked him whether any brahmin had ever seen Brahma face-to-face. Since God is invisible and unknowable, Vasettha was obliged to reply: "No." In that case, countered Gotama, any claim about a path that leads to union with Brahma must be groundless. "Just as a file of blind men go on, clinging to each other, and the first one sees nothing, the middle one sees nothing, and the last one sees nothing, so it is with the talk of these brahmins. Their talk is laughable, mere words, empty and vain." He then compared a passionate believer in God to a man who declares that he is in love with the most beautiful girl in the land, but on being asked what she looks like is forced to admit that he has never once set eyes on her.

When the wanderer Udayin was asked by Gotama what doctrine he followed, he replied: "Our doctrine teaches: 'This is the Perfect Splendor, this is the Perfect Splendor!'" "But what is that Perfect Splendor, Udayin?" asked the Buddha. "That Splendor is the Perfect Splendor which is unsurpassed by any other Splendor higher or more sublime!" replied Udayin. Each time Gotama asked him to clarify what he meant, Udayin simply added another superlative to his declaration. "Udayin," said Gotama. "You could go on like this for a long time." With both Vasettha and Udayin, Gotama enjoyed poking fun at the absurdity of their claims. He exposed belief in an unknowable God as an irrational claim, unsupported by either experience or reason, based solely on the assertion of a teacher or a scripture that is reverently repeated.

In a similar vein, the Buddha told of a certain monk who wanted to know the answer to the metaphysical question "Where do the four great elements—earth, water, fire, and air—cease without remainder?" After failing to get an answer from the minor gods, the monk made his way to see Brahma, the greatest god of all. On being asked the question, Brahma replied: "Monk, I am Brahma, Great Brahma, the Conqueror, the Unconquered, the All-Seeing, All-Powerful, the Lord, the Maker and Creator, the Ruler, Appointer and Orderer, Father of All that Have Been and Shall Be." The monk said: "But that is not what I asked." Brahma took the monk by the arm and led him aside. "Look," he said. "My attendant gods believe there is nothing I do not know. That is why I did not speak in front of them. Monk, I don't know where the four great elements cease without remainder."

On the few occasions in the Canon such as these, where Gotama explicitly addressed the question of God, he is presented as an ironic atheist. The rejection of God is not a mainstay of his teaching and he did not get worked up about it. Such passages have the flavor of a diversion, a light entertainment, in which another of humanity's irrational opinions is gently ridiculed and then put aside. This approach is in contrast to the aggressive atheism that periodically erupts in the modern West. Advocates of such atheism are outraged that educated and intelligent people still persist in holding what, to them, are patently false and scarily dangerous ideas. Their position is premised on a denial of God every bit as fervent as the believer's affirmation of Him. It would be more accurate to call this "anti-theism." Then "atheism" would be free to recover its original meaning of simply "nottheism." Gotama was not a theist but nor was he an anti-theist. "God" is simply not part of his vocabulary. He was an "atheist" in the literal sense of the term.

Siddhattha Gotama was concerned with the systematic turning of one's attention to "this ground: this-conditionality, conditioned arising." Of course, for some, this might entail that one stop seeking God, but for others, like myself, who have never had the God habit, the sole task is to find ways of focusing unwaveringly on the suffering world as it presents itself in all its messiness, ambiguity, and specificity here and now. Gotama emphasized opening one's attention to the complexity and plurality of experience rather than narrowing it upon a single privileged religious object such as "Consciousness." When training in mindfulness, once you have stabilized attention by concentrating on the inbreath and outbreath, you extend it to include bodily sensations, feelings, mental states, and, finally, whatever is occurring within your field of awareness at a given moment. This is the exact opposite of what is taught in the Upanishads, which describes yoga as "the firm holding back of the senses" in order to achieve a state of "thoughtlessness" that prepares one for union with the Absolute.

The practice of mindfulness aims for a still and lucid *engagement* with the open field of contingent events in which one's life is embedded. All events are ontologically equivalent: mind is not more "real" than matter, nor matter more "real" than mind. When Gotama learned that Sati, one of his monks, had been saying that one's consciousness survives death and goes on to another life, he asked Sati to come and see him. He said: "Misguided man, when have you ever heard me teach that? Have I not repeatedly said that consciousness is conditionally arisen?"

Consciousness is what happens when an organism encounters an environment. If an eye is struck by light reflected off a colored shape, then visual consciousness occurs. But as soon as the object passes out of the field of vision or one shuts one's eyes, that consciousness ceases. This is true of every kind of consciousness. "Just as a fire," Gotama explained to Sati, "is reckoned by the particular condition dependent on which it burns—a log fire, a grass fire, a dung fire and so on—so too, consciousness is reckoned by the particular condition on which it arises." Consciousness is an emergent, contingent, and impermanent phenomenon. It has no magical capacity to break free from the field of events out of which it springs.

There are no wormholes in this intricate and fluid field through which one can wriggle out, either to reach union with God or move on to another existence after death. This is a field in which one is challenged to act; it is your actions alone that define you. There is no point in praying for divine guidance or assistance. That, as Gotama told Vasettha, would be like someone who wishes to cross the Aciravati River by calling out to the far bank: "Come here, other bank, come here!" No amount of "calling, begging, requesting or wheedling" will have any effect at all.

Buddhism has become for me a philosophy of action and responsibility. It provides a framework of values, ideas, and practices that nurture my ability to create a path in life, to define myself as a person, to act, to take risks, to imagine things differently, to make art. The more I prize Gotama's teachings free from the matrix of Indian religious thought in which they are entrenched and the more I come to understand how his own life unfolded in the context of his times, the more I discern a template for living that I can apply at this time in this increasingly secular and globalized world.

I am fully aware that the passages to which I am drawn in the Canon are those that best fit my own views and biases as a secular Westerner. Critics have accused me of "cherry picking" Buddhist sources, of extracting only those citations that support my position while either ignoring or explaining away everything else. To this objection, I can only point out that *it has ever been thus*. Each Buddhist school that has emerged in the course of history has done exactly the same. Chinese Buddhists selected the texts that best fitted their needs as Chinese, just as Tibetan Buddhists chose those that best fitted theirs. If Buddhism is a living tradition for you, one to which you turn for clues as to how to lead your life here and now rather than for cold impersonal facts, then how could it be otherwise? In this respect, I confess that what I am doing is not an objective study of Buddhism, but what I can only call *theology*—albeit theology without *theos*.

Ever since my time as a monk in Switzerland, I have been inspired by the work of liberal Protestant theologians. On first reading a book by Paul Tillich—I think it was *The Courage to Be*—I felt a powerful affinity with the tone and style of the prose. This, I realized, was the way I too wanted to write. Here was a man who was struggling to resolve the same kinds of questions in the context of Christianity that I faced in my own attempt to come to terms with Buddhism. I had not turned to Tillich out of any particular interest in Christian ideas. I was interested in his theological *method,* particularly the way he made use of modern philosophy and psychology in order to articulate a fresh and provocative reading of biblical texts. His work was not abstract and speculative but infused with personal commitment. What he was writing about mattered to him. It was not until I came across the work of Nanavira Thera that I found a Buddhist voice that achieved an equivalent synthesis of critical rigor and existential passion.

In the mid-1990s I was given a book by the Anglican theologian Don Cupitt called *The Time Being.* I was immediately impressed by the incisive, playful, and intensely personal quality of the writing. I was also astounded to find that Cupitt drew unapologetically on Buddhist sources, in particular Nagarjuna and Dogen, to make his case. I soon learned that Cupitt was a controversial, if not heretical, figure in the Christian world. In 1980, he had published a book entitled *Taking Leave of God,* in which he explicitly rejected any idea of God as a metaphysical reality existing outside the realm of human thought and language. Since then his views have become increasingly radical as he ruthlessly strips away the last remaining consolations of traditional religious belief. I became a keen admirer of his work. I have a greater affinity with Don Cupitt than with any living Buddhist thinker.

"Our old religious and moral traditions," writes Cupitt in *The Great Questions of Life* (2005), "have faded away, and nothing can resuscitate them. That is why a tiny handful of us are not liberal, but radical, theologians. We say that the new culture is so different from anything that existed in the past that religion has to be completely reinvented. Unfortunately, the new style of religious thinking that we are trying to introduce is so queer and so new that most people have great difficulty in recognizing it as religion at all."

Much of what Siddhattha Gotama taught must have struck his contemporaries as equally "queer" and "new." At the age of eighty, in the final year of his life, he was denounced to the Vajjian parliament in Vesali by a former monk called Sunakkhatta, a man who had once served as his attendant. Sunakkhatta declared, "The recluse Gotama does not have any superhuman states, any distinction in knowledge and vision worthy of the noble ones. The recluse Gotama teaches a Dhamma hammered out by reasoning, following his own line of inquiry as it occurs to him; and when he teaches this Dhamma to anyone, it leads him when he practices it only to the ending of pain." On being told of this criticism, Gotama remarked: "Sunakkhatta is angry and his words are spoken out of anger. Thinking to discredit me, he actually praises me."

Much of what Gotama said was so at odds with the conventional religious behavior and language of the day that it remained baffling even for someone who had once been close to him. Just as the very idea of godless religion is contradictory and distasteful for many theists today, so Gotama's reasoned exposition of conditioned arising and the Four Noble Truths would have appeared bizarre and not even worthy of the name "religion" for many of his contemporaries.

# 15

# VIDUDABHA'S REVENGE

IMAGINE YOU ARE hacking your way through a jungle. All of a sudden you come across the ruins of a long-abandoned temple. The only parts of the structure that remain standing are overgrown with creepers and vegetation. Stones, figurines, pillars, and lintels lie scattered about the forest floor, some of them still in good condition, but mostly you find just shards and fragments covered with moss. Then you notice a carved frieze of images running along the remains of an outside wall. Some sections are still intact and you can make out what appear to be the scenes of a story. You search among the fallen masonry. There too you come across stones with additional scenes from the frieze, though many are damaged and worn, making it difficult to interpret them. And everything is muddled up. Worse still, you have no idea at all of what the frieze is trying to tell you.

To read the Pali Canon in order to uncover the man Siddhattha Gotama is like this. You hack your way through page upon page of edifying and, at times, numbingly repetitive discourses. Only occasionally do you come across a sustained section of biographical narrative. It is far more common to stumble upon an isolated sentence or paragraph, like a carved scene on a chipped stone, that offers a brief, tantalizing glimpse into his world. Rarely is such a scene placed in an intelligible context. Rarely is it explained who the characters are and at what period in Gotama's life the events they describe occur. If, like most readers for whom these texts were intended, you are more interested in the Dhamma, such passages seem at worst irrelevant, at best stage decor.

I believe that these passages are surviving fragments of a story that has not been fully told. This story has long been buried beneath the myth of the prince in his palaces who renounces his kingdom, realizes enlightenment, establishes his doctrine and community, then dies. The myth shows how one man's existential conflicts are resolved through a profound awakening. It neatly encapsulates the Buddhist vision of salvation, expressed in dramatic terms that anyone can understand. To the extent that you can identify with the existential dilemma the Buddha faced as a young man that drove him to abandon his family, you can appreciate the possibility of resolving the dilemma through a life-transforming spiritual awakening. As an inspiring narrative, however, the story ends there.

The untold story, however, *begins* with the awakening. It tells of a man who has had a radical insight into what human life and society could be, who then spends the remaining forty-five years of his life articulating that vision and creating a community to uphold it after his death. To achieve his goal, he faces opposition from the brahmin establishment as well as other non-orthodox traditions; he has to convince fickle kings like King Pasenadi to support the endeavor; and he has to deal with the consequences of actions committed by ambitious members of his family such as Devadatta and Mahanama. Unlike the myth, this story cannot be summarized in a few memorable phrases. It consists of many interwoven threads, involves a wide cast of characters, and takes place in distant countries and cities, most of which no longer exist today.

For nearly four hundred years, before it was first written down in Sri Lanka, the Pali Canon survived in the memories of those monks entrusted with the task of preserving the Buddha's teaching for posterity. The sole concern of these early compilers of the Canon was to preserve the Dhamma taught by the Buddha. They appear to have had no interest in the order in which Gotama delivered his teachings, or in recording the political and social circumstances of his time. They classified his discourses according to whether they were long, middle-length, connected by theme, or given as a numbered list. Any sense of chronology or setting was thereby lost. The surviving fragments of historical detail were scattered like needles in a huge haystack of text. Fortunately, the monks continued to recite these fragments along with everything else they had memorized, irrespective of whether they made much sense. Over time, no doubt, certain details were forgotten, omitted, or muddled up, and doctrinal passages were elaborated and refined.

Yet when you pick out these scattered shards of history from the Canon and try to put them together again in the order they occurred, you discover an extraordinary consistency and coherence. I have yet to find a fragment that doesn't further illuminate the whole or is significantly inconsistent with any of the other pieces. As each chipped and weathered stone finds its place in the frieze around the temple wall, the sublime tragedy of Siddhattha Gotama's life begins to unfold before one's startled eyes.

Nonetheless, old habits die hard. In my quest for the historical Buddha, I still keep catching myself in search of a perfect person: one who can do no wrong, whose every thought, word, and deed springs from infallible understanding. But Gotama cannot be perfect because he is not God. He did not exempt himself when he said that all things are impermanent, suffering, unreliable, and contingent. He tried to respond as best as he could to the situation at hand. When I try to imagine myself in *his* present moment, I have to cancel everything I know about what happened in the centuries that separate his time from mine. He had no inkling of the worldwide spread of Buddhism that would occur after his death. In the fractious environment of his time, he did not know whether he, his community, or his teaching would survive even for another day.

Prince Vidudabha, the son of King Pasenadi and "Lady" Vasabha, was sixteen when he first visited his maternal homeland of Sakiya. As befitted one of his rank, the heir to the throne of Kosala would have ridden into Kapilavatthu on an elephant at the head of a procession of officials, soldiers, and retainers. Since he was a boy, he had been pressing Vasabha to allow him to visit his grandfather, Mahanama, in Sakiya. He was puzzled why, unlike the other boys at Pasenadi's court in Savatthi, he never received any gifts of toy horses or elephants from his mother's father. Vasabha explained that this was because Sakiya was such a long way away, though, in fact, it was only eighty miles to the east and connected by the North Road. In the end, after repeated requests, she relented and allowed him to go.

On arriving at Kapilavatthu, Vidudabha's party was welcomed warmly by the Buddha's cousin Mahanama and lodged in the royal guesthouse. The young prince could not understand why, apart from his grandfather, only one uncle had turned out to greet him. He was told that all the younger noblemen had gone to the country. Nonetheless, for the rest of his stay he was lavishly entertained and shown great hospitality. Just after he and his entourage departed, one of his soldiers realized he had forgotten a sword in the guesthouse and went back to retrieve it. On going inside, he noticed a woman scrubbing with milk the seat that Prince Vidudabha had used and overheard her mutter contemptuously: "This is where the son of that slave-woman Vasabha sat!" When he reported what he had heard to General Karayana, the army commander, there was an uproar. The young prince, who would have been deeply humiliated and compromised by this revelation, made a vow there and then: "These Sakiyans wash the seat on which I sat with milk; when I gain my throne, I will wash it with the blood of their throats!"

When King Pasenadi was told what had happened, he flew into a rage against the Sakiyans, stripped Vasabha and Vidudabha of their royal positions, cropped their hair, dressed them in sackcloth, and returned them to the condition of slavery. On hearing of Pasenadi's treatment of his wife and son, Gotama came to the palace to plead on their behalf. He admitted that the Sakiyans had behaved wrongly in deceiving the king, but argued that, in the case of both the queen and the prince, their mothers' status was irrelevant. "It is the family of the father," he said, "that affords the true measure of social position." Since Vasabha was fathered by Mahanama, who was both a nobleman and a chief, and Vidudabha was fathered by Pasenadi himself, that was what mattered. The king, who was emotionally attached both to wife and son, was persuaded by this reasoning and restored them to their former positions.

Gotama and Pasenadi would have been in their seventies at this time. Although the king still had the authority to reinstate Prince Vidudabha as heir to the throne, it is doubtful that others at court—particularly those faithful to the ways of the brahmin priests—would have accepted as the future king of Kosala a youth in whose veins ran the tainted blood of a slave. Pasenadi would have realized that there could now be little assurance of a peaceful succession. Gotama's position at Savatthi would likewise have been severely weakened by the exposure of Mahanama's deception. His enemies would have regarded him and those of his inner circle, which included Mahanama's brothers Ananda and Anuruddha, as sharing in the treachery of the Sakiyans. From that point onward, it appears that Gotama's idyll in Jeta's Grove was over.

While it is difficult to establish the exact sequence of events that follows, it seems likely that Gotama left Savatthi under a cloud and returned to Rajagaha. There too his fortunes had recently suffered a series of blows. When Gotama was seventy-two, his first patron, King Bimbisara, was forced to abdicate in favor of his son Ajatasattu. To prevent the old king from making a comeback, Ajatasattu had his father imprisoned and then starved him to death. Ajatasattu's mother, Queen Devi, the sister of King Pasenadi, collapsed on learning what had happened to Bimbisara and never recovered. At the same time,

Siddhattha's cousin Devadatta, who had become Ajatasattu's mentor, tried to seize control of the monastic order.

After unsuccessfully imploring the Buddha to retire on grounds of old age and pass the leadership of the community to him, Devadatta then sought to persuade his cousin to impose five additional rules on the monks. This would have required the monks (1) to live in forests, with (2) only the branches of trees for shelter, (3) no longer to enter the homes of laypeople for meals or (4) to accept gifts of cloth from them, and (5) only to eat vegetarian food. Gotama refused to institute any of these rules. Not only would they have severely restricted the social mobility of the monks, they would have transformed the order into an ascetic movement similar to that of the Jains. Nonetheless, Devadatta declared that he himself would adopt these rules and invited others to do likewise. A considerable number of younger monks joined him, thereby causing a schism in the community. Devadatta and his followers then departed for a forested hill outside the city of Gaya in order to pursue their strict regimen. It is also possible that Devadatta or his lay supporters made attempts on Gotama's life during this power struggle.

In the end, the schism was healed through the intervention of Gotama's disciples Sariputta and Moggallana, who persuaded the renegade monks to return to the fold. What happened to Devadatta after his failed bid for power is unclear. It seems that he regretted his actions and sought to reconcile himself with Gotama, but died before he could reach Jeta's Grove. The episode reveals tensions and disagreements among the inner circle of Gotama's followers. Devadatta may not have been the only senior monk to have had concerns that the monastic community was not sufficiently austere in its behavior. Gotama was an old man then, whose authority had been openly challenged.

When Gotama arrived in Rajagaha after the exposure of the deception in Savatthi, it may have been the first time he had returned to the Magadhan capital since the schism. He stayed with his retinue of monks in a circular pavilion in the mango grove owned by Jivaka, the

Takkasila-educated royal physician, instead of residing at Bamboo Grove. This may be an indication that he was ill and needed medical supervision. Then one full-moon night, at Jivaka's suggestion, Devadatta's former sponsor, King Ajatasattu, went to visit Gotama. The doctor had advised the king to talk to the Buddha in order to "bring peace to Your Majesty's heart." It seems that Ajatasattu was tormented by guilt and remorse over the death of his parents.

King Ajatasattu entered the pavilion to find Gotama seated against the central pillar, with a group of monks before him. "I have a question," the king said. "Consider the craftsmen I employ: elephant-handlers, cooks, soldiers, barbers, bakers, potters, accountants and so on. All of them can be seen, here and now, to enjoy the fruits of their labors. Not only are they rewarded by their skills, but so are their families and friends. Now what can you show me as a reward, visible here and now, as the result of leading the homeless life of a monk?"

"Suppose you had a slave," said Gotama, "who works for you unstintingly from dawn to dusk. Then one day he thinks: 'This is strange. King Ajatasattu is a man and I too am a man. But while he lives like a god, I live as a slave. What if I were to cut off my hair and beard, don a yellow robe and go forth into homelessness?' So he does just that and goes off to live in solitude, mindful and content with little. If someone reported this to you, would you say: 'That slave must come back immediately and work for me as before'?"

"No," said the king, "I would not. I'd honor and protect that man. I would provide him with robes, food, lodging and other requisites."

"Then, Your Majesty, would that not be a reward of the homeless life, clearly visible here and now?"

Siddhattha Gotama did not regard the value of what he taught as limited to invisible spiritual rewards, whether in this or a future life. By embracing his vision, people could also be liberated from the indignity of slavery, winning the respect and support of those they had previously served. His teaching had clear social implications. He saw his community as the microcosm of another kind of society, one in which rank, caste, and gender no longer define who you are. He compared his teaching and training to an ocean in which rivers merge and lose their identity. For as soon as you adopted them, you lost your identity of belonging to a particular social class. Instead, "just as an ocean is permeated by the taste of salt," his community was "permeated by the taste of freedom."

At the conclusion of their discussion, Ajatasattu brought himself to confess what had been tormenting him. "For the sake of the throne," he admitted, "I deprived my father, that good man and just king, of his life." Gotama accepted the king's confession. "He who acknowledges his transgression," he said, "and confesses it for betterment in the future, will grow in the noble discipline." Forgiveness emerges as the theme that unites these tragic events: Pasenadi forgave Vasabha and Vidudabha; Ajatasattu forgave the hypothetical runaway slave; Gotama forgave the parricidal king. Then Ajatasattu, relieved by and rejoicing in what Gotama had said, rose from his seat, bowed, and departed. As far as we know it was the last time the two men met face-to-face.

The final meeting between Siddhattha Gotama and King Pasenadi took place—probably a year or so later—in a town called Medalumpa, in Sakiya. King Pasenadi and his army commander, General Karayana, were staying at the nearby town of Nagaraka, from where they proceeded by state carriage to the park where Gotama was living. They dismounted at the end of the carriage track and followed a path into a grove where a number of monks were walking slowly up and down. When asked where they could find Gotama, a monk replied: "That is his dwelling, Your Majesty, the one with the closed door. Go up to it quietly, enter the porch, clear your throat, and tap on the panel. He will open the door for you." Pasenadi handed over his sword, turban, fan, parasol, and sandals to General Karayana and, bareheaded and unarmed, headed for the hut alone.

On entering the hut, Pasenadi collapsed at Gotama's feet, covered them with kisses, and caressed them tenderly, repeating: "I am King

Pasenadi of Kosala, venerable sir, I am King Pasenadi of Kosala." Gotama said: "But, Your Majesty, why are you honoring me like this? Why are you displaying such friendship?"

Pasenadi launched into a rambling eulogy of the Buddha, his teaching, and his monks. He spoke as a humiliated and broken man who has lost his hold on power and no longer commands respect. He complained that, as king, he was supposed to have the power of life and death over his subjects, but nowadays, when sitting in council, he did not even have the power to stop people from interrupting him when he was speaking. Yet when he had been to hear Gotama address a large gathering, he noticed that not a single person would be heard even to cough or clear his throat for fear of interrupting his discourse. "It is quite wonderful," he remarked ruefully, "how an assembly can be so well disciplined without the threat of force or weapons." In conclusion, he said: "And you ask me why I show you such honor and friendship? Because you are a nobleman and I am a nobleman; because you are a Kosalan and I am a Kosalan; because you are eighty years old and I am eighty years old. So now I must go. We are both busy and have much to do."

When the king stepped out of the hut, there was no sign of General Karayana; just a woman servant and a horse stood forlornly before him. The woman told Pasenadi that Karayana had taken the sword, turban, and other objects entrusted to him—the symbolic insignia of kingship—and was on his way to crown Prince Vidudabha as king of Kosala. Given what Pasenadi had just told Gotama, the old man could not have been entirely surprised by this plot between his general and his son. After waiting patiently for many years, Karayana had seized the opportunity to avenge his uncle Bandhula, the former army commander and chief justice, whom Pasenadi had murdered out of fear that Bandhula was planning to overthrow him. The king realized that his only option was to go to Rajagaha—more than two hundred miles to the south—and seek asylum and perhaps military support from his nephew, King Ajatasattu.

Since the Kosalan army was most likely already gathering on the borders of Sakiya, in preparation to attack Kapilavatthu in revenge for Mahanama's deception, King Pasenadi and General Karayana's visit to
Gotama looked as though it may have been just a cynical ruse engi-
neered by the general to dispose of the sentimental and feeble old
monarch. When the first battalion of troops, under the command of
the newly crowned King Vidudabha, approached the border, they
found Gotama waiting for them, seated in the shade of a small tree.
Initially, his presence and authority seemed to have been sufficient to
deter Vidudabha, who ordered the soldiers to retreat. After three such
standoffs, however, Gotama realized that he was powerless to prevent
what was about to happen. So he too, like Pasenadi, headed south for
Rajagaha, leaving Vidudabha's army to march on Kapilavatthu with orders to kill every Sakiyan they saw, "sparing not even infants at the
breast."

I picture Pasenadi slumped dejectedly in the saddle of his horse with
his woman servant walking alongside. As they make their way out of
Sakiya into Malla, the pre-monsoon sun beats down upon them merci-
lessly, flies buzz all around, while hot winds blow the dust of the North
Road onto their sweating faces. Without his sword, turban, fan, parasol, or sandals, Pasenadi is just another tired old man making a long
journey at the worst time of year.

Pasenadi's willingness to entrust himself to his nephew, King
Ajatasattu of Magadha, is a clear sign of the deposed monarch's des-
peration. On learning that Ajatasattu had starved her husband Bimbisara to death, Devi, the former queen and Pasenadi's sister, had broken
down and died of grief. To avenge her death, Pasenadi had launched a
war against Ajatasattu in order to regain the strategic villages near
Baranasi on the northern bank of the Ganges, which had been given
to Bimbisara as part of Devi's dowry. Neither side, however, was able to
gain a conclusive victory. To secure the peace, Pasenadi was obliged to
give his beloved daughter Vajiri in marriage to the man who had caused

his sister's death. Pasenadi was alone in the world. Mallika, his first queen and Vajiri's mother, had died some years before. He had no option but to place his hope for survival in the hands of a man with a very poor track record of caring for elderly relatives. The only ray of light would have been the prospect of seeing his daughter again. She alone might be able to prevail on Ajatasattu to take pity on him.

After crossing the Ganges, Pasenadi would have taken the highway Bimbisara had built to connect the port of Patali with the landlocked capital of Rajagaha. He arrived at the city at night. The gates were closed and the guards refused to admit this disheveled old man who claimed to be the queen's father. Exhausted from the journey, Pasenadi took a room at an inn outside the city walls. The following morning, his servant woman found him dead. On hearing the news, Ajatasattu insisted on conducting the funeral rites for his uncle and father-in-law himself. And they were performed with much pomp and solemnity, as befitted the memory of such a great monarch as King Pasenadi of Kosala.

# 16

# GODS AND DEMONS   .

MY FRIEND FRED VARLEY died in late April or early May 1975; no one is sure of the date and a death certificate was never issued. He was a strapping twenty-five-year-old lad from Lancashire, with whom I had been chatting and laughing in Achala's tea shop in McLeod Ganj only a week before. The next day, at first light, my fellow monk Kevin Rigby and I walked in silence through the forest up to the Swiss clinic, an assortment of tidy buildings on the steep hillside between Forsyth Ganj and McLeod Ganj. Even at that hour, the pre-monsoon heat was becoming unbearable. The distressed and nervous young doctor showed us into an unlit storeroom with a tin roof, where Fred's body lay under a soiled sheet on a charpoy—a simple Indian rope bed. Glenn Mullin drew back the sheet and the vile stench of decomposition swept into my nostrils, making my stomach heave. I had never seen a corpse before. Fred was dressed in the same homespun cotton clothes he had been wearing when I last saw him.

Trijang Rinpoche, the junior tutor, had thrown a *mo* (a method of divination involving dice), which indicated that Fred should be cremated immediately rather than left for three days, the time Tibetans believe it takes for a departing consciousness to leave the body. The day before, he had dispatched Geshe Dhargyey to the clinic to perform the final rites of *powa*, a tantric procedure that propels a dying or recently deceased person's consciousness to a favorable rebirth. He had also stipulated that only six of Fred's male friends be present at the cremation. A stretcher had already been improvised and lay on the ground beside the charpoy. Our first attempt to raise the body only succeeded in releasing another nauseating wave of the smell of decomposition. I ran outside to retch. On the second attempt, we held our breath and somehow managed to heave the corpse onto the stretcher. We covered it with the sheet, then secured it to the stretcher with ropes. Glenn and three others hoisted Fred's dead weight onto their shoulders and we headed off down the hill to the cremation ground, chanting "*Om Mani Padme Hum*"—the mantra of Avalokiteshvara, the bodhisattva of compassion. As monks, Kevin and I, each bearing a smoldering bundle of musky Tibetan incense sticks wrapped in a white silk *katag,* led the four others who bore the stretcher on their shoulders.

The Tibetans were convinced that a singularly evil spirit was at loose in Dharamsala that summer. I had been told that a government official had already stabbed himself with a kitchen knife in Gangchen Kyishong and an old woman had been attacked by a swarm of bees while circumambulating the hill on which the Dalai Lama's residence stood. Both had died of their injuries. And now one of the *Injis* had been suddenly struck down by illness, driven violently insane and killed. There was no doubt in anyone's mind that these deaths were the work of a destructive but invisible entity of some kind. "Traps"—shallow boxes packed with *tsampa* dough in which were planted little masts of crossed sticks emblazoned with a diamond of brightly colored threads—were placed at crossroads and other strategic junctions in order to deflect the demon from its course.

Even the sultry gusts of wind that raised little eddies of dust on the main street of McLeod Ganj had a sinister air about them. The Tibetans were seized with a calm and resolute certainty about the seriousness of the threat. This destructive spirit was as real for them as if it had been a band of Mongol horsemen, stealthily stalking the village to launch sudden, deadly attacks. The fact that the spirit was invisible only served to confirm how powerful and dangerous it was. Viscerally, I found it impossible to resist the contagion of this collective belief. Sympathetic terror quivered through my body. At the same time my inner anthropologist stood back, observing what was happening with detached curiosity. And yet another part of myself stood even further back, noting the tug-of-war between conflicting aspects of my psyche.

A few days after Fred's cremation, monks from Gyuto, the Upper Tantric College, who specialized in exorcizing spirits of this kind, arrived in Dharamsala from Dalhousie in three jeeps piled high with rolled carpets, long bundles of scripture in orange cloth, and brocade-wrapped accoutrements. They conducted their rituals in secret. All we could hear were the distant pounding of drums, the clashing of cymbals, and the ringing of bells. Then, to the palpable relief of the community, it was announced that the demon had been captured inside a triangular box, which was then sealed with *vajras* and buried deep in the earth. An Englishwoman who lived near to where the rituals were performed said that she saw the spirit descend like a flash of forked lightning into the box. At this point, secure in the knowledge that the spirit had been vanquished, the world returned to its normal routines. And there were no more violent deaths that summer.

Most Buddhists throughout Asia are and always have been polytheists. They believe in the existence of a range of spirits and gods whose worlds intersect with our own. These entities do not have a merely symbolic existence; they are real beings with consciousness, autonomy, and agency, who can grant favors if pleased and wreak havoc if offended. It is very much in our interest to keep on the right side of them. But since many of these spirits are fickle beings like ourselves, they cannot ultimately be trusted. On formally becoming a Buddhist, one "takes refuge" in the Buddha, Dharma, and Sangha, thereby renouncing reliance on these beings. But the spirits and gods are only downgraded, not abolished. They continue to play a role in one's personal and social life. This is the thought-world one finds throughout the Pali Canon. Siddhattha Gotama did not reject the existence of the gods, he marginalized them. He may have mocked their conceits but he acknowledged their presence. At times they even functioned as inspirational voices that prompted him to act.

However tempting it is for me to dismiss the existence of gods and spirits as outdated nonsense, I need to be aware of the equally tenuous foundations of my own beliefs. If challenged, I would be incapable of persuading someone who does not already share my view of the universe or human life that my beliefs about them are true. I once spent a couple of hours trying to persuade a learned and intelligent Tibetan lama that the world is spherical in shape—but with little success. I would have had even less success had I tried to convince him of other beliefs I held: those about the Big Bang, evolution by natural selection, or the neural foundations of consciousness. I believed these things on much the same grounds that he believed in disembodied gods and spirits. Just as I unquestioningly accepted the authority of eminent scientists, so he accepted the authority of eminent Buddhist teachers. Just as I trusted that what the scientist claims to be true can be backed up by observation and experiment, so he trusted that what his teachers claim to be true can be backed up by direct meditational insight. I had to recognize that many of my truth-claims were no more or less reasonable than his.

I know very little with anything approaching certainty. I know that I was born, that I exist, and that I will die. For the most part, I can trust my brain's interpretation of the data presented to my senses: this is a rose, that is a car, she is my wife. I do not doubt the reality of the thoughts and emotions and impulses I experience in response to these things. I know that if there is smoke coming out of a chimney, then there will be a fire that produced it. And I possess a miscellany of remembered facts and figures: Borobodur is in Java; water boils at 100 degrees Celsius (at sea level). Yet apart from these primary perceptions, intuitions, inferences, and bits of information, the views that I hold about the things that really matter to me—meaning, truth, happiness, goodness, beauty—are finely woven tissues of belief and opinion. These views enable me to get by in my workaday world but would not stand up to a great deal of scrutiny from someone who was not sympathetic to them. Depending on how crucial they are to my integrity and credibility, I am prepared to defend some of them with greater vigor and passion than others. I drift and swim through life on a tide of derivative beliefs that I share with others who belong to the same kind of cultures as myself.

As I was writing this, a copy of a quarterly newsletter from a Buddhist publisher arrived on my desk. On the front page was an extract of a text written by Karma Lingpa—the fourteenth-century revealer of the Tibetan Book of the Dead—translated, as luck would have it, by my old friend Glenn Mullin. It boldly declares, "If when dying, one's hands shake back and forth and one babbles meaninglessly, and if the bodily warmth first withdraws from under the right armpit, this indicates rebirth as a titan." (For a believer in rebirth, this is an entirely reasonable claim: if consciousness "leaves" the body, it has to leave from somewhere.) This information is presented as a matter-of-fact description of something that occurs in the world. There is not the slightest hint of irony. As I read it, I felt myself rejecting it as naturally as a body would reject a piece of foreign tissue. How could such a claim ever be validated or falsified? I reject it not because it is "wrong" or "incorrect" (how could one ever know?) but because it is so completely at variance with other views of the world that I have found to be of value.

Following the example of William James, John Dewey, and Richard Rorty, I have relinquished the idea that a "true" belief is one that corresponds to something that exists "out there" in or beyond reality somewhere. For pragmatist philosophers such as these, a belief is valued as true because it is useful, because it works, because it brings tangible benefits to human beings and other creatures. Siddhattha Gotama's Four Noble Truths are "true" not because they correspond to something real somewhere, but because, when put into practice, they can enhance the quality of your life. In the context of the worldview and sociopolitical organization of medieval Tibet, belief in spirits worked to the extent that it provided explanations for natural events. It also "worked" in that it enabled practices that sometimes seemed to resolve the ensuing problems spirits caused. At the time it may have been one of the better theories around. In the secular world of twenty-first-century Europe and America, such beliefs are less likely to attract adherents and less likely to work, because they are increasingly difficult to mesh with a worldview composed of other beliefs that have shown a remarkable ability to produce desired effects in people's lives.

The strongest argument against gods, spirits, and tantric divination is found in the existence of the electricity grid, brain surgery, and the Declaration of Human Rights. Irrespective of whether the truth-claims made by Newton or Voltaire can be shown to correspond with reality or not, they have become part of an understanding of the person and the world that has led to numerous benefits and freedoms that I for one would not be prepared to exchange for a life in a pre-modern Buddhist society. This is not to say that modern liberal democratic societies are perfect. Far from it. The fundamental human suffering that Buddha addressed in *Turning the Wheel of Dhamma* is no different today than it was two and a half thousand years ago. What draws me to Buddhism is not that it has a more convincing explanation of the nature of reality than other religions, but that it offers a methodology which might actually work in addressing the question of suffering.

I left Dharamsala for Switzerland in the autumn of 1975. With me I carried Fred's ashes in a tin of Amul milk powder, which I delivered, along with a Tibetan *thangka* (scroll painting), to his distraught and uncomprehending father. As I sought to console this self-effacing man by explaining some of the Buddhist beliefs his son had adopted, I was conscious of how alien and hollow my words must have sounded. For Mr. Varley the only consolation was to know that Fred had left him a grandson. At the time of Fred's death, his estranged girlfriend was five months pregnant with their child. The baby had been born on

August 19, shortly before I left India. I was not to see Dharamsala again for another eighteen years.

I returned to McLeod Ganj on March 12, 1993, to attend a four-day meeting of Western Buddhist teachers with the Dalai Lama. I was thirty-nine years old and living at Sharpham. There were twenty-two of us, representing Tibetan, Zen, and Theravada schools of Buddhism. Some of us were either monastics or bore a religious title of some kind; others, like Martine and myself, were laypeople. What bound us together was that we were all engaged full-time in teaching Buddhism in Europe or America. Some of us had published books. Some had founded or were directing Buddhist centers and communities. It was nonetheless an eccentric sampling. A number of widely followed Buddhist schools were not represented at all. From his side, the Dalai Lama had also invited several prominent Tibetan lamas to attend, but only three relatively obscure figures showed up.

A great deal had changed since I was last in McLeod Ganj. The place had been transformed from an idyllic Indian hill-station into a congested, polluted little township ("Muck Load Ganj" in the words of one local Indian wit). The broad main street had been divided down the middle with shops selling Tibetan knickknacks, which forced jeeps, trucks, Maruti Suzuki taxis, motorbikes, and pedestrians to squeeze through the narrow lanes to either side. We were lodged in a multistoried concrete hotel called the Surya Resorts, precariously perched on the hillside at the edge of the village and managed by enterprising Indians. Since I had last been there, plastic bags and bottles had become widespread in India and now lay discarded like slurry down the hillside.

The Dalai Lama was fifty-eight. Since being awarded the Nobel Peace Prize in 1989, he was fast becoming a global spiritual superstar. This meant that he spent less and less time in Dharamsala as he traveled the world teaching Buddhism and ceaselessly campaigning on behalf of his people for greater freedom and justice in Tibet. The Chinese authorities remained as obdurate as ever. The prominence given to the

Dalai Lama in the Western media and the sympathetic concern for his cause occasionally voiced by world leaders had had no discernible effect on the situation in Tibet.

On returning to McLeod Ganj, I sensed that Buddhism too had somehow lost its innocence. Since I had first arrived here twenty years earlier, Buddhist centers, communities, and publishing houses had sprung up and proliferated all over Europe, America, and Australia. This was largely due to the efforts of Westerners who had returned home from their studies in Asia and then invited their Buddhist teachers to come over and establish centers. The popularity of Buddhism had soared. It was no longer perceived as a quaint spiritual pastime of aging hippies but was being enthusiastically absorbed into mainstream Western culture. Inevitably, it was also becoming more institutionalized. In a very short time, Buddhist groups had acquired extensive properties and wealthy benefactors. The heady mix of "enlightened masters," devoted students, and grandiose spiritual ambition can easily lead to sectarianism and the abuse of power. These were the key issues that the twenty-two of us had come to Dharamsala to discuss in person with the Dalai Lama.

After two days of preparation, we were ushered into a high-ceilinged, chilly room in the palace for the first of our eight two-hour sessions with the Dalai Lama. We had prepared a number of topics: the adaptation of Buddhism to the West, tradition versus culture, sectarianism, psychotherapy, monks and laity, and the monster that kept rearing its head: sexual relations between teachers and students.

The discussions proceeded awkwardly at first, no one quite sure of where we were heading or what to expect. As he listened to our brief presentations, the Dalai Lama emanated an almost restless energy, switching effortlessly from intense inner reflection to bubbling laughter. His face flooded you with a gaze of such warmth and openness that it was hard not to avert your eyes. When excited, the pitch of his voice rose to the verge of a shriek, and the staccato firing of English syllables broke into a torrent of Tibetan; his hands chopped the air with conviction. Then he would pause—silence—laugh, grin, and beam at his interlocutor: "Yes? All right. Next?"

When it came to my turn, I offered the Dalai Lama a brief history of Buddhism as a way of showing how, over time, it had responded to the needs of different Asian cultures, but in so doing, had itself been transformed by the encounter. This appeared so self-evident to me that I worried my presentation might be too simplistic. Yet to my surprise, the Dalai Lama listened with a slightly puzzled look on his face, as though the idea was novel and rather dubious. He asked for some concrete examples. I suggested he consider how the image of the Buddha in Japan looks Japanese, while in Tibet it looks Tibetan. He swung around and pointed at a Tibetan *thangka* behind him: "But look, this Buddha: he is *Indian*." It was difficult to know what to say. The image he was pointing to looked, as Martine put it afterward, "no more Indian than my *mémé*"—her eighty-four-year-old granny in Bordeaux.

Again I was forced to recognize that no matter how intelligent the person to whom one is talking may be, his or her view of the world might be based on entirely different premises. What seems obvious to me as a modern Westerner may not be at all obvious to a Tibetan lama—even one who in so many other respects seems to have embraced and understood the modern world. And whereas I found the study of history to be a vivid illustration of the Buddhist teachings on impermanence and conditioned arising, this did not appear to strike the Dalai Lama as particularly significant. I realized with an unsettling jolt that the "historical consciousness" I so take for granted was a peculiar feature of my own upbringing and conditioning. As this exchange indicated, someone from another background might perceive the same sensory data quite differently.

During the 1980s a number of scandals had erupted in the Western Buddhist world, usually involving sexual relations between teachers and their students. The Dalai Lama told us that he had received several letters from Western women who alleged that their Buddhist teacher had coerced them into having sex on such grounds as "it would purify their negative karma." He was very upset about what he heard. He worried that the media attention given to such incidents damaged the reputation of Buddhism and weakened its potential as a force for peace and good in the world. In the course of our discussions, he kept returning to this theme. It soon became clear that one of the reasons he was being so generous with his time was that he wanted us to help him tackle this problem in an effective way.

As our discussions drew to a close, he suggested that we compose an "open letter" in which we summarized some of the conclusions we had drawn from our meeting. I was selected to be the scribe. After we had worked through several drafts, I read the letter aloud to the Dalai Lama. He listened attentively and constantly suggested changes in wording and emphasis. For the first time, I witnessed his sharply honed political intelligence at work. In the crucial paragraph concerning teachers' ethics, we had written: "Each student must be encouraged to take responsible measures to confront teachers with unethical aspects of their conduct. If the teacher shows no sign of reform, students should not hesitate to publicize any unethical behavior of which there is irrefutable evidence." This was the point the Dalai Lama was most keen to get across. He hoped that such public exposure would enable the victims to be heard and the malefactors to be shamed, thus breaking any cycle of abuse.

It took weeks for the Dalai Lama's private office to ratify the document. And when it was finally returned to us for publication, it was unchanged except for one thing: the sentence in which the Dalai Lama personally endorsed the text had been deleted. Without his endorsement, the open letter gave the impression that twenty-two self-selected Western teachers had taken it upon themselves to issue a decree to the entire Buddhist community. From the moment the Dalai Lama first suggested writing an open letter, I had assumed that I was drafting a joint statement that would be released by the Dalai Lama and our group. I fully agreed with the content of the letter we published, but the whole experience left me with the slightly unpleasant taste of having been used. The Dalai Lama had succeeded in communicating his concerns and proposing a solution, but by removing his endorsement from the letter, his staff ensured that he did not have to take any responsibility for what it said. Once again, I became aware of how what appeared on the surface to be a shared cause between Tibetans and Westerners could also conceal conflicting agendas and expectations.

The encounter between Tibet and the 1960s was like a midair collision of two sets of conflicting desires. We were both exiles, fleeing in opposite directions. The Tibetans were escaping from Chinese Communism; we were running away from broken homes, the Cold War, and the military-industrial complex. We smashed into each other over India like particles in an accelerator. Neither side really understood or appreciated the needs of the other. I looked to the Tibetans for the lofty insights of Buddhism to help resolve my existential anxieties; they looked to me for the support they needed to survive as refugees in an uncomprehending and hostile world. As I came to understand, my painful struggle with Geshe Rabten revolved entirely around this issue in particular, as it played out in the crisis that continued to simmer around allegiance to the protector god, Dorje Shugden.

When I had sought the Dalai Lama's advice on this issue in 1985, he had told me, through his private secretary, that it was an internal Tibetan matter and had no need to be aired in the Western media. Since then, the dispute had steadily heated up. The Dalai Lama persisted in making public statements that denounced this protector as a dangerous and evil spirit. He encouraged Tibetans to abandon its practice in favor of that of another protector god called Dorje Drakden, who traditionally advises the government through the State Oracle. He ordered public images of Dorje Shugden to be removed from monasteries and temples. He stopped short of trying to ban the practice outright but forbade anyone who continued to do it from attending his teachings and initiations. It was claimed that those employed by the Tibetan government in exile had to sign a declaration renouncing allegiance to the god.

Most Tibetans appeared to follow the Dalai Lama's instructions, but a number of senior lamas in the Geluk school, including Geshe Rabten, refused to do so. The close disciples of Trijang Rinpoche, the junior tutor and leading proponent of the practice, were unwilling to compromise their loyalty to a teacher who had, after all, been the mentor of the Dalai Lama himself. Trijang's authority carried more weight for them than that of the man they considered his pupil. The conflict reflected a tension between the *ancien régime* of old Tibet, represented by Trijang and his followers, and the new order the Dalai Lama was seeking to establish in the post-1959 Tibetan diaspora community. The Dalai Lama felt that this refusal to follow his advice in the matter of Dorje Shugden amounted to a rejection of his leadership of Tibet in exile and thus a betrayal of his efforts to secure Tibetan freedom.

The first visible sign of a fracture between the two camps occurred in 1991, two years before our meeting in Dharamsala, when Geshe Kelsang Gyatso, the lama with whom I had worked for a month at Manjushri Institute in 1978 on my first trip back to England, announced the formation of the New Kadampa Tradition (NKT). This effectively created a schism within the Geluk order, yet it took place not among exiled Tibetans in India but in the rolling hills of Cumbria. Apart from Geshe Kelsang, every member of this new Buddhist school was a Westerner. Images of the Dalai Lama were banned in all NKT centers and his books removed from their libraries. Yet rather than fizzle out as an eccentric sect of malcontents, the NKT thrived; the organization now claims to have more than 1,100 centers worldwide. When the Dalai Lama arrived in England on a teaching tour in 1996, he found himself confronted by crowds of maroon-robed Western monks and nuns with placards bearing slogans such as "Your Smiles Charm—Your Actions Harm," as they shouted denunciations that accused him of being a ruthless dictator who repressed the religious freedom and infringed on the human rights of his own people.

According to the Indian police, on the evening of January 31, 1997, six Tibetan youths left New Delhi in a taxi. They headed north through the night until they reached the town of Kangra, where they lodged in the Grand Hotel for three days. On the night of February 4, some or all of the youths made their way the short distance up to Dharamsala. They headed for the Institute of Buddhist Dialectics, located about two hundred yards from the Dalai Lama's palace. Once there, they burst into the quarters of the resident teacher Gen Lobsang Gyatso, who was sitting in his room with two young monks. The youths launched a frenzied attack with knives, repeatedly stabbing the three monks and cutting their throats. In the struggle, Lobsang Gyatso managed to wrest an Adidas backpack from one of the attackers, which was later recognized by staff at the Grand Hotel as belonging to the youths. The bag contained documents that helped identify two of the suspected assailants, as well as literature advocating the practice of Dorje Shugden.

On February 17, the London *Independent* revealed that "a wrathful deity is the main suspect for three murders in Dharamsala, the Himalayan capital of Tibet's Government-in-Exile." The story was widely reported throughout the media, thereby bringing an issue the Dalai Lama saw as an internal Tibetan matter to the attention of an uncomprehending global public. Efforts by the Indian police failed to apprehend the suspects, Tenzin Choezin, twenty-five, and Lobsang Choedrak, twenty-two. Both young men came from Chatreng, a region in Tibet known for its allegiance to Dorje Shugden. They had traveled to India some years previously to enroll as monks in Tibetan monasteries in South India. It was believed they had probably slipped back into Tibet via Nepal. Their photographs were published, Interpol was alerted, but the pair are still at large.

I did not know Gen Lobsang Gyatso well, but I had met him on several occasions while living in Dharamsala in the 1970s and later translated part of a textbook he had written on Buddhist psychology. He impressed me as a kind and learned man, though I was aware that he had become one of the Dalai Lama's most outspoken allies in the controversy around Dorje Shugden. But who were Tenzin Choezin and Lobsang Choedrak, his alleged assassins? Were they, as the Tibetan government in exile suspected, hit men sent by the Dorje Shugden Society, an organization established in Delhi in June 1996 to protest against the Dalai Lama's policies? Or were they just a pair of fanatical hotheads, rogue monks who got carried away by a sense of injustice? Or could they have been Chinese agents, dispatched to India to fan the flames of a dispute that was dividing the Tibetan community abroad? We will probably never know. Both the Dorje Shugden Society and the NKT strongly condemned the murders and insisted that they had had no part in them.

In October of the same year I returned to Tibet to work on the second edition of *The Tibet Guide*. In a small square in the heart of the old city of Lhasa, I discovered a recently reopened shrine called Trode Khangsar, which, to my surprise, was dedicated to Dorje Shugden. The main image on the altar was that of Tsongkhapa, the founder of the Geluk school. To his left stood a new statue of Trijang Rinpoche, the junior tutor, while cabinets on the right of the room housed the revered images of Shugden himself. (One block south of the shrine I found the Trijang Labrang, the junior tutor's former residence, which had been converted to apartments and offices.) More recently, Tibet watchers have observed a large image of Dorje Shugden displayed behind the Chinese-backed Panchen Lama in official photographs of the young man. It is not surprising that the Communist authorities are eager to promote the veneration of a god that the Dalai Lama believes "does great harm to the cause of Tibet and endangers the life of the Dalai Lama."

Shortly before I left Dharamsala, Ani Jampa, an English Buddhist nun, asked me to translate for her in an interview with Ling Rinpoche, the senior tutor of the Dalai Lama. She explained to Rinpoche that she would shortly be leaving India to visit other countries in Asia and asked if he could provide her with a *sung-du*—a knotted protection string—to ward off the influence of harmful spirits. Ling Rinpoche chuckled and said that all she needed to do was take refuge in the Buddha, Dharma, and Sangha (community). If she sincerely entrusted herself to these three guiding principles, which are commitments common to all Buddhists, that would be sufficient to protect her against whatever harmful influences she might encounter. I was struck by this simple answer, which seemed so straightforward in contrast to all the fuss about spirits and protectors that so animated the Tibetan community. In retrospect, I can see that this advice was characteristic of the senior tutor, who consistently kept himself out of the fray around Dorje Shugden.

This dispute marks another phase in the breakdown and disintegration of the Tibetan state. The gods don't work anymore. However you explain it, Tibet's *ancien régime* failed in its primary duty as a government: to guarantee the integrity of the state and ensure the security of its people. The lamas were convinced that powerful and invisible protectors safeguarded Tibet against its enemies. Geshe Dhargyey solemnly told our class at the Library in the early 1970s that the occupying Chinese army in Lhasa was almost defeated when the protectors caused an outbreak of dysentery among the troops. In reality, though, the Tibetans' occult defense shield was useless against dialectical materialism and the guns of the People's Liberation Army. With few exceptions, the rulers of Tibet failed to appreciate how fundamentally the nature of geopolitics in central Asia had changed during the course of the twentieth century. Now, fifty years later, the exile community—supported by a fervent body of Western Buddhists—is still squabbling over which protector god has the greatest clout.

On August 26, 1999, I returned to my old monastery Tharpa Choeling (now called Rabten Choeling) for the first time since Geshe's death in 1986. I ascended the steep slope of Le Mont-Pèlerin in the bright red funicular from the shore of Lake Geneva with a mixture of nostalgia and trepidation. In the end, the monastery Geshe had founded in 1977 quietly severed its connections with the Dalai Lama and affirmed its allegiance to Geshe's root teacher, the junior tutor. The center did not align itself either with Geshe Kelsang's NKT or other pro-Shugden factions and had remained independent. But because of its refusal to toe the Dalai Lama's line, it was largely shunned by the rest of the Tibetan community in Switzerland and elsewhere.

I was warmly greeted by Gonsar Rinpoche, Geshe's successor and director of the center, whom I had known since my earliest days in Dharamsala. Photos of the Dalai Lama were still displayed on the walls and his writings were available in the bookstore. There seemed to be no personal animosity against him. Then I was introduced to the young Tibetan boy who had been identified as Geshe's reincarnation. Rabten Tulku Rinpoche was a delightfully bashful eleven-year-old, who seemed as curious and awkward about this encounter as I was. I had no idea of how to relate to this bright, smiling child, whom I was supposed to regard as my former teacher. Despite myself, I kept looking for a glimmer of mutual recognition in the boy's eyes. But throughout our halting conversation he showed not the slightest hint of knowing who I was.

With the serrated peaks of the Dents du Midi visible through the window behind us, I chatted and laughed with Gonsar for a couple of hours over endless cups of tea and a large bowl of Tibetan nibbles. As we reminisced about the past and he explained to me how well the monastery was now doing, I was acutely conscious of the elephant in the room that we both took great care not to mention.

How well had I really known Geshe Rabten? As I look back and try to reconstruct what happened between us, things I failed to understand at the time begin to make more sense. Geshe left India for Switzerland in the autumn of 1975, the year of Fred Varley's death. This was also the year in which the crisis around Dorje Shugden first erupted in Dharamsala. I wonder now whether Geshe's move to the West might have already been prompted by his need to distance himself from the Dalai Lama. I can also see other reasons why Geshe may not have wanted his Western students to get too close to the Dalai Lama during the visit I helped organize in 1979. He may have been concerned that one of us would innocently raise the issue of Dorje Shugden with the Dalai Lama, thereby forcing out into the open a rift that was threatening to tear the Geluk order apart but so far had not been made public. More troubling, though, is the dawning recognition that Geshe Rabten did not really trust me.

In the summer of 1978, Geshe was invited to Madison, Wisconsin, to teach for the first (and only) time in the United States. He asked three Western monks to accompany him and left me behind in Switzerland to help oversee the running of the monastery during their absence. While in Madison, he arranged for the three of them to be initiated into the practice of Dorje Shugden by the eminent Geluk lama Song Rinpoche. After the initiation, he explained to one of them, Ven. Helmut: "This manifestation of the Buddha has no equal. If you are determined to tame your mind, then he will even give you his heart in order to help you." Although Geshe depended on me to work for him, he never once mentioned Dorje Shugden in my presence, which suggests that he did not regard me as a suitable vessel for the practice. It seems that he knew me far better than I thought.

However much I empathize with the plight of Gonsar Rinpoche and the Rabten Tulku in their solitude on Le Mont-Pèlerin, their impenetrable world of gods and demons is one to which I cannot return. Since then, I have had no further contact with the Dalai Lama. Nor have I been back to Tibet.

# 17

# TREAD THE PATH
# WITH CARE

UNBEKNOWN TO ME, the key to unraveling the complexities of Siddhattha Gotama's life lay hidden in the pages of a book that I had long heard about but for which I could see no good reason to spend the sum of £111 ($165) to purchase. The book was titled *A Dictionary of Pali Proper Names*, written by the Sri Lankan scholar and diplomat Dr. G. P. Malalasekera, and was first published in 1938 under the auspices of the British Raj. It was only in 2004 when my colleague Andy Olendzki in Massachusetts reached behind him to take his copy from a bookshelf in order to cross-check a detail about the Buddha's life that I first set eyes on it.

A *Dictionary of Pali Proper Names* is not a dictionary at all. It is a densely printed, three-volume encyclopedia of 1,370 pages, with an entry on every proper name, (i.e., person, place, or text) that appears anywhere in Pali literature. Look up *Pasenadi*, for example, and you will find six pages of text that give a biography of the king, referencing every occasion in the Canon where he is mentioned and highlighting in bold every other character to whom he is connected and for whom the "dictionary" has an entry. This invaluable sourcebook saved me a huge amount of time. Instead of having to trawl through numerous discourses in search of a mention of one of my characters—Mahanama, Mallika, Bandhula, etc.—all I had to do was look the person up in the

DPPN, then go straight to the relevant text in the Canon. Yet despite having accumulated this extraordinary wealth of data, Malalasekera appears to have had no interest in organizing it into a single chronological narrative of the Buddha's life. My task, therefore, has largely been one of joining up Malalasekera's dots.

The image that emerges from the Pali Canon of this man Siddhattha Gotama is inconsistent. In some of the earliest passages of the Canon, one has the impression that Gotama was a solitary figure, wandering alone "like a rhinoceros" in remote forested areas of the Gangetic Plain. In other texts he is presented as a heroic public figure, revered by kings and queens and financed by bankers, preaching to vast audiences of devotees and monks, his every word carrying immense authority. Or he is depicted as the supremely accomplished meditator, capable of entering at will the most refined states of absorption. Or he appears as miracle worker with supernormal powers such as walking through walls and flying through the sky like a bird. Elsewhere he is presented as the messianic "Great Man," endowed with superhuman physical marks—a fleshly growth on the top of his head, Dhamma-wheels on the palms of his hands and the soles of his feet, a tongue that can lick both ears, a penis that can be retracted inside his pelvis. Yet in other passages he is depicted as just an ordinary-looking monk, harassed by the ambitions of his family, frustrated by disputes among his followers, who spent his time walking up and down the North Road tirelessly trying to get his message across and prevent his community from fragmenting.

Gotama also had a sense of humor. When the monk Pukkusati, a former nobleman from Takkasila, arrived in Rajagaha one day, he was lodged in the workshop of a potter. Later that evening another monk appeared and asked Pukkusati if he objected to his sharing the workshop with him. Pukkusati welcomed him and the two spent much of the night in meditation. The next morning, the monk asked Pukkusati who was his teacher. Pukkusati replied that he was a follower of Siddhattha Gotama, though he had not yet had the good fortune to meet him in person. "So where is this Gotama living now?" asked the other. "In Savatthi, a city to the north," replied Pukkusati. Only at this point did the other monk reveal that he had been pulling Pukkusati's leg. For this other monk was none other than Siddhattha Gotama, who then proceeded to offer the astonished Pukkusati a discourse on the elements of existence.

On leaving his homeland of Sakiya for the last time, the elderly and frail Siddhattha Gotama headed south to Rajagaha in the footsteps of his friend and patron King Pasenadi of Kosala. Sariputta, his chief disciple, appears to have been waiting for him at Vesali, the capital of Vajji. It was at this time that Gotama's former attendant Sunakkhatta, a nobleman of Vesali who had left the monastic order, denounced him to the Vajjian parliament as one who "does not have any superhuman states," who teaches a doctrine "hammered out by reasoning, following his own line of inquiry as it occurs to him," the only result of which is that it leads one to stop craving. "Sunakkhatta is angry," said Gotama to Sariputta. "Thinking to discredit me, he actually praises me." In the light of following events, however, it seems likely that Sunakkhatta's tirade to the parliament contributed to Gotama's loss of standing and support in Vesali.

Gotama and his followers decided to leave Vesali and the Vajjian republic. They headed south, took a ferry across the Ganges into Magadha, then followed the North Road to its terminus at Rajagaha. That long walk from Sakiya via Vesali to Rajagaha in the sweltering premonsoon weather would have taken them at least a month if not more. On reaching the Magadhan capital, they chose to stay in the caves on Vulture's Peak, which would have afforded some respite from the oppressive heat.

One morning, as Ananda stood behind Siddhattha fanning him, they saw a royal carriage approach on the road below. A man stepped out and started to climb up the hill. As he got closer, they realized it was Brahmin Vassakara, the prime minister of King Ajatasattu. He bowed, touched his forehead to Gotama's feet, sat down to one side, then said: "His Majesty wishes to inform you that he intends to strike down the Vajjians, who have become so powerful and strong. He intends to bring them to ruin and destruction. I am to report this to you, then return to the king with your response. He believes that a Buddha cannot lie."

Rather than offer any help to Gotama or the beleaguered Sakiyans, Ajatasattu had sent his prime minister to use the Buddha as a sounding board in his own preparations for war. In revealing his plans to attack the Vajjians, to whose parliament in Vesali Gotama had just been ridiculed, Ajatasattu was announcing that he would launch an invasion across the Ganges into their territory. Gotama had fled from the violent conflict in his homeland only to find himself confronted by the imminent outbreak of another. Ignoring the prime minister, he turned to his attendant: "Ananda, have you not heard that the Vajjians hold frequent and regular assemblies? As long as they do this and continue to conduct their business in harmony, keep to their ancient traditions, respect their elders, honor saints and do not abduct the wives and children of others, they may be expected to prosper and not decline."

Brahmin Vassakara, who had been listening carefully, said: "That is true. If the Vajjians keep to those principles, they will remain strong. In that case, we will not conquer them by force of arms but only by means of propaganda and setting them against each other." He got up from his seat, bowed, and headed back down the hill to his carriage.

Whatever slim hopes for sympathy and support that Gotama may have had in coming to Rajagaha would have been dashed, first on learning of the death of Pasenadi, and then being subjected to the cynical treatment just meted out on him by the prime minister. He asked Ananda to summon all the remaining monks in Rajagaha to Vulture's Peak, where he delivered what would be his final address to them. Taking the model of the Vajjian parliament, he urged his monks likewise to hold regular assemblies, to preserve harmony, to respect the elders of the community. Moreover, they should value the solitude of forest dwellings, maintain mindfulness at all times, be kind and benevolent to each other, share the alms they received, and pursue the eightfold path. He then announced that he was leaving Rajagaha for the nearby town of Nalanda. From there, he and Ananda headed back to the Ganges, following the same hot and dusty road by which they had come not long before.

Gotama's sense of failure would have been further compounded by the deaths of his two foremost disciples, Sariputta and Moggallana, which both occurred around this time. After returning from Vesali with Gotama, the elderly Sariputta died of illness at Nalaka, the village of his birth near Rajagaha, in the same room in which he had been born. Two weeks later, Moggallana was beaten to death by brigands while living in solitude on the Black Rock near Isigili, one of the hills surrounding Rajagaha. Although Ananda was distraught at the loss of these two leading figures of the community, Gotama berated him for not having taken his teaching on impermanence to heart and compared their deaths to large branches falling off a mighty tree.

By the time Gotama and Ananda reached the ferry port of Patali, the first clouds of monsoon would have started to gather, making the heat and humidity nearly intolerable. They stayed overnight in the rest house of some lay supporters in the town. Early next morning, Gotama noticed that fortifications were being erected along the riverfront. He was told that Prime Minister Vassakara was overseeing the construction of a fortress to protect the town against the Vajjians. Gotama realized that a new city was being founded. Then Vassakara himself called on the monks and invited them for a meal the next day. At the conclusion of that feast, their host declared that he would name the gate through which Gotama left Patali as the "Gotama Gate."

By not objecting to a city gate being named after him, was Gotama tacitly acknowledging that this newly emerging city might be that "ancient city in the forest" of which he spoke, "with parks, groves, ponds and ramparts, a delightful place," which, once renovated by the king, "would become successful, prosperous and filled with people once again"? Patali was located at the confluence where the Son River, from the south, and the Gandak River, from the north, joined the Ganges, making it ideally suited for commerce, military expeditions, and the administration of an empire. It would soon replace the mountain stronghold of Rajagaha as the capital of Magadha. One hundred and fifty years later, as Pataliputra (son of Patali), it would become, under Emperor Ashoka, the first capital of a unified India.

But all that lay in the future. Gotama's immediate concern was to cross the Ganges and go back to Vesali for the Rains, before continuing his return journey to his homeland of Sakiya.

As Mr. Khan and I pull into the compound of the PWD Inspection Bungalow in Vaishali (the current Sanskritized name for Vesali), the sun, a brilliant pink orb reflected in the water of a great rectangular man-made pool beside the road, is sinking behind the horizon of trees. A flustered *chowkidar*—caretaker—stumbles out of the building, alarmed at the prospect of a guest, and hurries to prepare a room, repeating: "Rajiv Gandhi sleep here, sahib," as though this mantra would dispel any misgivings I might have about the dark, dank place with neither electricity nor running water. I go outside. The pilgrimage industry, with all its attendant hawkers and beggars, has yet to reach Vaishali. It is wonderfully quiet. A solitary monk from the Japanese Peace Pagoda across the water—the sole temple in the area—beats a handheld drum as he walks around the tank, chanting, *"Nam-myo-ho-renge-kyo!"* It sounds like a lament.

Nothing is left of the great three-walled city of Gotama's time. Modern Vaishali consists of but a few farming villages and fields. Excavations have uncovered the foundations of what is thought to have been the Vajjian parliament as well as the primitive stupa in which the relic casket I saw in the Patna Museum was found. Nearby is another well-maintained park of lawns and flower beds belonging to the Archaeological Survey of India. Enclosed by its iron railings are a smaller rectangular water tank and numerous brick cores of stupas of varying sizes. From the center of these ruins rises an intact Ashokan column, on top of which crouches a magnificent stone lion. As I stand at its base, I can just make out the name "H.W. Finch" carved into its surface some feet above my head. When the British first arrived here, the tank and all the stupas would have been buried, leaving only the upper section of the column exposed, onto which bored company officials or soldiers could scratch their names.

It would have taken Gotama three days to walk from the northern shore of the Ganges to Vesali. Word of his impending arrival in the city preceded him. On learning that he had reached the village of Koti, the courtesan Ambapali drove down in her luxurious carriage to meet him. That grand lady, who had once been the mistress of King Bimbisara and had a son by him, invited Gotama to stay at her mango grove in Vesali and take his meals there. Just as she was leaving, a group of young noblemen rode into Koti on their chariots. They seemed to be involved in an elaborate, perhaps erotic, game with Ambapali. Each youth was clothed, made-up, and ornamented in a different color: some were in all green, some in all yellow, some in all red, some in all white. "Look at them," said Gotama to his monks, "the gods have arrived." They too asked Gotama to dine with them when he got to the city the next day. "But I've promised Ambapali to take my meal with her," he replied. In unison, the young men snapped their fingers and sang: "Beaten by the mango woman! Cheated by the mango woman!" Then they raced back to the city.

This was a society descending into decadence and frivolity as the armies of its powerful enemy assembled across the river in preparation for war. The color-coded dandies were a parody of "the Vajjians who have become so powerful and strong" that King Ajatasattu and his prime minister had vowed to attack and destroy. Ambapali's invitation suggested that Gotama had also lost favor with his patrons in Vesali, which may have been a result of his having been denounced to the parliament by Sunakkhatta. Rather than go to his usual base in the city— the Gabled House in the forest—he accepted an invitation to stay in the mango grove of a high-class woman of pleasure. And when the

Rains began, Gotama chose to spend that time alone in a village called Beluva, outside the city walls, and told his monks: "Go anywhere in Vesali where you have friends or acquaintances or supporters and spend the Rains there."

In the course of these Rains, Siddhattha Gotama was "attacked by a severe sickness, with sharp pains as if he were about to die." He recovered but was badly weakened. "I am worn out," he said to Ananda. "My body is only kept going by being strapped up like an old cart." Ananda urged him to make a final statement about the order of monks. "What does the order of monks expect of me?" he retorted. "I have taught the Dhamma without making any distinction between 'outer' and 'inner' teachings. I am not someone who has a closed fist in regard to what I teach. If there is someone who thinks 'I shall take charge of the order,' then let him make some statement. I do not think in such terms. Ananda: you should live as islands to yourselves, being your own refuge, with no other as your refuge, with the Dhamma as an island, with the Dhamma as your refuge, with no other refuge."

In other words: when the chips are down, the only thing you can rely on is whatever values and practices you have managed to integrate into your own life. Neither the Buddha nor the Sangha (community) will be of any help. You are on your own.

Once the Rains were over, Gotama asked Ananda to summon all the monks in Vesali to the Gabled House, where he would bid them farewell. He incited them to "learn, practice, and cultivate" the eightfold path he had discovered, "so that out of compassion for the world, this way of life may endure for a long time and be for the happiness and benefit of many." He concluded by announcing that he did not expect to live for more than a few months.

When Gotama left Vesali, only his Sakiyan cousins Ananda and Anuruddha, "Big" Cunda, the younger brother of Sariputta, and a Kosalan monk called Upavana accompanied him. Since he was gravely ill, it is likely that some younger monks went with them as litter-bearers. They headed northwest, along the North Road, in the direction of

Sakiya, and passed through the villages of Bhanda, Hatthi, Amba, Jambu, and Bhoganagara, none of which are identifiable today. It is only when they got to the town of Pava that we can locate them on a modern map: in Fazilnagar, eighty miles northwest of Vaishali.

Fazilnagar is a charmless Indian town of dilapidated concrete buildings, with a single street of shops and sagging stalls that sell everything from bridal accessories to tractor parts. I head down a dark alley off the main street until I reach an open area dominated by a great mound of packed earth. Sections of brickwork are visible where the earth has crumbled away. A bent and battered sign, against which a water buffalo scratches its neck, declares the mound to be a "Protected National Monument." Useless remnants of posts and fencing can be seen here and there. The mound serves as an open-air toilet, where ragged children cluster in groups and goats and dogs feed on refuse. At its base is a mint-green Muslim shrine, before which kneel three women, keening and wailing, swinging their long black hair up and down, writhing in what could be either ecstasy or unbearable grief.

Inside this mound is the stupa that marks the spot where Gotama received his final meal of tenderized pork at the house of a man called Cunda the Smith. From the moment it was offered to him, it seems that Gotama suspected something was amiss with the food. "Serve the pork to me," he told his host, "and the remaining food to the other monks." When the meal was over, he said to Cunda: "You should now bury any leftover pork in a pit." Then he "was attacked by a severe sickness with bloody diarrhea, which he endured mindfully without any complaint." His only response was to say to Ananda: "Let us go to Kusinara," which, under the circumstances, sounds like *Let's get out of this place.*

Was someone trying to poison Gotama? If so, who? And why? He had no shortage of enemies. Pava was one of the two principal towns of Malla, the Kosalan province adjoining Sakiya. Karayana, the general of the Kosalan army now laying waste to Sakiya, came from Malla, possibly from Pava itself. Pava was also where Mahavira, the ascetic founder of Jainism, is said to have died a few years earlier, after which his followers "were split into two parties, quarreling and disputing, fighting and attacking each other." On hearing of this, Gotama dismissed Mahavira's teaching as "ill-proclaimed, unedifyingly displayed and ineffectual in calming the mind because its proclaimer was not fully awake." When captured, the brigands who murdered Gotama's senior disciple Moggallana in Rajagaha confessed to having been hired by some of Mahavira's followers to kill the old monk. When the ailing Gotama arrived at Pava on his final journey, he entered a place that could already have become a shrine to his principal rival.

But what could be gained by poisoning an old man who is already dying? A more likely motive would have been to poison those who would carry on his legacy into future generations. Whether someone wanted to punish Gotama for his apparent complicity in his cousin Mahanama's deception of Pasenadi by giving the king a slave girl as a bride or to ensure that the Buddha's ideas would not survive to compete with their own teacher's doctrine, the most effective way would have been to kill Ananda, the faithful attendant who had stored in his memory everything Gotama taught. By insisting that he alone be served the pork and the leftovers buried, Gotama prevented Ananda from eating it. He may therefore have hastened his own death in order that his teaching would survive.

Without my noticing it, a throng of fifty or sixty boys, each smiling and gazing with blank, innocent eyes, has gathered around me on the top of the earthen mound. Whenever I make a movement, the crowd, without a blink in its collective stare, adjusts sympathetically, as if it were a giant organism studying an unknown creature held gently but warily in its embrace. When I decide at last to leave, a passageway opens for me in the circle, and I return to the alleyway, accompanied by a straggle of the most courageous kids, who take it in turns to solicit pens and rupees.

On the outskirts of Fazilnagar, where the town gives way to farmyards and fields, I discover an imposing slab of white marble with the inscription 24th TIRTHANKAR 1008 BHAGWAN MAHAVIRJI. Beneath it a text, in English, explains: "This place is decided as the Nirvan place of Lord Mahavir by the historians and research scholars. A grand temple was constructed here by Digambar Jain society on this basis." This is the spot where Gotama's contemporary and rival Mahavira is believed—at least by some members of the strict Digambara sect of Jainism—to have died.

As I look about for the "grand temple" mentioned in the inscription, I am once again encircled by a horde of village children. I suspect the temple must be behind the high brick wall adjacent to the marble slab. I walk along the wall until I find a gate, which is bolted and locked. I can just manage to hoist myself—to a delighted chorus of cheers and laughter—high enough up it to peer over the top. Apart from a single, rather desolate building to one side, the place is empty. What look like building materials lay scattered about, overgrown with grasses and weeds.

Today, ten miles of good road separate Fazilnagar (Pava) from Kushinagar (Kusinara). Gotama, being so ill, would have had to be carried on a litter. His small group of monks had stopped to bathe in the Kakuttha River, then Big Cunda laid out a robe for Gotama on the bank so that he could lie down and rest. Possibly they spent the night there. And, lo and behold, about halfway to Kushinagar Mr. Khan and I come to a river, now spanned by a concrete bridge, with a wide grass bank shaded by trees. But I have grown suspicious of rivers on alluvial plains and resist the inference that this must be the Kakuttha and that there, on its banks, the dying Gotama once lay.

Have I come any closer to this man Siddhattha Gotama? Have I gained anything by wandering around these archaeological sites, tracing his itinerary across Bihar and Uttar Pradesh, contemplating a soapstone casket that purportedly holds his ashes? On arriving at Vulture's Peak or standing upon a mound of earth in Fazilnagar, I initially experienced a brief, exhilarating rush of associations. For a few tantalizing moments it felt as though Gotama was nearly in reach of my straining fingertips. But as soon as the thrill wore off, mild indifference, even despondency, returned. I was forced to recognize the place for what it was: just another pile of bricks, just another hill, just another patch of earth.

We pull into the broad forecourt of the Lotus Nikko Hotel in Kushinagar. Mr. Khan switches off the engine, a servant in white pulls open my door, and the air explodes with the shriek of cicadas. *This is what remains:* the cicadas, the chipmunks, the cattle, the crows, the parakeets, the mange-ridden dogs, the *neem* trees, the green and yellow mustard fields in which women and girls in brilliantly colored saris are crouched in toil. These living, reproducing plants, birds, animals, and humans are all that have survived. I will never see what Gotama saw, but I can listen to the descendants of the same cicadas he would have heard when night fell in Kusinara all those years ago.

On arriving in Kusinara, Gotama told Ananda to take him to the *sal* grove of the local Malla people on the edge of the town. Once there, he asked him to prepare a bed between two *sal* trees. Knowing that he did not have long to live, Gotama explained how he should be cremated and what should be done with his remains. This was all too much for Ananda, who broke down in tears. "Do not weep and wail," said Gotama. "Have I not told you that all things pleasant and delightful are subject to change? How could it be that something compounded should not pass away?"

Ananda was not placated. "Don't die here," he pleaded, "in this miserable little town of wattle-and-daub, in this jungle in the back of beyond! If we could make it to a city like Rajagaha or Savatthi or Baranasi, your supporters there would provide for your funeral in the proper style." I imagine Gotama dismissing this absurd suggestion with a tired wave of his hand.

After the townsfolk of Kusinara had gone to the *sal* grove to pay their final respects, a wanderer called Subhadda appeared and asked Ananda if he could be allowed to see Gotama. Ananda refused. But Gotama overheard them and bade Subhadda to come to his side. Subhadda said, "Tell me who among the teachers of our time have realized the truth?" Gotama dismissed the question: "Never mind whether all, or none, or some of them have realized the truth. I will teach you the Dhamma." He explained that wherever the eightfold path—of appropriate vision, thought, speech, action, livelihood, effort, mindfulness, and concentration—can be found, there you will find people who have realized the phases of awakening. He then instructed Ananda to receive Subhadda into the order of monks.

It was late at night. Perhaps a clear autumn moon shone through the canopy of *sal* leaves. Gotama turned to the small group of monks present and said: "If anyone has an outstanding doubt about what I have taught, now is the time to ask." The monks remained silent. "If you are silent out of respect for me, then at least ask one another." Still no one said a word. Gotama said: "Then you must all be awakened. Listen: conditioned things break down, tread the path with care!" Then he too fell quiet. Those were his last words.

I feel strangely elated the next morning as I visit the shrine in Kushinagar that marks the place where Gotama died. A black stone statue of the reclining Buddha, draped with a yellow robe, lies along the length of the somber room. The shrine, a functional concrete edifice built in 1956, is the centerpiece of another well-tended park of trees and flower beds, excavated foundations of monasteries and brick stupa cores. This is where Gotama would have lain down between the *sal* trees, received Subhadda, and uttered his last words. And this is where those who had not yet achieved freedom of mind "wept and tore their hair, raising their arms, throwing themselves down, twisting and turning, crying: 'All too soon! All too soon! The Buddha has passed away!' While others endured it mindfully and said: 'All compounded things are impermanent—what is the use of all this fuss?' "

# 18

# A SECULAR BUDDHIST

IN 1996 I discovered the Internet. I was working at Sharpham as the director of the newly founded Sharpham College for Buddhist Studies and Contemporary Enquiry, which had just started running a yearlong residential program for up to twelve students. One of the students had previously worked in the computer industry and showed me how to use the Internet as a research tool. Out of curiosity, I typed in the name of my great-uncle Leonard Craske, the black sheep of our family, who had abandoned his wife and a career in medicine to pursue his vocation as an actor and artist in the United States.

The search produced a number of references, most of which were connected to a statue of a fisherman located on the shorefront of the city of Gloucester, Massachusetts. "The Man at the Wheel," as it is known, turned out to be Leonard's most famous work of sculpture. Commissioned by the city of Gloucester to commemorate the 300th anniversary of the founding of the city in 1623, the bronze statue was unveiled to the public and dedicated on August 23, 1925. It depicts a ten-foot-high fisherman in oilskins gripping the wheel of his boat as he steers it through a North Atlantic storm. Yet to my Buddhist eyes this monument commemorating heroic American individualism showed a man holding an eight-spoked Wheel of Dhamma. The seeker of cod was transformed into a bodhisattva in search of awakening, guiding the boat of his precious human body by means of the eightfold path through the treacherous seas of samsara.

According to the Ellis Island records, Leonard arrived in New York in 1913 at the age of thirty-four. He worked as an actor in Boston's Copley Theatre during the First World War, before taking up a career as a sculptor. He lived and worked in Back Bay, Boston, with a summer studio in the artist's colony at Rocky Neck, a few miles up the Cape Ann peninsula from Gloucester. He was "easily recognized by his prematurely white hair and ruddy complexion." He never remarried and appears to have lived alone. Judging from the dandyish poses in the photographs of him in the archives of the Cape Ann Historical Association, I wonder if he might have been gay. From the late 1920s Leonard turned his attention to color photography and was one of the first noncommercial photographers to work with color film. He died in Boston in 1950, two and a half years before I was born. "Money doesn't mean very much to me," he was quoted as saying in his obituary in the *Boston Herald*. "I do whatever I please, so I suppose I run counter to most people's patterns for a proper design for living. Personally, I think that most people are eccentrics, and I'm not. People follow the herd. I don't. Never have. Never will."

Like my great-uncle Leonard, I am one of those people who has to make things. I become restless and irritable if I am not actively involved in manufacturing something. Since 1995, I have been producing collages made from discarded materials—paper, cloth, plastic—that I find dropped on the street, blown into hedgerows, tossed into wastebaskets and dumpsters. Following strict formal rules, I cut up these useless, unwanted things with a scalpel and reassemble them as intricate, symmetrical mosaics. I have no idea why I do this. I have neither an aesthetic theory to prove nor any need for a product to sell. I am free to follow the silent intuitions that move me. I may spend months finding the right materials and organizing them into a collage. It is intensely satisfying to transform these scraps of waste into a composition that transcends each little piece but could not exist without every one of them.

I write books in this way too. Each book is a collage. Jackdaw-like, I pick and choose ideas, phrases, images, and vignettes that for some reason appeal to me. I am as likely to find them in a fragment of overheard conversation as in a Buddhist scripture. I do not work methodically. I sometimes discover what I am looking for by dreamily opening a book at random and stumbling across a sentence that jumps off the page as the answer to a question. Because I do not make systematic notes, I spend hours trying to retrieve a reference I have lost. Then I need to assemble all these little bits and pieces into tidily organized chapters. And I have to sustain the illusion of a self-assured narrator who has known from the outset what he wants to say and how he is going to say it. I experience the same tension between formal rules and arbitrary content as in making a collage.

After *Buddhism Without Beliefs,* I contracted with my publisher to write a book that would further develop my ideas about an agnostic approach to Buddhism. As usual I started writing notes, collating ideas, gathering quotes, reading relevant books and articles, designing chapter plans, toying with titles, and generally letting my mind wander as it would around the theme. Then I began to write. Within a week, I abandoned everything I had planned. The act of writing, following its own inscrutable logic, had guided me to the topic of the book: the devil. Nowhere in my copious notes did I mention the devil—or "Mara," as he is known in Buddhism. Yet I knew then that the germ of the entire book was contained in that single idea.

I spent the next three years writing *Living with the Devil.* This led me to another thread of ideas that runs through the Pali Canon but goes against the grain of much Buddhist orthodoxy. For traditional Buddhists, the Buddha has come to be seen as the perfect person. He is an example of what a human being can ultimately become through treading the eightfold path. The Buddha is said to have eliminated from his mind every last trace of greed, hatred, and confusion, so that they are "cut off at the root, made like a palm stump, so that they will never arise again." At the same time, the Buddha is believed to have acquired faultless wisdom and boundless compassion. He is omniscient and unerringly loving. He has become God.

Yet the many passages in the Pali Canon that depict the Buddha's relations with Mara paint a different picture. On attaining awakening in Uruvela, Siddhattha Gotama did not "conquer" Mara in the sense of literally destroying him. For Mara is a figure that continues to present himself to Gotama even *after* the awakening. He keeps reappearing under different guises until shortly before the Buddha's death in Kusinara. This implies that craving and the other "armies of Mara" have not been literally deleted from Gotama's being. Rather, he has found a way of living with Mara that deprives the devil of his power. To be no longer manipulated by Mara is equivalent to being free from him. The Buddha's freedom is found not in destroying greed and hatred, but in comprehending them as transient, impersonal emotions that will pass away of their own accord as long as you do not cling to and identify with them.

In Pali, *Mara* means "the killer." The devil is a mythic way of talking about whatever imposes limits on the realization of one's potential as a human being. As well as physical death, *Mara* refers to anything that wears you down or causes your life to be reduced, blighted, or frustrated. Craving is a kind of inner death because it clings to what is safe and familiar, blocking one's capacity to enter the stream of the path. Yet other kinds of "death" can be imposed by social pressures, political persecution, religious intolerance, war, famine, earthquakes, and so on. Mara permeates the fabric of the world in which we struggle to realize our goals and achieve fulfillment. Siddhattha Gotama was no more exempt from these constraints than anyone else.

If Mara is a metaphor for death, then Buddha, as his twin, is a metaphor for *life*. The two are inseparable. You cannot have Buddha without Mara any more than you can have life without death. This was the insight I gained from writing *Living with the Devil*. Instead of perfection or transcendence, the goal of Gotama's Dhamma was to embrace this suffering world without being overwhelmed by the attendant fear or attachment, craving or hatred, confusion or conceit, that come in its wake.

A clue to how this might be done is found in the parable of the raft. Gotama compares the Dhamma to a raft that one assembles from pieces of driftwood, fallen branches and other bits of rubbish. Once it has taken you across the river that lies in your way, you leave it behind on the bank for someone else and proceed on your way. The Dhamma is a temporary expedient. To treat it as an object of reverence is as absurd as carrying the raft on your back even though you no longer need it. To practice the Dhamma is like making a collage. You collect ideas, images, insights, philosophical styles, meditation methods, and ethical values that you find here and there in Buddhism, bind them securely together, then launch your raft into the river of your life. As long as it does not sink or disintegrate and can get you to the other shore, then it works. That is all that matters. It need not correspond to anyone else's idea of what "Buddhism" is or should be.

The Buddha died, exhausted and sick, in the company of Ananda and Anuruddha, his cousins and fellow Sakiyans. They had failed to reach their homeland, which lay a farther seventy-five miles northwest. At the time of his death, Siddhattha Gotama still may not have known what fate had befallen his countrymen at the hands of the Kosalan army. At least he had some supporters left in the Mallan town of Kusinara, where he lay down to die. Principal of these would have been Mallika, the elderly widow of Bandhula, the military commander and chief justice murdered many years before by King Pasenadi. On learning of the Buddha's death, the Mallans returned to the *sal* grove to pay their respects. They brought garlands and perfumes, assembled musicians, dressed in their finest clothes, and for seven days danced, sang, and played music before Gotama's corpse, over which Mallika had spread her finest jeweled cloak.

Just before the funeral pyre was to be ignited, a large group of monks arrived in haste from the direction of Pava. At their head was a monk called Kassapa the Great, who insisted that the cremation not take place until he had paid his last respects by touching his forehead to Gotama's feet. Kassapa and his group were a few days' march behind the dying Gotama and his small band. It seems likely that they left Rajagaha after the Rains as soon as they received word of Gotama's severe illness in Vesali.

Kassapa was a brahmin from Magadha, who became a monk as an old man during the last years of Gotama's life. He claimed to have a special relationship with Gotama. After their first encounter beneath a banyan tree on the road to Nalanda, Gotama had given Kassapa his "worn out hempen robe" in exchange for Kassapa's robe of fine cloth. This episode came to be seen as a transmission of authority. After the deaths of Sariputta and Moggallana, it seems that Kassapa considered himself as the most qualified person to succeed Gotama and lead the order of monks. In the Zen tradition, he is regarded as the "First Patriarch." He was the one who is said to have smiled when the Buddha held up a flower, thereby receiving the "mind-to-mind" transmission that transcends words and concepts.

As he lay dying, Gotama said to Ananda: "It may be that you will think that after my death you will have no teacher. It should not be seen like this, Ananda, for what I have taught and explained to you as the Dhamma and training will, at my passing, be your teacher." When Devadatta tried to seize control of the order, Gotama told his cousin: "I would not even ask Sariputta and Moggallana to head this community, let alone a lick-spittle like you." Gotama did not intend anyone to succeed him. He envisioned a community that would be governed after his death by an impersonal body of ideas and practices rather than by an enlightened monk. He modeled it on the system of parliamentary government that still survived in Vesali, not the kind of autocratic kingship that prevailed in Magadha and Kosala.

The arrival of Kassapa at the Buddha's funeral marks the beginning of a power struggle. On the one side is Kassapa: the mystic and ascetic, the stern elderly brahmin who adheres to the traditional Indian idea as taught in the pre-Buddhist Upanishads that spiritual authority is transmitted from guru to disciple. On the other side is Ananda: the faithful attendant, the secretary and memorist, Gotama's intermediary with the world, and a champion of women, who has entered the stream of the path but is not liberated from the rounds of rebirth. They embody two conflicting visions of what Gotama's legacy might be: another Indian religion controlled by priests, or a culture of awakening that could produce another kind of civilization.

Once Gotama's ash and bones had been parceled out to his followers in different parts of North India (with the notable exception of Savatthi), the monks agreed to Kassapa's proposal that a council be convened in order to formally establish what Gotama taught. Kassapa was entreated to select those elders whom he considered qualified to attend. His list of eligible candidates did not include Ananda, on the grounds that Ananda was only a "learner" and not "fully liberated." Only after pressure from the other elders did he relent and allow Ananda to participate. They decided to hold the council in Rajagaha during the next Rains. Apart from those designated by Kassapa, they agreed that no other monk would be allowed to reside in the city at that time.

So they set off for the south again, retracing their steps. One hundred and fifty miles of dusty roads and the River Ganges lay between Kusinara and Rajagaha. It was winter. They would have to endure cold ground mists that can linger all morning. This was the third time that Ananda had to make this journey since fleeing Sakiya the year before. He would have set off with a heavy heart. The person who meant everything to him was dead. And now he had to submit to the authority of this relative newcomer, Kassapa. It may have been around this time that he composed this verse:

> *They of old have passed away;*
> *The new men suit me not at all.*
> *Alone today this child doth brood,*
> *Like nesting bird when rain doth fall.*

He felt as bereft as a fledgling abandoned in its nest as the first heavy drops of monsoon rain begin to fall. His world had fallen apart. He had been co-opted by a group of monks with whom he had little in common. Like the bones and ash of the Buddha, he was a relic. He was a repository of information being escorted to Rajagaha so he could recite what he remembered.

At some point the party arrived at a nunnery and the nuns invited Kassapa to give them a discourse on the Dhamma. Kassapa tried to persuade Ananda to perform this duty, but Ananda insisted that it was Kassapa they wanted to hear. The next morning, with Ananda as his attendant, Kassapa went to the nuns' quarters and "instructed, exhorted, inspired and gladdened" the nuns with a lecture. As he was departing, he overheard a nun called Tissa say: "How can Kassapa even think of speaking on the Dhamma in the presence of Ananda? This is just as if a needle-peddler would think he could sell a needle to the needle-maker!"

Kassapa took Ananda aside and repeated to him what he had overheard. "How is it then, friend Ananda, am I the needle-peddler and you the needle-maker, or am I the needle-maker and you the needle-peddler?" Ananda tried to make light of the exchange. "Be patient, Kassapa," he said. "You know how foolish women can be." Kassapa was furious at Ananda's response. It suggested to him that Ananda was trying to justify the nun's comment rather than condemn it, thereby siding with her rather than him. "Careful, Ananda," he said. "Don't give the community of monks occasion to investigate you further," thus implying that Ananda had stood up for the nun because he may have been romantically involved with her.

As soon as the party arrived in Rajagaha, Ananda decided to go on a walking tour with some followers in an area called the Southern Hills. We are also told that a monk called Purana was walking through the Southern Hills around this time. The only thing we know about Purana is that after the council completed its work, he came to Rajagaha and was told by the elders to "submit" to their authorized record of what Gotama taught. But Purana refused. "I will bear in mind," he said, "only those teachings that I heard directly from the Buddha myself."

When Ananda returned to Rajagaha, he was summoned to see Kassapa. Kassapa had learned that while Ananda was in the Southern Hills, thirty of the young monks accompanying him had disrobed and returned to lay life. "Your retinue is breaking apart, Ananda," he said. "Your young followers are slipping away. You don't know your measure, boy."

"Are these not gray hairs growing on my head?" retorted Ananda. "You have no right to call me 'boy.' "

When the nun Nanda heard about this exchange, she came to Ananda's defense. "How," she asked, "can Kassapa, who was formerly a member of another sect, think to disparage Ananda by calling him a 'boy'?"

Kassapa then felt obliged to justify himself at length. He told the story of meeting the Buddha on the road to Nalanda, of being praised by him as an exceptional disciple, and then being given his old worn-out patched robe. "If one could say of anyone that he is born of the Buddha's breast, born of his mouth, born of the Dhamma, an heir to the Dhamma, a receiver of worn-out hempen rags," he insisted, "it is of me that one could rightly say this. . . . In this very life I enter and dwell in the taintless liberation of mind. One might as well think that a bull elephant could be concealed by a palm leaf as think that my direct knowledge could ever be concealed." The matter was closed. Nanda, the nun who had the nerve to challenge Kassapa, disrobed and returned to lay life.

The tension among Gotama's followers was raising questions among the officials and ministers at King Ajatasattu's court. While waiting for the council to begin, Ananda visited the office of a brahmin called Gopaka, where he found Prime Minister Vassakara. The two men asked him whether there was any monk in the community who possessed the same qualities as Siddhattha Gotama. Ananda said: "No." "Then is there any single monk who was appointed by Master Gotama as his successor?" "No." "So is there any monk who has been appointed by the community and elders as Master Gotama's successor?" "No." "But if you have no single monk as your refuge, then how can you hope to have concord in your community?" Ananda said: "But we do have a refuge, brahmin; we have the Dhamma as our refuge."

While at Gopaka's office, Ananda learned that the fortifications of Rajagaha were being strengthened in preparation for an attack on the city by the forces of King Pajjota, the ruler of Avanti, the kingdom to the west. As Ajatasattu concentrated his troops in Pataliputra in order to attack the Vajjians across the Ganges, Pajjota seemed to have taken the opportunity to launch a campaign against the poorly defended city of Rajagaha, purportedly to avenge the death of King Bimbisara. The whole of Ananda's known world, from Sakiya to Magadha, was on the verge of being engulfed in war.

The council took place in the Seven Leaf Cave in the mountains above the city. Now, as then, the path to the cave starts at the entrance to the hot springs across the road from Bamboo Grove. You climb up a steep stairway past pools packed with glistening bodies of bathers noisily reveling in the warm water that gushes from ancient stone pipes. From here, the path takes you up to the ridge that runs along the circle of hills enclosing Rajagaha. After about half a mile, a trail cuts off down to the right and emerges onto a large, flat ledge of rock. There is an almost sheer drop to the plain below. The Seven Leaf Cave is just an open fissure that extends some fifteen yards into the cliff behind. At most you could fit about thirty people inside.

And it was here, either huddled inside this cave or under an awning erected above the ledge, exposed to the lashing rain and wind of the monsoon, that a group of elderly monks listened attentively as Kassapa invited Ananda to recite from memory everything he had heard Gotama say.

That is how Buddhism began its life as an organized religion at what is now called the "First Council," held in the Seven Leaf Cave in Rajagaha around 400 BCE. Over the next fifteen hundred years the Dhamma spread from India throughout the rest of Asia, spawning numerous movements and schools and acquiring millions of adherents, before disappearing from its land of origin in the wake of Muslim invasions of the subcontinent from the eleventh century onward. The first informed accounts of Buddhism began to appear in the West in the middle of the nineteenth century, when scholars gained access to classical texts and started deciphering them. In 1881, T. W. Rhys Davids founded the Pali Text Society in London, which inaugurated the systematic translation of the discourses of Siddhattha Gotama and other writings preserved in Pali into English, an endeavor that continues to this day.

It was not until the early years of the twentieth century that the first Europeans traveled to Burma to receive ordination as Buddhist monks. Until the 1960s there were no more than a handful of Western Buddhists, some as monks in Asia, others as members of small lay Buddhist circles in Europe and America. Then, in 1959, came the exodus of the Dalai Lama and his followers from Tibet. This was followed shortly afterward by the cultural upheavals of the 1960s, which allowed a leisured generation of young people, who had largely lost faith in Christianity and Judaism, to travel to Asia—India, Nepal, Thailand, Burma, Sri Lanka, Japan, Korea—and explore new religious possibilities that would have been unthinkable for their parents. Since then, the West's fascination with Buddhism has continued unabated.

When he disbanded the Order of the Star in 1929, the young Jiddu Krishnamurti told his audience of three thousand followers: "You may remember the story of how the devil and a friend of his were walking down the street, when they saw ahead of them a man stoop down and pick up something from the ground, look at it, and put it away in his pocket. The friend said to the devil, 'What did that man pick up?' 'He picked up a piece of Truth,' said the devil. 'That is a very bad business for you, then,' said his friend. 'Oh, not at all,' the devil replied, 'I am going to let him organize it.' "

"I am living hemmed in by monks and nuns," thought Siddhattha Gotama to himself one day in the Ghosita Monastery near Kosambi, "by kings and ministers, by sectarian teachers and their followers, and I live in discomfort and not at ease. Suppose I were to live alone, se-cluded from the crowd?" So after returning from his alms-round, he ti-died his hut, took his bowl and robe, and, without informing anyone, set off unaccompanied for Parileyyaka, where he stayed alone in a for-est beneath a *sal* tree. Even the Buddha, it would appear, was oppressed by the organization he had created to uphold and spread his teaching.

But if his ideas had not been organized into orthodoxies and institu-tions, would they have survived at all? However much I sympathize with Ananda in his struggle with Kassapa, I have to recognize that without the aggressive leadership of a man like Kassapa at such an un-stable time, the Dhamma may have been forgotten within a generation or so of Gotama's death. If Sera Monastery and Songgwangsa had not existed for centuries as bastions of their respective Buddhist traditions, would I have been able to receive the kind of education and training that provided me a foundation on which to write about Buddhism as I do now? I very much doubt it. Whether I like it or not, the animating spirit of religious life and its formal organization appear—like Buddha and Mara—to be inextricably entwined with each other.

To reject organized religion in favor of a nebulous and eclectic "spirituality" is not a satisfactory solution either. As language users, we can no more cease trying to generate coherent theories and beliefs than a stomach can cease to digest food. As social animals we invariably organize ourselves into groups and communities. Without a rigorous, self-critical discourse, one risks lapsing into pious platitudes and un-examined generalizations. And without some sort of social cohesion, one's brilliant ideas are liable to perish. The point is not to abandon all institutions and dogmas but to find a way to live with them more iron-ically, to appreciate them for what they are—the play of the human mind in its endless quest for connection and meaning—rather than timeless entities that have to be ruthlessly defended or forcibly imposed.

"Religion today," says Don Cupitt, "has to become beliefless. There is nothing out there to believe in or to hope for. Religion therefore has to become an immediate and deeply felt way of relating yourself to life in general and your own life in particular." This is the spirit in which I have tried to understand what the Buddha was saying all those years ago. In attempting to recover Gotama's humanity and disentangle his ideas from the prevailing opinions of his time, I like to think that a sim-ilar perspective may have animated him as well. Whether or not you find my resulting collage to be a convincing portrait of the man and his ideas, it is one that works better for me as a layman in today's world than any of the alternatives proposed by traditional Buddhism.

What is it in Gotama's teaching that was distinctively his own? There are four core elements of the Dhamma that cannot be derived from the Indian culture of his time. These are

1. The *principle* of "this-conditionality, conditioned arising."
2. The *process* of the Four Noble Truths.
3. The *practice* of mindful awareness.
4. The *power* of self-reliance.

These four axioms provide a sufficient ground for the kind of ethi-cally committed, practically realized, and intellectually coherent way of life Gotama anticipated. They are the matrix that frames his vision of a new kind of culture, society, and *civitas*.

Yet Gotama's Dhamma is more than just a series of axioms. It is to be lived rather than simply adopted and believed in. It entails that one embrace this world in all its contingency and specificity, with all its ambiguity and flaws. It requires an unflinching honesty with oneself, a willingness to face one's deepest fears and longings, the courage to resist fleeing to the imagined safety of one's "place." In the midst of strife and confusion, it invites one to pay precise attention to what is happening, to resist the urge to follow habitual patterns of reaction, to respond from the still and sane perspective of one's "ground."

Gotama's Dhamma calls for a sensibility that infuses and transforms one's relationship with others. "Whoever would tend to me," he said, "should tend to the sick." To heed the injunction to embrace suffering leads to an empathetic identification with the plight of others. Their pain comes to be felt as one's own. Shantideva, writing more than a thousand years after the First Council, expands this further in his *A Guide to the Bodhisattva's Way of Life*. If the compassionate Buddha regarded others as himself, he argues, then as long as there was pain in the world, he suffered too. To "tend" to the Buddha entails that one heed the "call" (as Emmanuel Levinas, the philosopher I met in Fribourg many years ago, puts it) that silently issues from the face and eyes of the other, whose first mute syllables are these: "Do not kill me."

In 2000, after fifteen years of living and working at Sharpham, Martine and I left England and moved to southwest France. Four years earlier we had bought and started renovating the upper floor of Martine's family home in a medieval village near Bordeaux. We were faced with a choice. The Sharpham Trust had decided that the Sharpham College, of which I was the director and Martine the coordinator, needed to establish formal links with a British university in order that attendance at its courses would entitle students to receive credits toward a degree. Since we had no interest in taking the college in this direction and lacked the academic qualifications to do so, we decided to leave Devon and settle in our house in France, where we would have greater freedom to write and study, while also being able to accept the growing number of invitations to lead meditation retreats and teach Buddhist philosophy worldwide.

Our life in France soon settled into a rhythm. We now spend a total of about six months each year teaching retreats and courses across Europe and the United States and, occasionally, in Mexico, Australasia, and South Africa. The rest of our time is spent quietly at home, writing, taking care of the house and garden, and getting drawn into the dramas of Martine's extended family. We have deliberately not set up a meditation group or Buddhist study center in the locality. For the first time in more than thirty years we are able to enjoy an ordinary life in which we are not defined by our roles as "the Buddhists." It is strangely liberating.

My mother is ninety-six and lives in a residential care home in Shropshire. Over the years her reservations about what I was doing diminished in proportion as my work registered on her scale of success: an award-winning travel guide, contributions to radio programs, an occasional appearance on TV. As the Dalai Lama rose to become an international religious superstar, the prouder she became of her son for having known him in India when he was a relatively obscure refugee. She has never succeeded in reading more than a few pages of any of my books ("Far too clever for me, dear"), but has been heard to say that the only religion she feels any affinity for is Buddhism. My fierce ideological differences with my brother, David, evaporated long ago. He is now an artist and author living in London. In 2000 he published a book called *Chromophobia,* which became a cult bestseller. His work has been bought by collectors worldwide, commissioned for public buildings, and exhibited throughout Europe, Asia, and America.

Despite my abiding passion for the ideas and practices of the Dhamma, I am ambivalent about describing myself as a "religious" person. Whether prostrating myself before a gilded Buddha statue, intoning the *Heart Sutra* with my hands reverently placed together, or murmuring the mantra "Om Mani Padme Hum" in a crowd of faithful Buddhists, I feel like a bit of a fraud. Yet I love walking around ancient stupas, treading the ground on which the Buddha and his followers once stood, or sitting quietly in an old temple or shrine, just observing the inflow and outflow of my breath as I listen to the rustle of trees outside. If "secular religion" were not considered a contradiction in terms, I would happily endorse such a concept.

I no longer think of Buddhist practice solely in terms of gaining proficiency in meditation and acquiring "spiritual" attainments. The challenge of Gotama's eightfold path is, as I understand it, to live in this world in a way that allows every aspect of one's existence to flourish: seeing, thinking, speaking, acting, working, etc. Each area of life calls for a specific way of practicing the Dhamma. Meditation and mindfulness alone are not enough. Given the task of responding to the suffering that confronts me each time I open a newspaper, I find it immoral to relegate the demands of this life to the "higher" task of preparing oneself for a postmortem existence (or non-existence). I think of myself as a secular Buddhist who is concerned entirely with the demands of this age (*saeculum*) no matter how inadequate and insignificant my responses to these demands might be. And if in the end there does turn out to be a heaven or nirvana somewhere else, I can see no better way to prepare for it.

# APPENDIX I

## *The Pāli Canon*

The "Pāli Canon" refers to the body of texts attributed to Siddhattha Gotama preserved in the Pāli language. Pāli is an idiomatic form (*prakrit*) of Sanskrit, the language in which the classical works of Brahmanic civilization, such as the Vedas, the Mahabharata, and the Upanishads, are recorded. Pāli has a similar relation to Sanskrit as spoken Italian does to Latin. The form of Pāli that has come down to us is not, however, the language the Buddha spoke. Gotama is likely to have been familiar with a number of *prakrits*—Sanskrit-based dialects—that he would have used depending on where and to whom he was teaching. *Pāli,* which simply means "text," is a more literary version of these dialects, which evolved in the centuries after the Buddha's death while being employed by monks from different parts of India as a common language in which the Dhamma was recited and thereby remembered.

The Pāli Canon survived as an oral tradition, recited communally by groups of monks, for three or four centuries before it was first written down in Sri Lanka. There is no Pāli script. Wherever the texts of the Pāli Canon were written down, they were transcribed in the particular script of that country. In Sri Lanka, the Canon is written in Singalese script, in Burma, in Burmese script, and so on. Likewise, when it came to be studied in the West, it was transcribed and published by the Pāli Text Society in Roman script.

Discourses found in the Pāli Canon are also preserved in the canonical literature of other Buddhist traditions. The most complete collection of such discourses is found in a Chinese translation of a now-lost Sanskrit version of the Canon. This version, known as the Āgamas, is very close in content and organization to the version preserved in Pāli. Comparison of the Pāli Canon with the Āgamas shows that, although the two sets of texts are not word-for-word identical, they are recensions of the same primary materials. This points to the existence of a common body of early Buddhist texts, one of which was preserved in Pāli, which ended up in Sri Lanka, and another preserved in Buddhist "hybrid" Sanskrit, which was used in North India. That these two bodies of text are so similar, despite their adherents being physically separated for centuries, suggests that oral transmission is more reliable than those brought up in a culture of the written word would expect.

While a complete version of the early Buddhist canon was translated into Chinese, it was not translated into Tibetan. The Tibetan Buddhist canon (Kangyur) contains a relatively small number of the discourses found in the Pāli Canon and the Āgamas. It does, however, contain Tibetan translations of a body of monastic training texts (Vinaya), which is broadly similar to that found in the Pāli Canon.

The Pāli Canon is divided into "Three Baskets" (*Tipitaka*). These are (1) Sutta, i.e., discourses of the Buddha, (2) Vinaya, i.e., monastic training texts, and (3) Abhidhamma, i.e., exegetical treatises that seek to systematize and clarify the discourses. Traditionally all three "baskets" were accepted as the word of the Buddha. Nowadays, scholars regard the Abhidhamma as a later addition.

The discourses (sutta) found in the Pāli Canon are believed to have been delivered by Siddhattha Gotama, and on occasion by some of his eminent disciples, in different locations throughout North India during the Buddha's lifetime. Modern scholarship recognizes that not all these discourses are of equivalent antiquity, though the dating of the different strata of texts in the Canon is still to be resolved.

The discourses of the Pāli Canon are divided into five "Collections" (Nikāya):

1. Middle Length Discourses (*Majjhima Nikāya*)
2. Long Discourses (*Dīgha Nikāya*)
3. Connected Discourses (*Saṃyutta Nikāya*)
4. Numerical Discourses (*Aṅguttara Nikāya*)
5. Minor Discourses (*Khuddaka Nikāya*)—this collection includes the *Dhammapada, Udāna, Sutta Nipāta, Verses of the Elders (Theragāthā* and *Therīgāthā)*, and other texts.

Since the founding of the Pāli Text Society in 1881, all these discourses have been translated into English at least once and, in some cases, several times. New translations are continually being made. To give a sense of the size of the Canon, the English translation of all these discourses covers approximately 5,500 pages. There is, however, considerable repetition.

The monastic training texts (Vinaya) of the Pāli Canon are not as extensive in number as the discourses. In addition to the *Suttavibhanga,* which enumerates and explains the reason for each monastic rule, there are two main collections: the Greater Division (*Mahāvagga*) and the Lesser Division (*Cūlavagga*). These two Divisions include discussions about monastic life, accounts of key episodes in the Buddha's career, several discourses and homilies, stories of Gotama's encounters with disciples and supporters, and a wealth of information about daily life in North India in the fifth century BCE. Together, the Vinaya texts come to about 1,000 pages in English translation.

The discourses and monastic training texts of the Pāli Canon are the only sources I have used for the presentation of the Buddha's teaching in Part Two of this book.

My reconstruction of the Buddha's life is also primarily based on these same texts. Yet for certain episodes—notably the events that lead to the downfall of Sakiya—I have had to refer to the Pāli *Dhammapada Commentary* (*Dhammapadāṭṭhakathā*). This curious text takes each of the 423 verses of the *Dhammapada*—one of the best-loved Minor Discourses in the Canon—then follows it with a prose "commentary," which has at best a tenuous bearing on the meaning of the verse. It seems that the *Dhammapada,* a text many monks would have known by heart, is being used here as a mnemonic device, with each verse serving as a "peg" on which to hang a loosely related slab of prose. In common with other systems of memorization, recitation of the verse would act as a "cue" for the recollection of the prose passage. While some of these passages are elaborate legends that purport to explain the circumstances under which the verse was taught, others describe episodes from Gotama's life, which are either found in part or are absent from the discourses and monastic training texts. Since such episodes in the *Dhammapada Commentary* are consistent with the rest of the biographic material scattered through the Canon, it seems likely that they refer to the same original story, which, over time, was broken up, suppressed, or forgotten.

The coherence and consistency of the biographic episodes found throughout the discourses, monastic training texts, and the *Dhammapada Commentary* strengthen my confidence in the reliability of the Pāli Canon as a source of historical information about the Buddha and his teaching. The most economic explanation for such coherence and consistency is that these passages refer to historical persons and events. If, on the other hand, such passages are inventions that were later added to the Canon, one would have to answer the following questions:

1. In whose interest would it have been to add such a human and tragic account of the Buddha's life when the prevailing tendency—already ap-

parent even in some suttas—was to represent him as a perfect figure adorned with superhuman features?

2. And how would anyone have then managed to insert the details of this story in a scattershot manner throughout thousands of pages of text?

When Buddhists did later come to compose discourses and attribute them to Siddhattha Gotama, it is striking that the texts they produced (i.e., the Mahāyāna Sūtras) are devoid of any sense of historical, social, or geographic reality. Moreover, the Buddha they present as delivering these discourses is godlike in his perfection, thereby causing the reader to lose any sense of his being a human person living in a world of conflict and uncertainty.

The Sutta and Vinaya baskets of the Pāli Canon are to Buddhism what the New Testament is to Christianity and the Koran and Hadith are to Islam. While it would be naïve to consider the contents of these sections of the Pāli Canon as verbatim transcripts of what the Buddha said, they nonetheless provide a body of materials that brings us as close as we will ever get to the world in which Siddhattha Gotama lived and taught.

*For further information on the Pāli Canon and its formation, see Richard Gombrich.* What the Buddha Thought *and K. R. Norman.* A Philological Approach to Buddhism. *Many of the discourses of the Pāli Canon are available in English translation without charge at www.accesstoinsight.org. For the publications of the Pāli Text Society: www.palitext.com.*

# APPENDIX II

## *Was Siddhattha Gotama at Taxilā?*

How did Siddhattha Gotama come to acquire his distinctive tone of voice and doctrines, both of which are different from the tone of voice and doctrines of the pre-existent Indian culture as found, for example, in the Upanishads? By the time he started teaching at the age of thirty-five, Gotama appeared to have already established an informed yet critical, assured, and ironic distance from the brahmanic and other beliefs of his time. From the outset, he introduced notions (e.g., conditioned arising, mindfulness, the Four Noble Truths) that seem unprecedented among the traditions found in the Gangetic basin.

The Pāli Canon sheds very little light on this question. Before he left home at the age of twenty-nine, there is no mention of what kind of education Gotama received, what work or other duties he undertook, what questions and concerns animated him. There is a gaping hole in the narrative: we are simply not told what he did during his formative years. And in the six years between leaving home and the awakening, all we know is that he studied with two teachers, who taught him the absorptions on "nothingness" and "neither-perception-nor-non-perception" respectively (i.e., the seventh and eighth *jhānas*), and spent an unspecified period of time practicing self-mortification, all of which he rejected as inadequate. In despair at the failure of asceticism to resolve his dilemma, he recalls a time when he found himself sitting "in the cool shade of a rose-apple tree" while his "father the Sakiyan was occupied" and "entered and abided in the first *jhāna*, which is accompanied by applied and sustained thought, with rapture and pleasure born from seclusion" (M. 36, i. 246, p. 340). This memory leads him to believe that such a way is the path to awakening (though it is nonetheless puzzling for someone who has mastered the seventh and eighth *jhānas* to be unfamiliar with the first).

The canonical account expects us to believe that all Gotama did prior to his

245

awakening was master, then reject, two normative religious exercises—formless concentration and self-mortification—of his time. It gives no importance to the philosophical and religious topics he would have discussed with his fellow ascetics, thus providing us with no sense at all of the development of his ideas. The account serves the interests of those who insist that the Buddha's awakening is essentially a matter of private spiritual accomplishment, one that goes beyond the Upanishadic tradition but nonetheless remains at core an inner mystical experience. Mystical insight alone, however, seems insufficient to account for his distinctive tone of voice and doctrines. Traditionally, Buddhists believe that the bodhisatta had passed numerous lifetimes on his quest for full awakening and it was just a matter of time before he overcame the final hurdle to becoming a Buddha. For those who reject or are agnostic about reincarnation, however, this is not a satisfying answer either. One might as well say that his awakening was the result of God's grace, a theory that would have equivalent explanatory power.

If one does not accept these traditional accounts, then how can one explain the distinctive tone of voice and doctrines of Siddhattha Gotama? One hypothesis would be that during the years prior to the awakening, he was exposed to a high culture that was not exclusively brahmanic. At his time, the only place where he could feasibly have had such exposure was in the city of Taxilā (Pāli: Takkasilā). But is there any evidence in the Pāli Canon to support this claim?

## Taxilā

In the fifth century BCE, Taxilā was the capital city of Gandhāra, the easternmost satrapy (province) of the Persian Achaemenid Empire, the greatest world power of the day, whose territory spread as far west as Egypt. The city lay about seven hundred miles, a two-month caravan journey, from Kapilavatthu, where the Buddha was born. Lying at the crossroads of the major trade routes of Asia, Taxilā would have been populated by Persians, Greeks, and other peoples from the diverse Achaemenid Empire. This cosmopolitan city was the western terminus of the North Road, which started south of the Ganges in Rājagaha, capital of the kingdom of Magadha, and then passed through Vesālī, Kusinārā, Kapilavatthu, and Sāvatthi before reaching the border of the Persian Empire. Around the time of the Buddha's birth (c. 480 BCE), Indian soldiers from Gandhāra were fighting in the Persian army at the battle of Thermopylae, northwest of Athens. Despite primitive systems of transport, people were able and willing to travel great distances.

Taxilā was also renowned for its university, which made it the greatest center of learning in the region. Vedic lore as well as eighteen "sciences" (*vijja*) were reputedly taught in Taxila, though the only ones mentioned in the Canon are military skills, medicine and surgery, and magic. On admission to the university, students paid a fee to a teacher and would move into his household. They would be expected to perform chores for the teacher in return for the instructions they received, though it is likely that the wealthier students would have been accompanied by servants.

Some of the key figures in Siddhattha Gotama's life are known to have studied in Taxila. These include three contemporaries: King Pasenadi of Kosala, his friend and principal benefactor, who married the daughter of Siddhattha's cousin Mahānāma; Bandhula, a noble from Kusinara in the province of Malla, just south of Sakiya, who rose to become the commander of Pasenadi's army but was finally murdered by the king (Kusinara was also where the Buddha died); and Mahāli, a Licchavi prince from Vesāli, who interceded with King Bimbisāra of Magadha to invite the Buddha to the city. Two other well-known members of the Buddha's circle educated at Taxila were Aṅgulimāla, the son of a brahmin priest at Sāvatthi, who trained in the "black arts" at Taxila and then sought to murder a thousand people to repay the debt to his teacher there, and Jīvaka, the court doctor at Rājagaha, who studied medicine at Taxilā, treated Gotama when he was sick, and put him up in his mango grove toward the end of his life.

If you look at the map in Appendix IV, it is striking that a leading young nobleman from all but one of the major towns along the North Road in the northern Gangetic Plain (Sāvatthi, Kusinara, and Vesāli) was sent to the university of Taxila. The only major town from which a nobleman is *not* sent is Kapilavatthu, the home of Gotama, which lies halfway between Sāvatthi and Kusinara. It is difficult to imagine that Suddhodana, the Buddha's father, would not have considered sending his gifted son and heir to Taxila as well. For not only would Gotama have received an education there, he would have been trained alongside his peers (Pasenadi and Bandhula), who were being prepared to assume positions of power within the Kosalan state. The familiarity between Gotama and Pasenadi, which is apparent in the frank and intimate tone of their dialogues, would also be explained by the two men having known each other since a young age—possibly as fellow students at Taxila. Even if Gotama never set foot in Taxila himself, he would have spent time in the company of those who had and thus would have encountered ideas that came from beyond the Gangetic basin.

## Assalāyana

Moreover, we know from a dialogue with the brahmin scholar Assalāyana (M. 93, ii 149, pp. 764–5) that Gotama was familiar with the region of Gandhāra and its social customs. In this sutta, we find Gotama engaged in a debate with Assalāyana about the brahmins' claim that they are the highest caste. "What do you think, Assalāyana," says Gotama. "Have you heard that in Yona and Kamboja and in other outland countries there are only two castes, masters and slaves, and that masters become slaves and slaves masters?" "Yona" is the Pāli form of "Ionia," i.e., Greek Asia Minor (now Turkey). Here it refers to the region near Taxilā inhabited by the immigrant Greek communities that *preceded* Alexander the Great (they might have been exiled devotees of the god Dionysos). Kamboja is likewise a region in the same area of northwest India, possibly in Bactria, modern Afghanistan. It could be that Gotama, like Assalāyana, had only *heard of* these places, but their customs must have been well enough known to be used as an example in a learned debate. If he had been at Taxilā and visited these places himself, however, he would have gained firsthand knowledge of societies that did not assume the divine sanction of caste, which would have given him a strong empirical basis for his rejection of the caste system.

## The City

In another canonical passage (S. II, 105–7, pp. 603–4), Gotama says: "Suppose, monks, a man wandering through a forest would see an ancient path, an ancient road traveled upon by people in the past. He would follow it and would see an ancient city, an ancient capital that had been inhabited by people in the past, with parks, groves, ponds and ramparts, a delightful place." The parable continues with the man going to the local ruler and proposing that the ancient city he has found in the forest be renovated. The king accepts this proposal and rebuilds the city so that it again becomes "successful and prosperous, well populated, attained to growth and expansion."

The didactic value of a metaphor is to provide an example of something concrete and familiar to illustrate, by comparison, something less concrete and familiar. This passage, like the majority of the Buddha's discourses, was taught at Sāvatthi, i.e., on the northern Gangetic Plain. But at the time, there were no ruined roads and cities in the forests of the Ganges basin with which Gotama's audience could have been familiar. For the very first cities to emerge in this region were the ones that had been built in the last decades or so: Sāvatthi, Vesālī, etc. Moreover, these cities were constructed of perishable materials (sunbaked brick and wood), which would not survive for very long before they decomposed into the earth. Where and how, then, could Gotama's listeners have become familiar with the idea of imposing ruins of ancient roads and cities hidden in forests? There is only one possible answer: in Gandhāra, not too far from Taxilā, where the abandoned cities of the Indus Valley Civilization were to be found. This civilization flourished from 2600 to 1900 BCE, though some Harappan sites may still have been inhabited as late as 900 BCE, i.e., four hundred years before the Buddha. Unlike the buildings of the Gangetic basin, these ancient cities were made of kiln-fired bricks, a technology that had subsequently been lost in India and was not rediscovered until the Mauryan period, a century after the Buddha's death.

For Gotama to have used this metaphor does not entail that either he or his listeners had seen these ruins for themselves. But, as in the discussion with Assalāyana on caste, it implies that the ruined cities must have been well enough known by an educated public to serve as a didactic metaphor. It suggests that those living on the Gangetic Plain in crudely built towns of wattle and daub were conscious of a great, vanished civilization to the west that had built cities with strangely resilient materials that did not erode with each monsoon. By evoking this lost civilization, and comparing himself to a man who seeks, with the help of the king, to restore it, the Buddha implies that his eightfold path is a communal task that, if undertaken, could lead to a rebuilt city, i.e., a renewed civilization, comparable to the one in the Indus Valley that lay in ruins.

Yet if Gotama had indeed spent some years at Taxilā, it is possible that when he evoked this metaphor, he was recalling an experience he had had himself: of being in a forest, perhaps while out hunting with his friends Pasenadi and Bandhula, and stumbling across a ruined roadway that led them to an abandoned city. This may have left such an enduring and potent impression on the young man that he later used the memory of it as a rhetorical device to inspire his followers to realize the kind of "successful and prosperous, well populated" civilization to which he hoped his Dhamma might one day lead.

## Māra

Is there any specific doctrine within the Buddha's teaching that could plausibly have its origins outside the classical Indian sphere of ideas? If so, and particularly if the origin of that doctrine were to the west, then it would suggest not only that he may have been to Taxilā but also that he had been influenced by non-Indian ideas he encountered there.

The doctrine of Māra (the devil), which is already found in the *Sutta*

*Nipāta,* one of the earliest sections of the Pāli Canon, would be one such possibility. The canonical depiction of Māra as a trickster-like personification of evil has no precedent in the Indian tradition. Māra is not included among the numerous Indian gods. Only in Buddhism do we find this figure, who typically appears as a negative counterimage to the awakened person of the Buddha. Throughout Gotama's life, Māra is present as a kind of shadow that haunts the Buddha. Numerous dialogues occur throughout the Canon between the Buddha and Māra, most of which conclude with the Buddha recognizing Māra for what he is (i.e., the demonic play of either his own mind or the world), whereupon Māra disappears. Although Gotama is said to have overcome Māra on attaining awakening, Māra continues to interact with the Buddha until the end of his life. The two figures seem locked into a dance with each other, symbolizing a quasi-eternal struggle between the forces of good and evil.

The parallels between the Christian idea of Satan and the Buddhist concept of Māra have often been commented upon. It is likely that both traditions drew this idea from a common source that predated them: namely, Zoroastrianism, the religion founded by Zarathustra that came to prominence during the Persian Achaemenid Empire. Zarathustra taught how Ohrmazd (God) gave birth to twins. While one twin chose to follow truth, the other—Ahriman (the devil)—chose to follow lies. Zoroastrian texts describe Ahriman as "the destroyer . . . the accursed destructive spirit who is all wickedness and full of death, a liar and deceiver." (The word *Māra* literally means "the killer.") Ahriman's opposition to Ohrmazd is said to be the reason human existence is rooted in a primordial tension between the opposing forces of good and evil, light and darkness. While this kind of language is entirely foreign to the philosophy of the Upanishads, it is strikingly similar to the way in which the polarized figures of Buddha and Māra are described. If Gotama was influenced in his teaching by such ideas, where could he possibly have encountered them? Since, by his time, Zoroastrianism had become the court religion of the Persian emperors, it is likely that he picked them up either from those he knew who had been in Taxilā or from teachers he had met there himself.

### Conclusion

None of this provides sufficient evidence to establish conclusively that Siddhattha Gotama went to Taxilā. Given the absence of contemporary documents, one also cannot rule out the possibility that the passages I have cited from the suttas may have been added to the Canon at a later date, possibly by monks from the Gandhāra region, where we know that Buddhism subsequently flourished. Nonetheless, assuming these fragments of canonical evidence go back to the Buddha's time or shortly thereafter, when put together, they point to the possibility that during his formative years Gotama traveled to and studied in Taxilā.

Some years of study in Taxilā, followed, perhaps, by a period of working in a military or administrative capacity for the Kosalan state, would also explain why Gotama appears to have been absent from his homeland of Sakiya throughout his twenties. The Canon implies that he did not sire his first and only child until he was about twenty-eight, which is very late by the standards of a society where noblemen would have been married in their teens. If my hypothesis is correct, then another light is cast on the Buddha's departure from Sakiya at the age of twenty-nine (one of the few facts for which we have strong canonical authority: D. 16, ii 151, p. 268). Gotama's exposure to the wider world of the Persian Empire at Taxilā may have been the trigger that prompted him to pose questions about human life and society in terms broader than those he would have known in Sakiya. His return to Sakiya may have been simply in order to fulfill his duty to his family by providing an heir. For shortly after his son was born, he left again, though this time to the southeast rather than the northwest, to explore the spiritual traditions of the brahmins and other non-orthodox Indian teachers of the Gangetic heartland. His awakening is thus not a timeless mystical insight that appears out of the blue, but may have been the culmination of at least fifteen years of travel, study, reflection, discussion, meditation, and austerity.

# APPENDIX III

This appendix consists of my translation of the Buddha's first sermon, to which Chapter 12, "Embrace Suffering," provides a contemporary commentary.

## Turning the Wheel of Dhamma

This is what I heard. He was staying at Bārānasī in the Deer Park at Isipatana. He addressed the group of five:

"One gone forth does not pursue two dead ends. Which two? Infatuation, which is vulgar, uncivilized, and meaningless. And mortification, which is painful, uncivilized, and meaningless.

"I have awoken to a middle path that does not lead to dead ends. It is a path that generates vision and awareness. It leads to tranquillity, insight, awakening, and release. It has eight branches: appropriate vision, thought, speech, action, livelihood, effort, mindfulness, and concentration.

"This is suffering: birth is painful, aging is painful, sickness is painful, death is painful, encountering what is not dear is painful, separation from what is dear is painful, not getting what one wants is painful. This psycho-physical condition is painful.

"This is craving: craving is repetitive, it wallows in attachment and greed, obsessively indulging in this and that: craving for stimulation, craving for existence, craving for non-existence.

"This is cessation: the traceless fading away and cessation of that craving, the letting go and abandoning of it, freedom and independence from it.

"And this is the path: the path with eight branches: appropriate vision, thought, speech, action, livelihood, effort, mindfulness, and concentration.

" 'Such is suffering. It can be fully known. It has been fully known.'

" 'Such is craving. It can be let go of. It has been let go of.'

" 'Such is cessation. It can be experienced. It has been experienced.'

" 'Such is the path. It can be cultivated. It has been cultivated.'

"So there arose in me illumination about things previously unknown.

"As long as my knowledge and vision were not entirely clear about the twelve aspects of these Four Noble Truths, I did not claim to have had a peerless awakening in this world with its humans and celestials, its gods and devils, its ascetics and priests. Only when my knowledge and vision were clear in all these ways did I claim to have had such awakening.

" 'The freedom of my mind is unshakable. There will be no more repetitive existence.' "

This is what He said. Inspired, the five delighted in his words. While he was speaking, the dispassionate, stainless Dhamma eye arose in Kondañña: "Whatever has started can stop."

*According to tradition, Siddhattha Gotama delivered his first sermon,* Turning the Wheel of Dhamma, *in Isipatana (Sarnath) near Bārāṇasī (Varanasi) to his five former companions in asceticism several weeks after his awakening at Uruvelā (Bodh Gaya). Some seventeen versions of this discourse have been found in Pāli, Sanskrit, Chinese, and Tibetan. The preceding translation of the first sermon is based on that found in the Greater Division (*Mahāvagga*) of the monastic training texts (*Vinaya*) of the Pāli Canon (Mv. I, 9–10, pp. 15–17; cf. S. V, 420–4, pp. 1844–5).*

*I have translated* Turning the Wheel of Dhamma *in accordance with the principles outlined in this book. In seeking to uncover what is distinctive in the Buddha's teaching, I have removed from the text all passages that assume the multi-life worldview of ancient India. The most notable omissions are the classical names for the four truths: i.e., "the noble truth of suffering," "the noble truth of the origin of suffering," "the noble truth of the cessation of suffering," and "the noble truth that leads to the cessation of suffering." Instead, I present each truth in terms of what is most immediately pertinent about it. (1) suffering, (2) craving, (3) cessation, and (4) the path. Toward the end of the text, the Buddha concludes by saying: "The freedom of my mind is unshakable. This is the last birth. There will be no more repetitive existence." In my translation, I have removed the phrase "This is the last birth."*

# APPENDIX IV

The map on the following pages covers an area of 46,800 square miles in North India, where the Buddha was active from c. 480 to 400 BCE. The territory, now divided between the Indian states of Bihar and Uttar Pradesh, is the same size as the American state of Pennsylvania (46,058 square miles) and slightly smaller than England—*not* Great Britain—(50,337 square miles). The Himalayan peaks lie 80 miles to the north of Kapilavatthu. The Canon tells us that the Buddha sometimes stayed as far west as the city of Kosambī and as far east as the city of Campa, which are beyond the borders of this map. He also had a small community of followers in the city of Ujjeni, headed by the monk Mahākaccana, but is not recorded as having gone there himself. Several figures in the Canon are said to have studied at or come to see the Buddha from Takkasilā in the northwest (see Appendix II). The *Sutta Nipāta* (v. 977) recounts how sixteen students of the brahmin Bāvari traveled 1,000 miles to see the Buddha from the Godhāvarī River in South India (modern Andhra Pradesh).

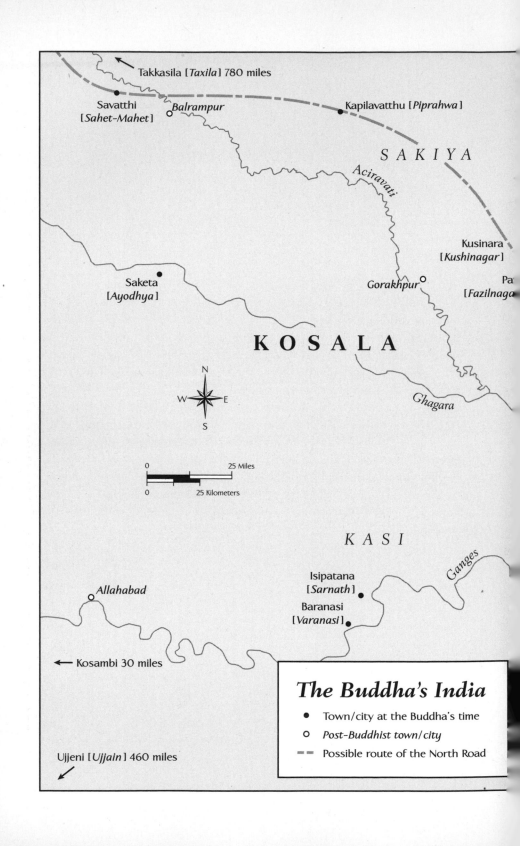

Takkasila [*Taxila*] 780 miles

Savatthi
[*Sahet-Mahet*]　　○ *Balrampur*　　Kapilavatthu [*Piprahwa*]

S A K I Y A

*Aciravati*

Kusinara
[*Kushinagar*]

Saketa
[*Ayodhya*]

Gorakhpur ○　　Pa
[*Fazilnaga*

K O S A L A

N
W · E
S

0　　　　　25 Miles
0　　　　　25 Kilometers

*Ghagara*

K A S I

*Ganges*

Isipatana
[*Sarnath*]
Baranasi
[*Varanasi*]

*Allahabad*

← Kosambi 30 miles

## *The Buddha's India*

- ● 　Town/city at the Buddha's time
- ○ 　*Post-Buddhist town/city*
- – – 　Possible route of the North Road

Ujjeni [*Ujjain*] 460 miles

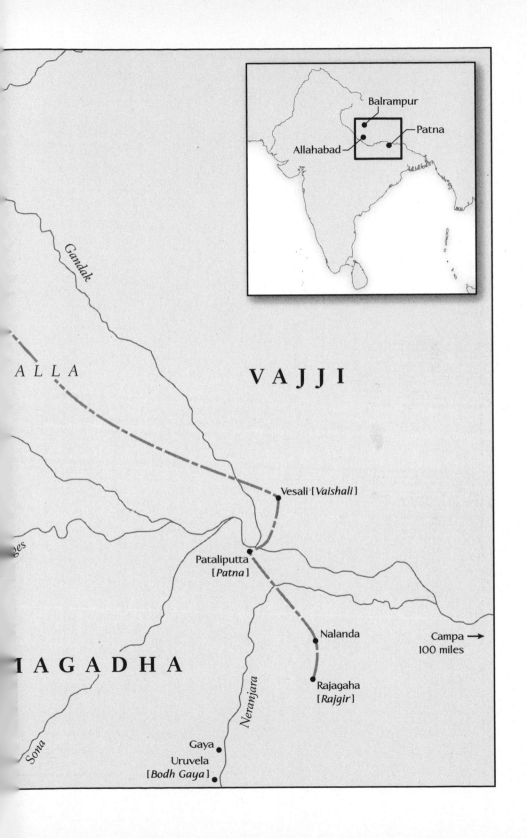

# NOTES

## Abbreviations for Texts in the Pāli Canon

NB: *The first letters and numbers that appear (e.g., M. 10, i. 56–63) refer to the Sutta (Discourse) number and pagination of the PTS edition in Pāli; this is followed by the page number of the English translation listed below in brackets (e.g., p. 145). I have often adapted the published English translations for conformity of terminology and consistency of style. For further information on the Pāli Canon, see Appendix I.*

| | |
|---|---|
| A | *Aṅguttara Nikāya (Tr. Nyanaponika/Bodhi, 1999)* |
| Cv | *Cūlavagga (Tr. Horner, 1952)* |
| D | *Dīgha Nikāya (Tr. Walshe, 1995)* |
| Dh | *Dhammapada (Tr. Fronsdal, 2005)* |
| DhA | *Dhammapadāṭṭhakathā (Tr. Burlingame, 1921)* |
| M | *Majjhima Nikāya (Tr. Nanamoli/Bodhi, 1995)* |
| Mv | *Mahāvagga (Tr. Horner, 1951)* |
| S | *Saṃyutta Nikāya (Tr. Bodhi, 2000)* |
| Sn | *Sutta Nipāta (Tr. Norman, 2001)* |
| Thag | *Theragāthā (Tr. Rhys Davids, 1909)* |
| Ud | *Udāna (Tr. Ireland, 1997)* |

## Opening Quotes

vii **There are not only one hundred** M. 73, i. 491, p. 597.

vii **Stories are impossible** Wim Wenders, *The Logic of Images*, p. 59.

PART ONE: MONK

## 2. On the Road

8 **From the monk's cell** The two standing Buddhas at Bamiyan were destroyed by the Taliban in March 2001.

17 **the Library of Tibetan Works and Archives** www.ltwa.net.

## 3. The Seminarian

19 **I learned that human life** This and the reflections that follow are characteristic of the Tibetan *lam rim* (stages on the path) literature. See Geshe Dhargyey's *Tibetan Tradition of Mental Development* (Dhargyey 1978), which consists of an edited transcript of lectures given at the Tibetan Library of Works and Archives in the early 1970s. Much of his teaching would have been based on Pabongka Rinpoche's *Liberation in the Palm of Your Hand* (Pabongka 1991). Geshe Dhargyey also taught Gampopa's *Jewel Ornament of Liberation* (Guenther 1970). For an example of Geshe Dhargyey's and Geshe Rabten's teaching in Dharamsala during the time I was there, see Geshe Rabten and Geshe Ngawang Dhargyey, *Advice from a Spiritual Friend.*

26 *Discourse on the Grounding of Mindfulness* M. 10, i. 56–63, p. 145 seq. For information on S. N. Goenka and his work: www.dhamma.org.

31 **Lama Yeshe** Lama Thubten Yeshe (1935–1984) and Lama Thubten Zopa (b. 1946) offered some of the first courses on Buddhism to Westerners in Kopan Monastery near Kathmandu and established the Foundation for the Preservation of the Mahayana Tradition (FPMT), now an international organization with centers worldwide. After Lama Yeshe's death, Osel Hita (b. 1985) was recognized as his reincarnation and educated in Sera Monastery, South India. Osel has left the monastic order and is currently studying film in Madrid. www.fpmt.org.

## 4. Eel Wriggling

33 **"Just as a goldsmith assays gold . . ."** The canonical source of this much quoted verse is not known.

33 **Tharpa Choeling, the monastery he founded** Tharpa Choeling was founded in 1977, two years after Geshe Rabten arrived in Switzerland. His post on leaving Dharamsala was abbot of the Tibetan Institute at Rikon, near Winterthur in the German-speaking part of Switzerland. Tharpa Choeling was renamed Rabten Choeling after Geshe's death in 1986. Several other "Rabten" centers have since been established in Europe. www.rabten.at/index_en.htm.

33 **the philosophy of Dharmakirti** The best account of Dharmakīrti and his philosophy in English is Georges Dreyfus's *Recognizing Reality.* For a

presentation of Dharmakīrti's epistemology as taught by Geshe Rabten in Switzerland, see Rabten, *The Mind and Its Functions,* pp. 19–95.

36 **This crisis erupted**  For the Dalai Lama's thoughts on the evidence for rebirth, including Dharmakīrti's proof cited here, see Dalai Lama, *The Universe in a Single Atom,* pp. 131–3.

39 **Geshe Rabten told us to subject the texts**  For another view on the role of critical inquiry in Geluk scholarship, see Dreyfus, *The Sound of Two Hands Clapping,* p. 267 seq.

41 **"eel wriggling"**  One of the wrong views listed in the *Brahmajāla Sutta.* "There are, monks, some ascetics and brahmins who are Eel-Wrigglers. When asked about this and that matter, they resort to evasive statements, and they wriggle like eels . . ." D. 1, i. 26, p. 80.

41 **Geshe Kelsang Gyatso**  Geshe Kelsang Gyatso (b. 1931) was invited by Lama Yeshe to be the resident teacher at Manjushri Institute in 1976. In 1991, he founded the New Kadampa Tradition, which has since become an international Tibetan Buddhist organization. See Chapter 16, "Gods and Demons," below. www.kadampa.org.

## 5. Being-in-the-World

46 **Dora Kalff**  Dora M. Kalff (1904–1990). For Frau Kalff's account of sandplay therapy, see Kalff, *Sandplay: A Psychotherapeutic Approach to the Psyche.* While undergoing sandplay therapy, I also attended lectures at the C. G. Jung Institute in nearby Küsnacht and studied the writings of Jung. Of the books I read in this field, one that spoke directly to my own situation was Marie-Louise von Franz's *Puer Aeternus.*

54 *The Eight Verses of Training the Mind*  A well-known Lojong (mind training) text of the Kadampa school of Tibetan Buddhism, composed by Geshe Langri Tampa (1054–1123). For a translation and commentary: www.buddhadharma.org/EightVerses.

55 **"Truth is a pathless land,"**  This and the following citation are from Krishnamurti's *Dissolution Speech:* http://bernie.cncfamily.com/k_path less.htm.

57 **Geshe Thubten Ngawang**  For information on Geshe Thubten Ngawang (1932–2003) and his work in the Tibetisches Zentrum in Hamburg: www.tibet.de (German language site).

## 6. Great Doubt

I have written about my move from Tibetan to Korean Buddhism in *The Faith to Doubt,* pp. 7–26. For a short history of Korean Buddhism, a sketch of life in Songgwangsa monastery, and a biographical portrait of Kusan Sunim, see the introduction to Kusan Sunim, *The Way of Korean Zen,* pp. 3–51. A detailed study of Korean Zen monastic life is in Buswell, *The Zen Monastic Experience.*

61 **Kalu Rinpoche** Kalu Rinpoche (1905–1989) was one of the foremost lamas of the Kagyu school to introduce Buddhism to Westerners in India, Europe, and the United States. The retreat center at the Château de Plaige is now called Dashang Kagyu Ling. www.mille-bouddhas.com.

67 **"questioning is the piety of thought."** Martin Heidegger, "The Question Concerning Technology," in *Basic Writings*, p. 317.

68 **"The purpose of Zen meditation . . ."** Kusan Sunim, *The Way of Korean Zen*, p. 60.

### PART TWO: LAYMAN

### 7. A Buddhist Failure (II)

88 **Gaia House, a Vipassana retreat center** www.gaiahouse.co.uk. For the Sharpham Trust: www.sharphamtrust.org. For Green Gulch Farm: www.sfzc.org/ggf/.

91 **It is too soon to tell whether the pressures of modernity** Crucial to the renewal of traditional monasticism would be the restoration of the *bhikkhunī* (nun) ordination in Southeast Asia and Tibet. At present women can receive full Buddhist monastic ordination only in Korea, China, and Taiwan. *Bhikkhunī* ordination has recently been reintroduced in Sri Lanka but is not yet fully accepted by the hierarchy of monks. See Bodhi, *The Revival of Bhikkhunī Ordination in the Theravāda Tradition*.

92 **The Kalachakra (Wheel of Time) tantra** For details on the Kālachakra tantra, the kingdom of Shambhala, and the Kālachakra initiation: http://kalachakranet.org/.

94 **the journal had published a review of *Kindness, Clarity, and Insight*** *The Middle Way: Journal of the Buddhist Society [London]*, Vol. 60, no. 1, May 1985, pp. 46–7.

94 **Dzogchen (Great Perfection) is a contemplative practice** In recent years many books have been published in English on Dzogchen by such authorities as Dilgo Khyentse Rinpoche, Urgyen Tulku, and Namkhai Norbu Rinpoche. For a comprehensive introduction and translation of a classic Dzogchen text, see Keith Dowman, *The Flight of the Garuda*.

95 **Dilgo Khyentse Rinpoche** Dilgo Khyentse Rinpoche (1910–1991) was one of the most accomplished lamas of the Nyingma school to have escaped Tibet in 1959. In exile he and his family were based in Bhutan. He taught extensively throughout Asia, Europe, and America. In 1987 he was appointed the head of the Nyingma school, a position he held until his death.

95 **Indeed, the concluding chapter of *Kindness, Clarity, and Insight*** The

chapter is titled "Union of the Old and New Translation Schools." Dalai Lama, *Kindness, Clarity, and Insight,* pp. 200–24.

## 8. Siddhattha Gotama

98 "It is proper for you, Kalamas, to doubt . . ." A. III, 65, p. 65.

99 "Suppose there is no hereafter . . ." A. III, 65, p. 67.

99 Is the universe eternal or not eternal? These "undeclared" questions and the parable of the man wounded by an arrow are in M. 64, i. 432–7, p. 537 seq.

99 Does one continue to exist after death or not Since this question literally reads "Does *the Tathāgata* continue to exist after death or not," it tends to be understood as referring to Gotama's refusal to speculate only about whether a Buddha continues to exist or not after physical death, not an ordinary, unawakened person. There are a number of problems with this interpretation. (1) Since the term *Tathāgata* is often the word Gotama uses to refer to himself, it could simply mean "I," or "one." (2) In *Turning the Wheel of Dhamma* and elsewhere, Gotama describes the effect of his awakening with the words: "this is the last birth," i.e., having become an *arhant,* he will *not* exist after death—thereby decisively answering the question. (3) In some passages, e.g., Ud. 6.4, we find non-Buddhist "brahmins and ascetics" who spend their time discussing questions such as "Does the Tathāgata continue to exist after death or not?" But why would those who are not followers of the Buddha be debating whether a Buddha exists after death or not? (4) In the case of this passage [Ud. 6.4] and elsewhere, the Pāli Commentaries themselves state that "Tathāgata" simply means *atta,* i.e., "self," or "one." (5) The context of the other questions Gotama refuses to answer—"Is the universe eternal or not eternal?" "Is the mind the same as or different from the body?" etc.—suggests that he is addressing the large imponderable questions that trouble all human beings, not specific issues of Buddhist theology.

99 a group of blind men who are summoned by a king Ud. 6.4, p. 86 seq.

102 when he calls his cousin Devadatta a "lick-spittle" Cv. VII, 187, p. 264. Horner translates the Pāli *kheḷāsika* as "vomited like spittle" and "Ñāṇamoli renders it as "a gob of spit." K. R. Norman argues that the term means "lick-spittle," i.e., a toady. Norman, *A Philological Approach to Buddhism,* p. 207.

104 "The Sakiyans are vassals of the King of Kosala," D. 27, iii. 83, p. 409.

104 the story of the four sights is related by Gotama D. 14, ii. 21–30, pp. 207–10.

105 "slaves, servants and workers, spurred on by punishment . . ." S. I, 75, p. 171.

106 "So, Master Gotama, how can you, who are still so young . . ." S. I, 68–70, pp. 164–6.

107 "a bucket measure of rice and curries" S. I, 81–2, pp. 176–7.

107 "I was sitting in the law court," S. I, 74, p. 170.

109 "an ancient path traveled upon by people in the past." S. II, 105–7, pp. 603–4.

### 9. The North Road

111 "The pursuit of meditation and photography," and following quote: Stephen Batchelor, "Photographer's Note," in Martine Batchelor, *Meditation for Life,* pp. 159–60.

114 **Kiln-fired bricks were unavailable in India at that period** Although kiln-fired bricks were widely used in the Indus Valley Civilization in Gandhāra centuries before, by the Buddha's time the technology had been lost. It was not reintroduced into India until the Mauryan period, around a hundred years later.

114 **"a massive sandstone coffer in a state of perfect preservation . . ."** and following quotes: Charles Allen, *The Buddha and the Sahibs,* pp. 274–5.

115 **At the time of Gotama's birth (c. 480 BCE)** Traditionally, the Buddha's dates are given as 563–483 BCE. Contemporary scholars, notably Heinz Bechert and Richard Gombrich, now agree on a later dating: c. 480–400 BCE. See Norman, *A Philological Approach to Buddhism,* pp. 50–1. F. R. Allchin states that such dating "provides a much better fit with every aspect of the archaeological record." See Allchin, *The Archaeology of Early Historic South Asia,* p. 105.

116 **One of the few events he recounts of his childhood** M. 36, i. 246, p. 340.

118 **"deathless supreme security from bondage,"** M. 26, i. 163, p. 256.

118 **"Though my mother and father wished otherwise,"** *Ibid.*

119 **"In a home, life is stifled in an atmosphere of dust. . . ."** Sn. III, v. 406, p. 50.

122 **"You are young and tender, in the prime of your life, . . ."** and following quotes: Sn. III, v. 420–4, p. 51.

123 **All we know is that he spent some time in the communities of two teachers** Gotama's stay with these teachers is recounted at M. 26, i. 163–6, pp. 256–9.

123 **"I took very little food,"** and following quotes: M. 36, i. 245–7, pp. 339–41.

## 10. Against the Stream

127 "This Dhamma I have reached," M. 26, i. 167, p. 260.

130 "When a monk breathes out long," M. 10, i. 56–7, pp. 145–7.

130 "who delight and revel in their place," M. 26, i. 167, p. 260.

131 "One who sees conditioned arising," M. 28, i. 191, p. 283.

131 "Let be the past," M. 79, ii. 32, pp. 655–6.

133 "The ignorant go after outward pleasures," *Katha Upanishad* 2.1. 2. See Max Müller, *The Thirteen Principal Upanishads*, p. 11.

133 "And therefore while we live," Plato, *Phaedo*, 67 a, p. 13.

134 "against the stream." M. 26, i. 168, p. 260.

134 He compared the meditator to a skilled woodturner M. 10, i. 57–8, pp. 146–8.

135 "those with little dust on their eyes," M. 26, i. 169, p. 261.

## 11. Clearing the Path

Extensive materials on Ñāṇavīra Thera, including his entire known written output, are available at www.nanavira.org. My earlier study of Ñāṇavīra Thera's life and work: *Existence, Enlightenment and Suicide: The Dilemma of Nanavira Thera* (first published in Tadeusz Skorupski [ed], *The Buddhist Forum Volume IV*. London: School of Oriental and African Studies, 1996) is also posted at this site.

NB. In the notes below, the book *Clearing the Path* is abbreviated as *CTP*. "L. 134," etc., means Letter number 134.

136 "How irritating the Buddha's teaching . . ." and following quotes: *CTP*, L. 134, p. 458.

137 "I do not *deny* that we may have . . ." *CTP*, L. 135, p. 459.

138 "the influence on European faiths . . ." Evola, *The Doctrine of Awakening*, p. 17.

138 "feelings of the inconsistency and vanity . . ." and following quote: Evola, *Le Chemin du Cinabre*, pp. 12–13.

139 "Whoever thinks: 'extinction is mine,' . . ." *Ibid.*, pp. 13–14. "Extinction" is Evola's rendering of "nirvana." The source is M. 1, i. 4, p. 87.

139 "like a sudden illumination. . . ." *Ibid.*, p. 14.

139 "recaptured the spirit of Buddhism in its original form," *Ibid.*, p. ix.

140 "the best treatise on Buddhism . . ." and following citations are from Ñāṇamoli's correspondence to Susan Hibbert, quoted in Maurice Cardiff, *A Sketch of the Life of Ñāṇamoli Thera (Osbert Moore)*. http://pathpress.wordpress.com/other/a-sketch-of-the-life-of-nanamoli-thera-osbert-moore/.

141 "the desire for some definite non-mystical . . ." *CTP*, L. 91, p. 368.

141 "The Buddha's Teaching is quite alien . . ." *CTP*, L. 101, p. 390.

141 "roll about on [his] bed . . ." Maugham, *Search for Nirvana*, p. 198.

141 A turning point in Nanavira's thinking The dialogue between the Buddha and Sīvaka is found at S. IV, 229–31, pp. 1278–9.

142 "came as a bit of a shock . . ." *CTP*, L. 149, p. 486.

142 "No other Pali books whatsoever," *CTP*, Preface, fn. a, p. 5.

143 HOMAGE TO THE AUSPICIOUS ONE . . . *CTP*, note to L. 1, p. 495.

143 "there was no longer anything for me . . ." *CTP*, L. 99, p. 386.

143 "a slightly displeasing air about them . . ." *CTP*, L. 42, fn. a, p. 255.

143 "were not written to pander . . ." *CTP*, L. 70, p. 323.

144 "are not one day going to get up . . ." *CTP*, L. 131, p. 452.

144 "to interest the professional scholar . . ." *CTP*, Preface, p. 5.

144 "would never reach the point of listening . . ." *CTP*, Preface, p. 11.

145 "I am quite unable to identify myself . . ." *CTP*, L. 62, p. 310.

146 "Under the pressure of this affliction," *CTP*, L. 19, p. 216.

146 "given up all hope of making . . ." *CTP*, L. 32, pp. 240–1.

146 "It was, and is, my attitude . . ." *CTP*, L. 60, p. 305.

147 "There is a way out," *CTP*, L. 128, p. 444.

147 "Do not think that I regard suicide . . ." *CTP*, L. 49, p. 279.

148 "an emaciated Edwardian gentleman . . ." Peter Maddock, personal communication, April 21, 2009.

148 "Man must never cease to transcend . . ." Robert Brady to Katherine Delavenay, November 11, 1965. The full text of this letter is available at www.nanavira.org.

149 " 'dry' and intellectual path . . ." and following quote: Julius Evola, *Le Chemin du Cinabre*, pp. 142–3.

### 12. Embrace Suffering

151 "Just as a farmer irrigates his fields," Dh. v. 80, p. 21.

152 "By action is one a farmer, . . ." Sn. v., 651–3, p. 84. This is Ñāṇavīra Thera's translation.

153 "the ultimate tasks for a man's performance." and example of Alice in Wonderland: Ñāṇavīra Thera, *Clearing the Path*, letter 42, pp. 258–9.

154 it was the last thing he spoke of D. 15, ii. 151, p. 268.

155 "Those who hold training as the essence," Ud. 6.8, p. 92.

156 As Nietzsche claimed "My formula for greatness in a human being is *amor fati*: that one wants nothing to be different, not forward, not back-

ward, not in all eternity. Not merely bear what is necessary, still less conceal it—all idealism is mendaciousness in the face of what is necessary—but *love* it." Friedrich Nietzsche, *Ecce Homo: How One Becomes What One Is,* section 10.

158 **"When you have neither father nor mother . . ."** Mv. VIII, 301, p. 432.

161 **Siddhattha Gotama compared himself to a man** S. II, 105–7, pp. 603–4.

### 13. In Jeta's Grove

165 **"gone beyond doubt, gained intrepidity . . ."** Mv. I, 36, p. 49. Despite Bimbisāra's initial enthusiasm and generosity, which are much celebrated in Buddhist sources, it does not appear that the king particularly favored Gotama over the other teachers who had groves and retreat centers in Rājagaha. He seems to have been equally supportive of Gotama's contemporary and rival Nātaputta (Mahāvīra), the ascetic founder of Jainism. (Today, the modern town of Rājagaha—called Rajgir—is a pilgrimage site for Jains.) Unlike with King Pasenadi of Kosala, there are no dialogues recorded in the Canon between Bimbisāra and Gotama. Nor does Bimbisāra ever pose a moral or philosophical question for Gotama to answer in the form of a discourse. The only times the king appears in the Canon is to ask Gotama not to accept into his community either civil servants or former residents of his prisons, and for the monks to hold formal gatherings at fixed times each month. Gotama agrees to all these requests without demur. Bimbisāra is a man who takes for granted the right to determine how the communities under his patronage conduct their affairs.

165 **"spitting hot blood."** Mv. I, 41, p. 55.

165 **Then one day Anathapindika** The story of Anāthapindika and the founding of Jeta's Grove is recounted in Cv. VI, 154–8, pp. 216–23.

165 **In the meantime, Gotama returned to Kapilavatthu** The Buddha's return to his homeland and reconciliation with his family is told in Mv. I, 54, pp. 103–4.

166 **The following year, several Sakiyan noblemen** This episode is recounted in Cv. VII, 181–3, pp. 256–9.

166 **On a subsequent visit home, he settled a dispute** DhA., iii. 254–6, vol. 3, pp. 70–2. See also the verses the Buddha is said to have spoken on this occasion: Sn. IV, v. 935–9, p. 122.

166 **Numerous Sakiyans asked to join the community** The account of the ordination of Pajāpatī and the first nuns is found at Cv. X, 252–5, pp. 352–6.

166 **After the death of Suddhodana, the governorship of Sakiya** Canonical evidence of this is found at M. 53, i. 354, p. 461.

166 He appears to have conspired with his mother Cv. VII, 179–81, pp. 253–6.

167 "monks' cells, dormitories, attendance halls. . . ." Cv. VI, 158, p. 223.

168 At one point, we find the two of them observing S. I, 77–9, pp. 173–4.

169 Pasenadi used to spy on Mallika in her bath DhA., iii. 119–20, vol. 3, p. 340. Confusingly, there are two Mallikās, the other Mallikā being the wife of Bandhula, the general of Pasenadi's army who was promoted to chief justice and then murdered on suspicion of plotting a coup.

169 Gotama too was accused of sexual improprieties Ud. 4.8, pp. 61–3.

170 In the end, it was Ananda's personal avowal M. 88, ii. 112–4, pp. 723–4.

170 Eventually, Mallika became pregnant S. I, 86, p. 179.

170 "Should anything happen to her," M. 87, ii. 110, p. 721.

170 King Pasenadi needed another wife The story of Pasenadi's marriage to Vāsabhā and the birth of her son are told at DhA., i. 344–6, vol. II, pp. 36–7.

## 14. An Ironic Atheist

175 "a civil but ferociously felt argument" *Time* magazine, October 13, 1997, pp. 80–1.

177 "I rather find myself at a loss . . ." Ñāṇavīra Thera, *Clearing the Path,* letter 144, p. 475.

178 "This is the only straight path," and following quotes: D. 13, i. 235–44, pp. 187–90.

178 "Our doctrine teaches: 'This is the Perfect Splendor . . .'" and following quotes: M. 79, ii. 32–5, pp. 654–6. Vāseṭṭha and Udāyin echo the *Katha Upanishad,* 2.3. 12, which says of God: "He cannot be reached by speech, by mind, or by the eye. How can He be apprehended except by him who says: 'He Is'?" See Max Müller, *The Thirteen Principal Upanishads,* p. 15.

178 In a similar vein, the Buddha told of a certain monk D. 11, i. 211–22, pp. 175–9.

180 "the firm holding back of the senses" *Katha Upanishad,* 2.3. 11. See Max Müller, *The Thirteen Principal Upanishads,* p. 14.

180 "Misguided man, when have you ever . . ." and following quote: M. 38, i. 256–60, pp. 349–51.

181 "Come here, other bank . . ." D. 13, i. 244, p. 190.

182 "Our old religious and moral traditions," Don Cupitt, *The Great Questions of Life,* pp. 11–12.

183 "The recluse Gotama does not have any superhuman states . . ." M. 12, i. 68–9, p. 164.

## 15. Vidudabha's Revenge

187 **Prince Vidudabha, the son of King Pasenadi** The following story of Vidudabha's humiliation is found in DhA., i. 347–9, vol. II, pp. 37–9.

188 **When Gotama was seventy-two, his first patron, King Bimbisara** The circumstances of Bimbisāra's abdication are told in Cv. VII, 189–90, pp. 267–8. The account of Bimbisāra's death is only found in later Pāli commentaries.

188 **At the same time, Siddhattha's cousin Devadatta** Devadatta's attempt to gain control of the monastic order is found in Cv. VII, 187–8, p. 264, and Cv. VII, 196–7, pp. 276–9.

189 **When Gotama arrived in Rajagaha** The meeting between Gotama and Ajātasattu is found in D. 2, i. 47–86, pp. 91–109.

190 **"Consider the craftsmen I employ . . ."** D. 2, i. 51, p. 93.

190 **"Suppose you had a slave,"** D. 2, i. 61–2, pp. 98–9.

191 **He compared his teaching and training to an ocean** Ud. 5.5, pp. 71–4.

191 **"For the sake of the throne,"** D. 2, i. 85, pp. 108–9.

191 **The final meeting between Siddhattha Gotama and King Pasenadi** This is described in M. 89, ii. 118–25, pp. 728–33.

192 **When the king stepped out of the hut** The following events are recounted in DhA., i. 356–9, vol. 2, pp. 42–5.

193 **"sparing not even infants at the breast."** DhA., i. 358, vol. 2, p. 44.

193 **To avenge her death, Pasenadi had launched a war** S. I, 82–5, pp. 177–8.

194 **The following morning, his servant woman found him dead** DhA., i. 356, vol. 2, p. 43.

## 16. Gods and Demons

195 **My friend Fred Varley died in late April** Mike H. gives an account of the death of Fred Varley in Tomory, *A Season in Heaven*, pp. 67–8.

199 **"If when dying, one's hands shake back and forth . . ."** *Snow Lion: Buddhist News and Catalog*, vol. 22, no. 4, Fall 2008, p. 1.

201 **I returned to McLeod Ganj on March 12, 1993** Another account of the meeting with the Dalai Lama can be found in my essay "The Future Is in Our Hands" at www.stephenbatchelor.org/future.html.

204 **As our discussions drew to a close** The open letter was published in *Tricycle: The Buddhist Review,* vol. 3, no. 1, Fall 1993, pp. 80–1.

205 **allegiance to the protector god, Dorje Shugden** For the background to the Dorje Shugden crisis, see Georges Dreyfus, "The Shuk-den Affair: Origins of a Controversy," at www.tibet.com/dholgyal/shugden-origins .html and my "Letting Daylight into Magic" in *Tricycle: The Buddhist Review,* vol. 7, no. 3, Spring 1998.

207 **I did not know Gen Lobsang Gyatso well** His textbook on Buddhist psychology is *Rigs lam che ba blo rigs kyi rnam gzhag nye mkho kun btus* (Dharamsala, 1975). Lobsang Gyatso's presentation of "mind and mental events" in this work formed the basis for Part Two of Geshe Rabten, Tr. Stephen Batchelor, *The Mind and Its Functions.*

208 **In October of the same year I returned to Tibet** For my description of Trode Khangsar, see *The Tibet Guide,* 2nd ed., pp. 74–5.

211 **"This manifestation of the Buddha has no equal. . . ."** www .dorjeshugden.com/articles/HelmutGassner01.pdf.

## 17. Tread the Path with Care

213 **wandering alone "like a rhinoceros"** See Sn. I, 3, v. 35–75.

213 **appears as miracle worker with supernormal powers** The stock text in the Pāli Canon that describes these says: "Having been one, he becomes many; having been many, he becomes one; he appears and vanishes; he goes unhindered through a wall as though through space; he dives in and out of the earth as though through water; he walks on water without sinking as though it were earth; seated cross-legged, he travels in space like a bird; with his hand he touches and strokes the moon and sun so powerful and mighty; he wields bodily mastery even as far as the Brahma-world." See, for example, M. 12, i. 69, p. 165.

213 **endowed with superhuman physical marks** The thirty-two marks of the Great Man are described throughout the Canon. See, for example, D. 14, ii. 16–19, pp. 205–6.

213 **When the monk Pukkusati, a former nobleman from Takkasila** This episode is found in M. 140, iii. 237–9, pp. 1087–8.

214 **Sariputta, his chief disciple, appears to have been waiting** The episode of Sunakkhata's denunciation can be dated to the last year of the Buddha's life by the statement toward the end of the discourse: "I am now old, aged, burdened with years, advanced in life, and come to the last stage: my years have turned eighty." M. 12, i. 82, p. 177.

214 **"Sunakkhatta is angry,"** M. 12, i. 68, p. 164. The rest of the text goes on at length to show how in fact the Buddha possesses every superhuman power under the sun.

214 **One morning, as Ananda stood behind Siddhattha fanning him** This is the opening passage of D. 16—the *Mahāparinibbāna Sutta (The Great*

*Discourse on the Passing)*—which provides a chronological account of the last months of the Buddha's life.

215 **"His Majesty wishes to inform you . . ."** D. 16, ii. 72, p. 231.

215 **"Ananda, have you not heard . . ."** D. 16, ii. 72–5, pp. 231–2.

215 **"That is true. If the Vajjians keep . . ."** D. 16, ii. 75–6, p. 232.

215 **Taking the model of the Vajjian parliament** D. 16, ii. 76–81, pp. 233–4.

216 **Gotama's sense of failure** The death of Sāriputta is recounted at S. V, 161–2, pp. 1642–4. The canonical account has the Buddha staying at Jeta's Grove when the death of Sāriputta occurs, but from context this must be incorrect. The death of Moggallāna is found in DhA., iii. 65–6, vol. 2, pp. 304–5.

216 **compared their deaths to large branches** S. V, 164, p. 1645.

216 **By the time Gotama and Ananda reached the ferry port of Patali** This episode is recounted at D. 16, ii. 87–8, pp. 237–8.

216 **"ancient city in the forest"** S. II, 105–7, pp. 603–4.

216 **Patali was located at the confluence where the Son River** Since the Buddha's time the course of the Son (Sona) has shifted twenty-five miles to the west.

218 **On learning that he had reached the village of Koti** Mv. VI, 29–30, pp. 315–8. I have taken the account of the meeting with Ambapāli and the Licchavi youths from the version given in the Vinaya, which differs from that in *Mahāparinibbāna Sutta* (D. 16, ii. 95–7, pp. 242–3) only in the locations where the events took place. In D. 16 the meeting with Ambapāli and the Licchavi youths occurs in Vesālī.

219 **"Go anywhere in Vesali where you have friends . . ."** D. 16, ii. 99, p. 244.

219 **"attacked by a severe sickness, with sharp pains . . ."** and following quotes: D. 16, ii. 99–101, pp. 244–5.

219 **"learn, practice, and cultivate"** D. 16, ii. 119–20, p. 253.

220 **"Serve the pork to me,"** D. 16, ii. 126–8, pp. 256–7. See DhA., i. 125–6, vol. 1, pp. 225–6, which tells of another (or could it be the same?) Cunda, the "pork butcher," and his method of tenderizing pork. Some modern commentators (e.g., Maurice Walshe, D. 16, n. 417, p. 571) have preferred to interpret the Buddha's final meal as consisting of mushrooms or truffles rather than pork. The Pāli term *sūkara-maddava* literally means "tender" (*maddava*) "pig" (*sūkara*). It is clear from the Canon that the Buddha was not a vegetarian. He rejected his cousin Devadatta's suggestion that vegetarianism be imposed as a rule on the monastic community. He had no objection to his monks eating meat,

provided that the animal had not been "seen, heard or suspected" to have been specifically killed for them (Cv. VII, 196, p. 277).

221 **"were split into two parties, quarreling and disputing . . ."** D. 29, iii. 117–8, p. 427. See also M. 104, ii. 243–5, p. 853–4. Both texts have the Buddha staying in Sakiya when this occurs.

221 **When captured, the brigands** DhA., iii. 66–7, vol. 2, p. 305.

221 **On the outskirts of Fazilnagar** Most Jains, however, consider Pawapur in Bihar, not far from Nalanda and Rajgir, as the place where their founding teacher Mahāvīra died. Today Pawapur is an important, well-maintained Jain pilgrimage site. The word *Pawapur* means "Pawa-town." *Pawa* appears to be a variant of the Pāli *Pāvā*.

222 **His small group of monks had stopped to bathe** D. 16, ii. 134, pp. 260–1.

223 **"Do not weep and wail,"** D. 16, ii. 144, p. 265.

223 **"Don't die here,"** D. 16, ii. 146, p. 266.

224 **"Tell me who among the teachers . . ."** D. 16, ii. 150–1, p. 268.

224 **"If anyone has an outstanding doubt . . ."** D. 16, ii. 154–5, p. 270.

224 **". . . conditioned things break down, tread the path with care!"** D. 16, ii. 156, p. 270.

224 **"wept and tore their hair . . ."** D. 16, ii. 157–8, p. 272.

## 18. A Secular Buddhist

225 **The search produced a number of references** The "Man at the Wheel" appeared in the movie *The Perfect Storm* (2000), starring George Clooney. The film was based on the book of the same name by Sebastian Junger, a dramatic account of the final journey of the *Andrea Gail,* a fishing boat from Gloucester lost with all hands in a North Atlantic storm in October 1991.

226 **"easily recognized by his prematurely white hair . . ."** From "Fisherman's wife statue—idea hailed then spurned," an article in the *Gloucester Daily Times* by James Shea, July 31, 1971.

226 **From the late 1920s Leonard** *Ibid.* Shea says that Craske "had a remarkable collection of color slides of Cape Ann and other scenes." I have been unable to trace them.

228 **"cut off at the root, made like a palm stump . . ."** A common metaphor found throughout the Canon. See, for example, M. 36, i. 250, p. 343.

228 **"armies of Mara"** These are sensual pleasure, discontent, hunger and thirst, craving, sloth and torpor, fear, doubt, hypocrisy and obstinacy, gain, renown, honor and fame, extolling oneself and disparaging others. Sn. III, v. 436–8.

229 **A clue to how this might be done** The Buddha's parable of the raft is found in M. 22, i. 134–5, pp. 228–9.

229 **The Buddha died, exhausted and sick** As for the rest of his family, his son, Rāhula, is mentioned in the Canon on a couple of occasions but is not a prominent figure. It is not known what became of him. His wife Bhaddakaccānā is said to have become a nun, but nothing further is reported about her in the Canon. His cousin Mahānāma, the leader of the Sakiyans, was spared during the ethnic cleansing of Sakiya at the command of his grandson King Viḍūḍabha and captured. While being taken to Sāvatthi (to stand trial?), he asked permission to take a bath. This wish was granted and Mahānāma committed suicide by drowning himself in the water. Viḍūḍabha returned with his army to Sāvatthi. Before arriving in the city, he and his troops camped in the dry riverbed of the Aciravatī. But there was a flash flood and he too was drowned. (See DhA., i. 357–60, vol. 2, pp. 44–5.) Nothing is known about the fate of "Lady" Vāsabhā, Viḍūḍabha's mother and Mahānāma's daughter with the slave Nāgamundā. As far as we know, the Buddha's cousins Ānanda and Anuruddha spent the rest of their lives as monks.

229 **At least he had some supporters left in the Mallan town of Kusinara** D. 16, ii. 159–61, pp. 273–4. The account of Mallikā spreading her jeweled cloak over the Buddha's body is not found in the Canon. It is recounted in Buddhaghosa's *Sumangalavilasini,* his commentary to the *Dīgha Nikāya,* ii. 597.

230 **Just before the funeral pyre was to be ignited** The arrival of Kassapa the Great and his followers: D. 16, ii. 162, p. 274.

230 **Kassapa was a brahmin from Magadha** A series of connected discourses relating to Kassapa are found in S. V, 194–225, pp. 662–81.

230 **"It may be that you will think that after my death you will have no teacher . . ."** D. 16, ii. 154, pp. 269–70.

230 **"I would not even ask Sariputta . . ."** Cv. VII, 187, p. 264. However, Sn. III, v. 556–7 implies that the Buddha may have regarded Sāriputta as his successor at an earlier stage in his teaching career.

231 **Once Gotama's ash and bones had been parceled out** D. 16, ii. 164–6, pp. 275–7.

231 **Kassapa was entreated to select those elders** Cv. XI, 284, pp. 394–5.

232 **They of old have passed away** Thag., v. 1036. The commentary to the *Theragāthā* explains that Ānanda composed this verse when he heard of the death of Sāriputta.

232 **At some point the party arrived at a nunnery** This episode is found in S. II, 214–7, pp. 674–6. The text maintains that it took place in Jeta's Grove at Sāvatthi, but this seems unlikely given the context.

232 "How can Kassapa even think of speaking . . ." and the following exchange: S. II, 215–7, pp. 675–6.

233 As soon as the party arrived in Rajagaha S. II, 217, p. 676.

233 We are also told that a monk called Purana Cv. XI, 288–9, pp. 401–2.

233 "Your retinue is breaking apart . . ." and the following exchange: S. II, 218–9, pp. 677–9.

234 The tension among Gotama's followers was raising questions The episode in Gopaka's office is found in M. 108, iii. 7–10, pp. 880–2.

235 the Pali Text Society www.palitext.com.

235 It was not until the early years of the twentieth century that the first Europeans The Englishman Allan Bennett was ordained as Ven. Ānanda Metteyya in Rangoon in 1901, followed in 1904 by the German Anton Gueth, who became Ven. Ñāṇatiloka—the founder of Island Hermitage in Ceylon and preceptor of Harold Musson (Ñāṇavira) and Osbert Moore (Ñāṇamoli). See my *The Awakening of the West*, pp. 307–8.

236 "You may remember the story of how the devil . . ." Krishnamurti, *Dissolution Speech:* http://bernie.cncfamily.com/k_pathless.htm.

236 "I am living hemmed in by monks and nuns . . ." Ud. 4.5, pp. 58–9.

237 "Religion today," says Don Cupitt Don Cupitt, *The Great Questions of Life*, p. 18.

238 "Whoever would tend to me," Mv. VIII, 301, p. 432.

238 If the compassionate Buddha regarded others as himself Shāntideva, *A Guide to the Bodhisattva's Way of Life*, VI: 126. I have simplified the text by referring it to the historical Buddha alone whereas Shāntideva talks of "the compassionate ones" and "the buddhas" in the plural.

238 "Do not kill me." See the chapter "The Face" in Emmanuel Levinas, *Ethics and Infinity*, pp. 85–92.

# GLOSSARY

**Aciravatī**  (Pāli) A river on the banks of which stood the city of Sāvatthi at the time of the Buddha.

**Ajātasattu**  (Pāli) Son of King Bimbisāra of Magadha and Queen Devi (sister of Pasenadi); after Bimbisāra's abdication in his favor, King of Magadha; disciple of Devadatta.

**Ānanda**  (Pāli) First cousin of the Buddha (on his father's side); brother of Mahānāma and Anuruddha; the Buddha's attendant for the last twenty-five years of his life; the monk who reputedly memorized all that the Buddha taught.

**Anāthapindika**  (Pāli) Wealthy merchant from Sāvatthi who donated the Jeta's Grove to the Buddha.

**Anuruddha**  (Pāli) First cousin of the Buddha (on his father's side); brother of Mahānāma and Ānanda.

**Arhant**  (Pāli) A "worthy one": a Buddhist saint who has achieved complete liberation from the cycle of death and rebirth.

**Ātman**  (Sanskrit) Literally "self"; in the non-Buddhist brahmanic tradition it refers to the pure consciousness that is the core of one's true being; identical in nature to Brahman (God).

**Avalokiteshvara**  (Sanskrit) The Bodhisattva of Compassion in Mahāyāna Buddhism.

**Bandhula**  (Pāli) Nobleman from Kusinārā; general of King Pasenadi's army; chief justice of Kosala; murdered with his sons by Pasenadi.

**Bimbisāra**  (Pāli) King of Magadha; husband of Devi (sister of Pasenadi); father of Ajātasattu; donated the Bamboo Grove in Rājagaha to the Buddha.

**Bodhisattva** (Sanskrit; Pāli = *bodhisatta*) One who has taken a vow to attain awakening for the sake of all sentient beings; one who aspires to become a Buddha.

**Bosalnim** (Korean) A Buddhist laywoman.

**Brahman** (Sanskrit) The impersonal, transcendent God or Godhead of Vedic and Upanishadic Indian tradition; the creative origin of the world and the essential nature of one's innermost self (*ātman*).

**Chuba** (Tibetan) A long formal dress or gown.

**Dacoit** (Hindi) A member of a gang of robbers or bandits.

**Dāna** (Pāli) Literally "giving" or "gift"; traditionally the offerings of food, clothing, and other necessities donated by the Buddhist laity to monks and nuns.

**Deva** (Pāli) A god; in the mundane sense, a celestial being inhabiting one of the higher realms of samsāra; in the supramundane sense, a Buddha who assumes a divine form in Mahāyāna and Vajrayāna Buddhism.

**Devadatta** (Pāli) First cousin of the Buddha (on his mother's side); sought to replace the Buddha as head of the order of monks.

**Dhamma** (Sanskrit = Dharma) The teaching of the Buddha; the truths and practices to which the Buddha's teaching refers.

**Dharmakīrti** (Sanskrit) Circa seventh-century Indian Buddhist monk-scholar known for his foundational work on logic and epistemology.

**Djukpi** (Korean) Wooden clapper used for timekeeping in Korean Zen monasteries.

**Dorje Shugden** (Tibetan) Controversial protector god of the Geluk school of Tibetan Buddhism.

**Dzogchen** (Tibetan) Literally "great completion": a formless meditation practice of pristine awareness taught in the Nyingma school of Tibetan Buddhism.

**Gandhāra** (Pāli) At the Buddha's time, a country in the west of the Indian subcontinent that was part of the Persian empire; its capital was Takkasilā; territorially equivalent to much of modern Pakistan.

**Geluk** (Tibetan) The order of Tibetan Buddhism founded by Tsongkhapa in the fourteenth century; the school in which the Dalai Lama was trained.

**Gho** (Bhutanese/Tibetan) Traditional knee-length robe worn by men in Bhutan.

**Hīnayāna** (Sanskrit) The "Lesser Vehicle" of Buddhism; a pejorative term coined by followers of the Mahāyāna to describe the selfish path of the *arhant* in contrast to the altruistic way of the bodhisattva.

**Ibseung Sunim** (Korean) A monk or nun who is appointed leader of a meditation hall, responsible for timekeeping and discipline.

**Inji** (Tibetan) Slang for "Westerner," a corruption of "English."

**Jhāna** (Pāli) Meditative absorption; traditionally there are eight jhānas: the first four are achieved through concentrating on a formal object, and the next four are achieved through concentrating on a formless object.

**Kagyu** (Tibetan) School of Tibetan Buddhism founded in the eleventh century by Marpa, Milarepa, Gompopa, and their followers.

**Kālachakra** (Sanskrit) Literally "Wheel of Time": multilimbed Vajrayāna deity associated with the mythical kingdom of Shambhala.

**Kangyur** (Tibetan) Literally "translations of the word": the section of the Tibetan Buddhist canon containing the discourses attributed to the Buddha.

**Kapilavatthu** (Pāli) The principal town of the Kosalan province of Sakiya where the Buddha was raised as a child; the modern village of Piprahwa.

**Kassapa** (Pāli) Also known as Mahākassapa (Kassapa the Great); prominent disciple of the Buddha who convened the First Council after Gotama's death.

**Katag** (Tibetan) White silk offering scarf used as a respectful greeting.

**Kira** (Bhutanese/Tibetan) Traditional ankle-length dress worn by women in Bhutan.

**Kosala** (Pāli) The Indian kingdom to the north of the Ganges at the Buddha's time; its capital was Sāvatthi and its king Pasenadi.

**Kusināra** (Pāli) One of the two principal towns of Malla (the other was Pāvā); the fief of Bandhula; the place where the Buddha died; now called Kushinagar.

**Madhyamaka** (Sanskrit) The Buddhist "middle way" philosophy of emptiness, founded by Nāgārjuna in the second century; also followed by Shāntideva and Tsongkhapa.

**Magadha** (Pāli) The Indian kingdom to the south of the Ganges at the Buddha's time; its capital was Rājagaha and its king Bimbisāra, then Ajātasattu.

**Mahānāma** (Pāli) First cousin of the Buddha (on his father's side); brother of Ānanda and Anuruddha; rose to become the governor of Sakiya; father of Vāsabhā.

**Mahāyāna** (Sanskrit) The "Greater Vehicle" of Buddhism, which encourages the bodhisattva's aspiration to become a Buddha for the sake of all beings; a polemical term contrasted to the Hīnayāna.

**Malla** (Pāli) Eastern province of the kingdom of Kosala to the south of Sakiya; its principal towns were Kusinara and Pāvā.

**Mallikā** (Pāli) 1. First wife of King Pasenadi of Kosala; mother of Vajīrī, who was married to Ajātasattu; 2. wife of Bandhula.

**Mañjushrī** (Sanskrit) The Bodhisattva of Wisdom in Mahāyāna Buddhism.

**Māra** (Pāli) The Buddhist devil; literally "the killer," i.e., whatever obstructs the path to awakening.

**Maru** (Korean) Raised wooden walkway outside the doors of traditional Korean buildings.

**Moggallāna** (Pāli) With Sāriputta, one of the two senior disciples of the Buddha; he was a brahmin from Magadha and became renowned for his meditative and psychic powers.

**Moktak** (Korean) Small handheld wooden drum beaten with a short stick; often used to keep time while chanting and performing Buddhist rituals.

**Mudrā** (Sanskrit) The symbolic hand gestures of figures, such as the Buddha, depicted in iconographic statues and paintings.

**Nirvāna** (Sanskrit; Pāli = nibbāna) The "blowing out" of the "fires" of greed, hatred, and delusion.

**Nyingma** (Tibetan) The "ancient" school of Tibetan Buddhism founded in the eighth century during the first phase of the dissemination of Buddhism in Tibet.

**Pāli** (Pāli) The Middle Indo-Aryan language used to record the Buddha's teaching as found in the canonical literature of the Theravāda school.

**Pasenadi** (Pāli) King of Kosala during the Buddha's lifetime.

**Pātali(putta)** (Pāli) Ferryport on the south bank of the Ganges in Magadha; by the end of the Buddha's life it was being developed into a fortified town; the future capital of Emperor Ashoka; the modern city of Patna.

**Pāvā** (Pāli) One of the two principal towns of Malla (the other is Kusinara); the place where the Buddha ate his last meal; also the place where Mahāvīra, the founder of the Jain religion, is believed to have died; the modern town of Fazilnagar.

**Pūjā** (Sanskrit) Literally "offering": a formal, often communal, religious service with chanting.

**Rājagaha** (Pāli) Capital city of Magadha; the modern town of Rajgir.

**Sādhana** (Sanskrit) A practice of Vajrayāna Buddhism that entails the daily recitation of a ritual text related to a tantric deity.

**Sakiya** (Pāli) Eastern province of the kingdom of Kosala where the Buddha was born; its capital was Kapilavatthu.

**Samsāra** (Pāli) The painful and repetitive cycle of death and rebirth.

**Sāriputta** (Pāli) With Moggallāna, one of the two senior disciples of the Buddha; he was a brahmin from Magadha and was renowned for his intelligence and wisdom.

**Sarīra** (Pāli) Bodily relics of an accomplished Buddhist teacher; often found among cremated remains in the form of small crystalline drops.

**Sāvatthi** (Pāli) Capital city of the kingdom of Kosala; the Jeta's Grove was nearby; the modern town of Sahet-Mahet / Śrāvastī.

**Shāntideva** (Sanskrit) Eighth-century Indian Mahāyāna Buddhist monk; author of *A Guide to the Bodhisattva's Way of Life (Bodhicaryāvatāra)*.

**Siddhattha Gotama** (Pāli) Personal name of the Buddha, the "Awakened One."

**Sonpang** (Korean) Meditation hall.

**Stupa** (Sanskrit) A funerary mound where the relics of cremated monks were enshrined; it later evolved into the preeminent architectural symbol of Buddhism.

**Suddhodana** (Pāli) The Buddha's father.

**Sunim** (Korean) A monk or nun; used as a polite form of address for monastics.

**Sutta** (Pāli) A discourse delivered by the Buddha or, on occasion, one of his prominent disciples.

**Takkasilā** (Pāli) Taxilā, the capital of Gandhāra and major center of learning at the Buddha's time.

**Tengyur** (Tibetan) Literally "translation of the commentaries," i.e., the division of the Tibetan Buddhist canon that contains the commentaries to the Buddha's teachings found in the Kangyur.

**Theravāda** (Pāli) Literally "the teaching of the elders": the school of Buddhism found today in Sri Lanka and Southeast Asia that is based on the Pāli Canon and the commentaries of Buddhaghosa.

**Tsampa** (Tibetan) Ground roasted barley flour, a traditional staple food in Tibet.

**Tsongkhapa** (Tibetan) Tibetan monk, scholar, and yogi (1357–1410) who founded the Geluk school of Tibetan Buddhism.

**Upanishad** (Sanskrit) A class of non-Buddhist religious-philosophical literature that explores the ways to achieve union with Brahman (God); also known as Vedanta, i.e., the "end" or "culmination" of the Vedas.

**Uruvelā** (Pāli) The place in Magadha where the Buddha achieved awakening; known today as Bodh Gaya.

**Vajji** (Pāli) The last surviving republic of the Buddha's time, located to the north of the Ganges and south of Malla; its capital city was Vesālī.

**Vajra** (Sanskrit) A five- or nine-pronged scepter used in tantric rituals.

**Vajrayāna** (Sanskrit) The "Diamond Vehicle": the path of tantric Buddhism that emerged in India around the third century; involves the use of mantra, visualization, and yogic exercises; it is widely practiced in all schools of Tibetan Buddhism.

**Vāsabhā** (Pāli) Or Vāsabhākhattiyā, i.e., "Lady Vasabha," daughter of Mahānāma and the slavewoman Nāgamundā; second wife of King Pasenadi; mother of Viḍūḍabha.

**Veda** (Sanskrit) A class of brahmanic, non-Buddhist religious literature, composed mainly of hymns to the gods; the earliest expression of Aryan culture in India prior to the Upanishads.

**Vesālī** (Pāli) Capital city of Vajji; the modern village of Vaishali.

**Viḍūḍabha** (Pāli) Son of King Pasenadi and Vāsabhā; briefly ruled as king of Kosala after the overthrow of Pasenadi.

**Vihara** (Pali) A monastery or nunnery.

**Vinaya** (Pāli) Literally "discipline": the moral rules and codes of conduct of Buddhist monks and nuns; the body of literature in the Pāli Canon that describes monastic life and practice.

**Vipassanā** (Pāli) Literally "insight": Buddhist meditation that is concerned with investigating the nature of experience, as opposed to *samatha* ("stillness"), i.e., quieting the mind through concentration on a single object.

**Yamantaka** (Sanskrit) Wrathful, bull-headed, multilimbed deity of Vajrayāna Buddhism.

# BIBLIOGRAPHY

Allchin, F. R. *The Archaeology of Early Historic South Asia: The Emergence of Cities and States*. Cambridge: Cambridge University Press, 1995.

Allen, Charles. *The Buddha and the Sahibs: The Men Who Discovered India's Lost Religion*. London: John Murray, 2003.

Bailey, Greg, and Ian Mabbett. *The Sociology of Early Buddhism*. Cambridge: Cambridge University Press, 2003.

Batchelor, David. *Chromophobia*. London: Reaktion Books, 2000.

Batchelor, Martine. *Meditation for Life*. London: Frances Lincoln, 2001.

———— and Son'gyong Sunim. *Women in Korean Zen: Lives and Practices*. Syracuse, N.Y.: Syracuse University Press, 2006.

Batchelor, Stephen. *Alone with Others: An Existential Approach to Buddhism*. New York: Grove, 1983.

————. *The Tibet Guide*. London: Wisdom Publications, 1988.

————. *The Faith to Doubt: Glimpses of Buddhist Uncertainty*. Berkeley, Calif.: Parallax, 1990.

————. *The Awakening of the West: The Encounter of Buddhism and Western Culture*. London: Aquarian, 1994.

————. *Buddhism Without Beliefs: A Contemporary Guide to Awakening*. New York: Riverhead, 1997.

————. *Living with the Devil: A Meditation on Good and Evil*. New York: Riverhead, 1997.

Bodhi, Bhikkhu, trans. *The Connected Discourses of the Buddha (Samyutta Nikāya)*. Somerville, Mass.: Wisdom Publications, 2000.

————. *The Revival of Bhikkhunī Ordination in the Theravāda Tradition*. Penang, Malaysia: Inward Path, 2009.

Buber, Martin. *I and Thou*. Translated by Walter Kaufmann. Edinburgh: T. T. Clark, 1979.

Burlingame, Eugene Watson, trans. *Buddhist Legends (Dhammapada Commentary)*. 3 vols. Oxford: Pali Text Society, 1995. [First published in 1921.]

Buswell, Robert E. *The Korean Approach to Zen: The Collected Works of Chinul*. Honolulu: University of Hawaii Press, 1983.

———. *The Zen Monastic Experience*. Princeton: Princeton University Press, 1992.

Cupitt, Don. *The Time Being*. London: SCM Press, 1992.

———. *The Great Questions of Life*. Santa Rosa, Calif.: Polebridge Press, 2005.

Dalai Lama. *Kindness, Clarity, and Insight*. Ithaca, N.Y.: Snow Lion, 1984.

———. *Freedom in Exile: The Autobiography of the Dalai Lama of Tibet*. London: Hodder and Stoughton, 1990.

———. *The Universe in a Single Atom: The Convergence of Science and Spirituality*. New York: Morgan Road Books, 2005.

Dawkins, Richard. *The God Delusion*. London: Bantam, 2006.

Dhargyey, Geshe. *The Tibetan Tradition of Mental Development*. Dharamsala, India: Library of Tibetan Works and Archives, 1978.

Dowman, Keith, trans. and compiler. *The Flight of the Garuda*. Boston: Wisdom Publications, 1994.

Dreyfus, Georges B. J. *Recognizing Reality: Dharmakīrti's Philosophy and Its Tibetan Interpreters*. Albany: State University of New York Press, 1997.

———. *The Sound of Two Hands Clapping: The Education of a Tibetan Buddhist Monk*. Berkeley and Los Angeles: University of California Press, 2003.

Evola, Julius. *The Doctrine of Awakening: A Study on the Buddhist Ascesis*. Translated by H. E. Musson. London: Luzac, 1951. [Republished by Inner Traditions, Rochester, Vermont, in 1996.]

———. *Le Chemin du Cinabre*. Milan: Arche-Arktos, 1982. [First published in Italian in 1972. An English translation, *The Path of Cinnabar: An Intellectual Autobiography*, was published in 2009 by Integral Tradition Publishing, London.]

Fronsdal, Gil, trans. *The Dhammapada*. Boston and London: Shambhala, 2005.

Gombrich, Richard F. *How Buddhism Began: The Conditioned Genesis of the Early Teachings*. London: Athlone, 1996.

———. *What the Buddha Thought*. London/Oakville, Conn.: Equinox, 2009.

Grimmett, Richard, and Tim Inskipp. *Birds of North India*. Princeton and Oxford: Princeton University Press, 2003.

Guenther, Herbert V., trans. *Jewel Ornament of Liberation*. London: Rider, 1970.

Harris, Sam. *The End of Faith: Religion, Terror and the Future of Reason*. New York: Norton, 2004.

Heidegger, Martin. *Being and Time*. Translated by John Macquarrie and Edward Robinson. Oxford: Blackwell, 1962.

———. *Basic Writings*. Edited by David Farrell Krell. London: Routledge, Kegan and Paul, 1978.

Horner, I. B., trans. *The Book of Discipline, Vol. IV (Mahāvagga)*. Oxford: Pali Text Society, 1951.

———, trans. *The Book of Discipline, Vol. V (Cūlavagga)*. Oxford: Pali Text Society, 1952.

Ireland, John D., trans. *The Udāna and the Itivuttaka*. Kandy, Sri Lanka: Buddhist Publication Society, 1997.

Junger, Sebastian. *The Perfect Storm: A True Story of Man Against the Sea*. London: Fourth Estate, 1997.

Kalff, Dora. *Sandplay: A Psychotherapeutic Approach to the Psyche*. Santa Monica, Calif.: Sigo Press, 1980.

Kusan Sunim. *Nine Mountains: Dharma-Lectures of the Korean Meditation Master Ku San*. Seung Ju Kun, Korea: Songgwangsa Monastery, 1976.

———. *The Way of Korean Zen*. Boston and London: Weatherhill, 2009. [First published in 1985.]

Levinas, Emmanuel. *Ethics and Infinity*. Translated by Richard A. Cohen. Pittsburgh: Duquesne University Press, 1985.

Ling, Trevor. *The Buddha: Buddhist Civilization in India and Ceylon*. London: Temple Smith, 1973.

Macquarrie, John. *An Existentialist Theology*. London: Pelican, 1973.

Malalasekera, G. P. *Dictionary of Pāli Proper Names*. 3 vols. Oxford: Pali Text Society, 1997. [First published in 1938.]

Marcel, Gabriel. *Being and Having: An Existentialist Diary*. Translated by Katherine Farrer. Gloucester, Mass.: Peter Smith, 1976.

Maugham, Robin. *Search for Nirvana*. London: Allen and Unwin, 1975.

McEvilley, Thomas. *The Shape of Ancient Thought: Comparative Studies in Greek and Indian Philosophies*. New York: Allworth Press, 2002.

Müller, F. Max, trans. *The Thirteen Principal Upanishads*. Revised by Suren Navlakha. Ware, U.K.: Wordsworth, 2000.

Nakamura, Hajime. *Gotama Buddha: A Biography Based on the Most Reliable Texts*. 2 vols. Tokyo: Kosei Publishing, 2000 and 2005.

# Bibliography

Ñāṇamoli, Bhikkhu. *The Life of the Buddha*. Kandy, Sri Lanka: Buddhist Publication Society, 1978.

Ñāṇamoli, Bhikkhu, and Bhikkhu Bodhi, trans. *The Middle Length Discourses of the Buddha (Majjhima Nikāya)*. Boston: Wisdom Publications, 1995.

Ñāṇavīra Thera. *Clearing the Path: Writings of Ñāṇavīra Thera (1960–1965)*. Colombo, Sri Lanka: Path Press, 1987.

―――. *Notes on Dhamma (1960–1965)*. Nieuwerkerk a/d Yssel, Holland: Path Press Publications, 2009.

Norman, K. R., trans. *The Group of Discourses (Sutta-Nipāta)*. Oxford: Pali Text Society, 2001.

―――. *A Philological Approach to Buddhism*. Lancaster, U.K.: Pali Text Society, 2006.

Nyanaponika Thera. *Great Disciples of the Buddha: Their Lives, Their Works, Their Legacy*. Edited by Hellmuth Hecker and Bhikkhu Bodhi. Somerville, Mass.: Wisdom Publications, 2003.

Nyanaponika Thera and Bhikkhu Bodhi, trans. *Numerical Discourses of the Buddha: An Anthology of Suttas from the Anguttara Nikāya*. Walnut Creek, Calif.: Alta Mira Press, 1999.

Pabongka Rinpoche. *Liberation in the Palm of Your Hand*. Edited by Trijang Rinpoche. Translated by Michael Richards. Boston: Wisdom Publications, 1991.

Plato. *Phaedo*. Translated by David Gallop. Oxford: Oxford University Press, 1999.

Rabten, Geshe. *The Life and Teaching of Geshe Rabten*. Translated and edited by B. Alan Wallace. London: Allen and Unwin, 1980.

―――. *Echoes of Voidness*. Translated by Stephen Batchelor. London: Wisdom Publications, 1983.

―――. *The Song of the Profound View*. Translated by Stephen Batchelor. London: Wisdom Publications, 1989.

―――. *The Mind and Its Functions*. Translated and edited by Stephen Batchelor. Le Mont-Pèlerin: Editions Rabten Choeling, 1992. [First published in 1978.]

――― and Geshe Ngawang Dhargyey. *Advice from a Spiritual Friend*. Translated and edited by Brian Beresford with Gonsar Tulku and Sharpa Tulku. Somerville, Mass.: Wisdom Publications, 1996. [First published in 1977.]

Rhys Davids, Caroline A. F. *Psalms of the Early Buddhists*. Oxford: Pali Text Society, 1980. [*Theragāthā* was first published in 1909; *Therīgāthā* in 1937.]

Schettini, Stephen. *The Novice: Why I Became a Buddhist Monk, Why I Quit and What I Learned*. Austin, Tex.: Greenleaf Book Group Press, 2009.

Schumann, H. W. *The Historical Buddha: The Times, Life and Teachings of the Founder of Buddhism*. Translated by Maurice Walshe, London: Arkana, 1989.

Shāntideva. 1. *A Guide to the Bodhisattva's Way of Life*. Translated from Tibetan by Stephen Batchelor. Dharamsala, India: Library of Tibetan Works and Archives, 1979. 2. *The Bodhicaryāvatāra*. Translated from Sanskrit by Kate Crosby and Andrew Skilton. Oxford and New York: Oxford University Press, 1996. 3. *A Guide to the Bodhisattva's Way of Life*. Translated by Vesna Wallace and B. Alan Wallace from Sanskrit and Tibetan. Ithaca, N.Y.: Snow Lion, 1997.

Thomas, Edward J. *The Life of the Buddha as Legend and History*. London: 1927.

Tillich, Paul. *The Dynamics of Faith*. New York: Harper and Row, 1958.

———. *The Courage to Be*. London: Fontana, 1962.

———. *Systematic Theology*. 3 vols. in 1. Chicago: University of Chicago Press, 1967.

Tomory, David. *A Season in Heaven: True Tales from the Road to Kathmandu*. London: Thorsons, 1996.

Von Franz, Marie-Louise. *Puer Aeternus*. Santa Monica, Calif.: Sigo Press, 1970.

Walshe, Maurice, trans. *The Long Discourses of the Buddha (Dīgha Nikāya)*. Boston: Wisdom Publications, 1995.

Wenders, Wim. *The Logic of Images*. London: Faber, 1991.

# ACKNOWLEDGMENTS

I am indebted to all those people, past and present, who are mentioned or alluded to in the preceding pages and without whom *Confession of a Buddhist Atheist* could not have been written. I thank Darius Cuplinskas, Chris Desser, Antonia Macaro, John Peacock, Marjorie Silverman, Mark Vernon, and Gay Watson, who read through the book in manuscript form and offered many helpful suggestions for improvement; Allan Hunt Badiner and Shantum Seth, for showing me the Buddha's India; Richard Gombrich, for initiating me into the mysteries of Pāli; Stephen Schettini, for blazing the autobiographical trail; Peter Maddock, for his recollections of Ñāṇavīra Thera; Ilona Wille, for her memories of Fred Varley; Anne Amos and Mike Smith, for cooked breakfasts beyond the call of duty; my agent Anne Edelstein, for her enthusiasm for this book from its inception; and my editor Cindy Spiegel, for having enabled it to reach its final form.

# INDEX

# Index

# ABOUT THE AUTHOR

Stephen Batchelor was born in Scotland in 1953 and grew up near London. At the age of eighteen he left England and joined the community around the Dalai Lama in Dharamsala, India. He was ordained as a Buddhist monk in 1974. After formal training in both Tibetan and Zen traditions of Buddhism, he disrobed in 1984. As a layman he has focused increasingly on the early teachings of the Buddha as found in the Pali Canon. He is the author of several books, including the bestselling *Buddhism Without Beliefs*. Known for his agnostic and secular approach, he teaches Buddhist philosophy and meditation worldwide. He lives with his wife, Martine, near Bordeaux in southwestern France. For further information: www.stephenbatchelor.org

## ABOUT THE TYPE

This book was set in Fairfield, the first typeface from the hand of the distinguished American artist and engraver Rudolph Ruzicka (1883–1978). Ruzicka was born in Bohemia and came to America in 1894. He set up his own shop, devoted to wood engraving and printing, in New York in 1913 after a varied career working as a wood engraver, in photoengraving and banknote printing plants, and as an art director and freelance artist. He designed and illustrated many books, and was the creator of a considerable list of individual prints—wood engravings, line engravings on copper, and aquatints.